SPACE FORCE

OUR STAR TREK FUTURE

Also by DR. MICHAEL SALLA

Rise of the Red Dragon
Origins & Threat of China's Secret Space Program

– Book Five of the Secret Space Programs Series –

US Air Force Secret Space Program
Shifting Extraterrestrial Alliances and Space Force

– Book Four of the Secret Space Programs Series –

Antarctica's Hidden History
Corporate Foundations of Secret Space Programs

– Book Three of the Secret Space Programs Series –

The U.S. Navy's Secret Space Program & Nordic Extraterrestrial Alliance

– Book Two of the Secret Space Programs Series –

Insiders Reveal Secret Space Programs & Extraterrestrial Alliances

– Book One of the Secret Space Programs Series –

Kennedy's Last Stand
Eisenhower, UFOs, MJ-12 & JFK's Assassination

Galactic Diplomacy
Getting to Yes with ET

Exposing U.S. Government Policies on Extraterrestrial Life

Exopolitics
Political Implications of Extraterrestrial Life

SPACE FORCE

OUR STAR TREK FUTURE

MICHAEL E. SALLA, PH.D.

BOOK SIX OF THE SECRET SPACE PROGRAM SERIES

Hawaii, USA

SPACE FORCE
OUR STAR TREK FUTURE

Exopolitics Consultants
PO Box 478
Holualoa, HI 96725 USA

Printed in the United States of America

Cover Design: Rene McCann

ISBN 978-0-9986038-7-2

Dedication

For Angelika, my soulmate and best friend in life's journey of manifesting the True, the Good and the Beautiful.

Table of Contents

TABLE OF FIGURES

Preface

Prior to the official creation of the United States Space Force on December 20, 2019, the establishment of a military space corps was highly anticipated, but oddly, also strikingly opposed behind-the-scenes by senior Pentagon and White House officials. This opposition ignited back in June 2017, when two members of the US Congress proposed the creation of an independent military space service and placed it within the 2018 National Defense Authorization Act, which resulted in senior Pentagon and White House officials undermining it. Indeed, a gag order was put into force by the Secretary of the Air Force to prevent Air Force officers from rallying behind the Space Corps proposal, or to discuss space as a warfighting domain. Even the Air Force Chief of Staff, General David Goldfein, later admitted he was ordered to remain silent. When Lieutenant General Steven Kwast openly defied the gag order and repeatedly spoke about the need for an independent military space service, he was relieved of his command and forced into early retirement. Here was a modern-day reenactment of the famous 1925 Billy Mitchell incident, whereby a US Army brigadier general was court martialed and forced into early retirement for speaking out about the need for an independent Air Force. When President Donald Trump entered the debate in March 2018 championing the idea of a space force, he was opening the door to a discussion that had been stifled by senior Pentagon officials. The gag order stayed in place despite Trump's intervention and was only lifted after the responsible officials were forced to resign in 2019, after failing to persuade Trump to abandon the Space Force proposal.

Contrary to common opinion, however, Space Force is not an idea that originated with either President Trump in March 2018, or the two members of Congress in 2017. The proposal for a dedicated military space service dates back to January 11, 2001, when a report was delivered by a bipartisan high-level national security commission set up by President Bill Clinton. The "Space Commission Report" recommended the creation of a new military service, a Space Corps, within the Department of the US Air Force that would eventually become a separate department. Space Corps was deemed necessary to protect the US satellite grid from a future Space Pearl Harbor. The Space Commission Report identified China as the most likely foreign adversary capable of developing the capacity for undertaking such an attack. Indeed, China had already begun the task under its asymmetric military strategy in response to the US strategy of full spectrum dominance.

The newly installed Secretary of Defense in the George W. Bush administration, Donald Rumsfeld (2001-2006), was a strong supporter for the creation of Space Corps. In fact, Rumsfeld had chaired the bipartisan commission that recommended its formation. Secretary Rumsfeld's background is both intriguing and relevant as to why Space Corps was proposed towards the end of the Clinton administration. He had a long history on the UFO topic dating from July 29, 1968, when the House Science Aeronautics Committee held a symposium with the world's leading UFO researchers at the time. Multiple reports affirm that Rumsfeld was involved in highly classified reverse engineering projects connected to captured UFOs, which in turn directly led to the creation of a secret military space program. Was this in anyway related to his championing the creation of a space corps? Was Rumsfeld trying to 'white world'—bring out into the open—a secret military space program using reverse engineered alien technologies?

On September 10, 2001, Rumsfeld gave an extraordinary speech before the national press where he decried trillions of dollars missing from the Pentagon budget and a bloated Pentagon bureaucracy. This glaring shortfall prevented innovative military projects from going forward. Rumsfeld announced that he was about to send legislative proposals to Congress that would fund these innovative projects—among them was the launch of the Space Corps. It never happened. The very next day, the September 11 attacks occurred embroiling the US in a prolonged war on global terrorism. The war on terror took the Pentagon's attention firmly away from preparing for potential threats from the high ground of space. Instead, the Pentagon's best minds and resources were focused on finding underground locations in Afghanistan and other potential places where Islamic extremists were allegedly plotting the next terrorist strike. Was it just unfortunate timing or was September 11 a false flag event contrived by a mysterious "Deep State" determined to prevent the Space Corps from being birthed in order to facilitate a future Space Pearl Harbor?

What is truly intriguing about the creation of Space Force is its connection to the television and movie industry. After President Trump authorized the Pentagon to formally start the process of creating Space Force on June 18, 2018, key figures in the entertainment industry began developing ideas for a series to mock Trump's new branch of military service. This resulted in Netflix announcing a new sitcom featuring Steve Carrol as the first head of Space Force. The Netflix series aired on May 29, 2020, six months after Space Force's official launch. It depicted the new military service as the half-baked bungling afterthought of an erratic President. All laughs aside, the series had a very serious side effect. It appeared to set the foundation for Space Force to be defunded or even abolished as prominent Democratic Party activists called for the demise of Space Force during and after the 2020 Presidential Election. Was the Netflix series part of yet more opposition by "Deep State" officials to undermine Space Force's ongoing creation?

After choosing its logo, adopting a flag, acquiring its first recruits, gaining several space bases, and releasing core doctrinal documents, Space Force leaders decided on a name for its service members. They would henceforth be called "Guardians," allegedly to honor Air Force tradition dating back to 1983 with Air Force Space Command's motto of "Guardians of the High Frontier." Coming after the Netflix series, many jokingly thought the name was a nod to the pop culture classic film *Guardians of the Galaxy*. After the laughs subsided, one thing was clear about the name, it illustrated how the new service's members wanted to view themselves. Space Force's Guardians would in future protect the US and its allies from space threats, whether from foreign national adversaries such as China or Russia, or even alien life. While the Netflix series and "Deep State" opponents depicted Space Force as a joke, undeserving of serious funding or backing, the numerous space experts supporting it were very serious about Space Force's intrepid future.

This raises yet another intriguing pop culture reference concerning Space Force and what lies ahead. It involves its connection to a Star Trek future actively being planned by Pentagon officials. In a 'Space Futures Conference' convened by the US Air Force's Space Command in August 2019, eight possible futures were identified. The most optimal scenario was a "Star Trek future," and its main features were outlined for future planning efforts by the Air Force and space experts. Not surprisingly, the creation of a multinational military space alliance, a modern-day "Starfleet," was critical to bringing about the much desired Star Trek future. In 2020, the Artemis Accords and NATO took major steps towards the birthing of such a multinational space alliance under US leadership.

PREFACE

What makes the creation of a Star Trek future and a modern-day Starfleet even more fascinating is the possibility that Gene Rodenberry was given unofficial briefings in 1964-1965 about the imminent US Navy secret space program actively being planned at the time. Could Rodenberry have been secretly briefed about a future Navy space program that would operate much as was depicted in his *Star Trek* series? Was Rodenberry's fictional Starfleet actually modeled on projections of a Navy space program being designed and built in the 1960s and 1970s? Even more breathtaking, was the US Navy clandestinely working with human-looking extraterrestrials that were part of a Federation of Planets as multiple whistleblowers have claimed? Regardless of the answers to such questions, one thing is crystal clear: the creation of the US Space Force is part of a decades-long effort to create an independent military space service that would act as the fulcrum for a multinational space alliance to protect the US and its allies against space adversaries. Despite great opposition, Space Force is now an official part of the US military, and its emergence lays a solid foundation for our Star Trek future.

Michael Salla, Ph.D.
March 31, 2021

CHAPTER 1

2001 Commission Warns of Future Space Pearl Harbor

If the US is to avoid a 'space Pearl Harbor,' it needs to take seriously the possibility of an attack on US space systems.

— 2001 Space Commission Report

In July 2000, China's Xinhau news agency made the startling announcement that the People's Liberation Army was "developing methods and strategies for defeating the US military in a high-tech and space-based future war."[1] The official mouthpiece of China's Communist Party went even further by openly acknowledging that "for countries that could never win a war by using the method of tanks and planes, attacking the US space system may be an irresistible and most tempting choice."[2] The surprising statement from such an authoritative Chinese news source caught many US policy makers completely off guard. The dominant viewpoint held by President Bill Clinton, and shared by the earlier Bush and Reagan administrations, was that by giving China open access to US high-tech industries, commercial markets, and allowing tens of thousands of Chinese students to enroll in elite graduate schools, that China would gravitate towards a more open and democratic society. It was further hoped that such generous policies would lead to China peacefully cooperating with the US in managing global affairs.[3]

Unfortunately, the May 7, 1999 NATO bombing of Yugoslavia, that "accidently" struck the Chinese Embassy in Belgrade, Serbia, killing three Chinese journalists had put a dent in such hopes. China's authorities and general public were understandably furious. President Clinton apologized directly to China's President Jiang Zemin on May 14, and "called the bombing an isolated and tragic event and insisted it was not deliberate."[4] China's leaders, on the contrary, believed the bombing was a deliberate act designed to send China a clear message – stay in line with the emerging New World Order or else. Military strategists in the People's Liberation Army were henceforth encouraged to think of a long-term strategic approach that would enable China to adequately respond to future US military provocations. Consequently, the 1999 China Embassy bombing provides valuable context for understanding why, only a year later, China was boldly stating for all the world to see that it was looking for ways to exploit US strategic vulnerabilities in a future space war.

Developing a long-term national security response to the troubling Xinhua News Agency announcement became the immediate responsibility of the newly formed "Commission to Assess United States National Security Space Management and Organization" (aka Space Commission), which had been authorized in the National Defense Authorization Act for Fiscal Year 2000.[5] The Space Commission began meeting for the first time in July 2000, and quickly took note of China's announcement that it was now seeking to exploit US vulnerabilities in space.

Space Commission members had been appointed in a bipartisan basis by the ranking members from both parties sitting on the Armed Services committees of the House of Representatives and Senate, along with the Secretary of Defense and the Director of the CIA, both of whom were Clinton appointees. It would therefore be accurate to describe the Space Commission as a bipartisan attempt initiated by Congress and the Clinton Administration to develop a comprehensive roadmap to achieving space security, at a time when both China and Russia were boosting research and development of offensive space weapons designed to overwhelm the US satellite grid. Consequently, the origins of the United States Space Force (USSF) can be directly traced back to the final report written by the "Space Commission," which was delivered nine days before President Bill Clinton ended his second term of office on January 20, 2001.

In its January 11, 2001 report, the Space Commission unanimously agreed that US national interests were bolstered by ramping up space security to protect its vital assets:

> Therefore, it is in the U.S. national interest to:
>
> • Promote the peaceful use of space.
>
> • Use the nation's potential in space to support its domestic, economic, diplomatic and national security objectives.
>
> • Develop and deploy the means to deter and defend against hostile acts directed at U.S. space assets and against the uses of space hostile to U.S. interests.[6]

The Space Commission explained the vulnerability of US space assets and how these form attractive targets for hostile states:

> Those hostile to the U.S. possess, or can acquire on the global market, the means to deny, disrupt or destroy U.S. space systems by attacking satellites in space, communications links to and from the ground or ground stations that command the satellites and process their data. [7]

The Space Commission goes on to point out that a "Space Pearl Harbor" attack from a major adversary is not "an improbable act":

> An attack on elements of U.S. space systems during a crisis or conflict should not be considered an improbable act. If the U.S. is to avoid a "Space Pearl Harbor" it needs to take seriously the possibility of an attack on U.S. space systems. The nation's leaders must assure that the vulnerability of the United States is reduced and that the consequences of a surprise attack on U.S. space assets are limited in their effects.[8]

The Commission highlighted the July 2000 report from the Xinhua news agency on how China's asymmetric military strategy plans to leverage US space vulnerabilities "in a high-tech and space-based future war."[9] The Space Commission emphasized the danger in ignoring warning signs that China or another space adversary may take such action against US space assets in a surprise strike:

> History is replete with instances in which warning signs were ignored and change resisted until an external, "improbable" event forced resistant bureaucracies to take action. The question is whether the U.S. will be wise enough to act responsibly and soon enough to reduce U.S. space vulnerability. Or whether, as in the past, a disabling attack against the country and its people—a "Space Pearl Harbor"—will be the only event able to galvanize the nation and cause the U.S. Government to act.

> We are on notice, but we have not noticed.[10]

It is worth emphasizing that as early as 2001, US national security specialists were pointing out their concerns about China's rapid technological development, and it developing the capacity to launch a Space Pearl Harbor as part of its core military strategy. Many Space Commission members felt that these clear warning signs were not being heeded, and there was not enough preparation for a Space Pearl Harbor. In particular, General Ronald Fogleman, a newly retired USAF Chief of Staff (1994 -1997) and prominent Commission member was interviewed about the danger of a surprise attack in space:

> There was complete agreement among the commissioners that "we are going to see conflict in space," Fogleman noted. "Anybody who thinks we aren't has got his head in the sand." The US dependence on space is a "glaring vulnerability," he said. The nation hasn't done enough to prepare against an attack on US space assets, the commission decided. . . .

> However, the commission believed there would be a sudden move toward a Space Force if there was a "catastrophic event, . . . a potential Pearl Harbor in space," observed Fogleman. There would be immediate finger-pointing and a furious public, demanding to know, "Why did we not prevent this? Where did the failure occur? . . . Why were you not prepared for that? Why were weapons not developed?" Preparations should begin long before that happens, the commission warned.[11]

The Space Commission was very critical of how the US Air Force dealt with space operations. According to the reporter John

Tirpak who wrote about the Space Commission report for *Air Force Magazine* on March 1, 2001:

> The commission was launched by members of Congress who feel the Air Force is not paying sufficient attention to space, nor allocating enough resources to pursue a suitably strong military space presence. Some members, particularly Sen. Bob Smith (R-N.H.), consistently charged the Air Force with shortchanging space to keep money flowing to aircraft programs.
>
> The commission seemed to agree with this assessment.
>
> "Few witnesses before the commission expressed confidence that the current Air Force organization is suited to the conduct of these [space] missions," said the report. "Nor was there confidence that the Air Force will fully address the requirement to provide space capabilities for the other services. Many believe the Air Force treats space solely as a supporting capability that enhances the primary mission of the Air Force to conduct offensive and defensive air operations. Despite official doctrine that calls for the integration of space and air capabilities, the Air Force does not treat the two equally. As with air operations, the Air Force must take steps to create a culture within the service dedicated to developing new space system concepts, doctrine, and operational capabilities." [12]

In order to fully prepare for future contingencies in space, prevent any surprise attacks by China or another space adversary, and deal with the failure of the USAF to give space operations the proper attention they deserved, the Commission report provided five remedies. First, transforming US defense capabilities in space; second, strengthening intelligence collection capabilities; third, shaping international opinion to support weaponizing space for peaceful defense purposes; fourth, ensuring US technological dominance in vital aerospace industries; and finally, establishing a "cadre of Space Professionals." In the latter regard, the Space Commission recommended:

> Military space professionals will have to master highly complex technology; develop new doctrine and concepts of operations for space launch, offensive and defensive space operations, power projection in, from and through space and other military uses of space; and operate some of the most complex systems ever built and deployed.[13]

The Space Commission examined the idea of creating a Department for Space but decided the time was not yet ripe, and an intermediate position could be reached by making adjustments to the current Pentagon bureaucracy:

> The use of space in defense of U.S. interests may require the creation of a military department for space at some future date. A Space Department would provide strong advocacy for space and a single organization with the primary mission of providing forces for conducting both military and intelligence space operations. However, the Commission believes that the disadvantages of creating a department today outweigh the advantages for a number of reasons, including that

there is not yet a critical mass of qualified personnel, budget, requirements or missions sufficient to establish a new department. Meanwhile, near- and mid-term organizational adjustments should be fashioned so as to not preclude eventual evolution toward a Space Department if that proves desirable.[14]

The recommended organizational change was the creation of a "Space Corps" to become a military service within the Department of the Air Force that would eventually evolve into an independent Space Department:

> A Space Corps within the Department of the Air Force may be an appropriate model in its own right or a useful way station in the evolution toward a Space Department. One model is the Army Air Force's relationship to the Army during World War II. Existing Air Force space forces, facilities, units and personnel, and military space missions could be transferred to a Corps. A Space Corps could have authority for acquisition and operation of space systems, perhaps to include both DoD [Department of Defense] and Intelligence Community systems, while leveraging existing Air Force logistics and support functions.[15]

During World War II, it was decided that the Army Air Force needed complete autonomy from the US Army in order to optimize manpower and resources for the war effort. Consequently, both the Army and Army Air Force operated as separate military services under the Department of War until September 1947 when the National Security Act created a Department of the Air Force. Now the Air Force could compete on equal footing with the Army and the Navy in gaining congressional funding for future military projects and acquisitions.

The creation of a Space Corps would require adding a senior official within the Pentagon whose job would be to support the new service in gaining the necessary funding to meet its core responsibilities:

> An Under Secretary of Defense for Space, Intelligence and Information (USD (SII)) would provide policy, guidance and oversight for space in a single organization within the Office of the Secretary of Defense. . . . The USD (SII) would help ensure that space related issues are addressed in the Department at an appropriately influential level. This is particularly important in the near term to help advance the development of new space missions and associated forces.[16]

An approximate timeline of five to ten years was provided by the Commission for the creation of the Space Corps that would be highly contingent on circumstances:

> The Commission believes that once the realignment in the Air Force is complete, a logical step toward a Space Department could be to transition from the new Air Force Space Command to a Space Corps within the Air Force. This would be, in essence, an evolution much like that of the Army's air forces from the Army Air Corps, into the Army Air Forces and eventually into the Department of the Air Force. The timetable, which is not possible to predict,

would be dictated by circumstances over the next five to ten years. [17]

It is important to emphasize the critical role played by Donald Rumsfeld, who was appointed Chairman of the Commission, making its recommendations for a Space Corps. Rumsfeld's official background and multiple claims of his involvement in highly classified programs involving reverse engineering captured UFOs and other advanced technologies, provides important context for why he championed the creation of a Space Corps.

Donald Rumsfeld's UFO Background & its Relevance to a Space Corps

Rumsfeld was a former Secretary of Defense under President Gerald Ford (1975-1977) and was about to begin an unprecedented second term (2001-2006) with the George W. Bush administration. What is most intriguing about Rumsfeld's professional background and interest in outer space is that while serving in the US House of Representatives, he took an active interest in UFOs as both a scientific curiosity and a national security threat.

Rumsfeld's involvement in the UFO issue is a matter of the public record, and dates back to July 29, 1968 when he attended in an official capacity the Symposium on Unidentified Flying Objects that was held before the House of Representatives Committee on Science and Astronautics.[18] At the time, Rumsfeld was in his third term as a representative for the State of Illinois (1963-1969), and was serving as a member of Science and Astronautics Committee. His military experience as a naval aviator from 1955-1958, and subsequent service as a member of the US Naval Reserve where he reached the rank of Captain, made him an ideal candidate for the

Committee. Rumsfeld addressed the Committee featuring some of the most well recognized UFO experts of the era presenting the best available evidence about the reality of the phenomenon

Due to his naval aviator background, Rumsfeld was certainly aware that UFOs were treated by the Pentagon as much more than a mere scientific curiosity. As a Navy pilot, he was aware of Joint Army-Navy-Air Force Publication (JANAP) 146(c) that required pilots to report UFO sightings that had national security implications to the Canadian-United States Communications Instructions for Reporting Vital Intelligence Sights (CIRVIS) reporting system. Those UFO sightings with national security significance were relayed on to a joint Pentagon CIA entity for further action, while other UFO reports were sent to the Air Force's Project Bluebook for public release and debunking. This secret two-tiered UFO reporting system was revealed in a letter written by Brigadier General Bolender that was eventually released by the Freedom of Information Act in 1979.[19]

Rumsfeld left Congress in January 1969 to begin an appointment to head the US Office of Economic Opportunity and also serving as a counsellor to President Nixon from 1969 to 1973, where he had Cabinet level rank. Rumsfeld's position as a Counsellor to the President involved far more than merely economic advice. Rumsfeld played a key role in advising Nixon about UFOs, and what national security steps were being taken behind the scenes to deal with them. This is confirmed by Clark McClelland, who worked for multiple NASA contractors before being employed as a Spacecraft Operator (ground astronaut) in a 35-year NASA career that spanned from 1958 to 1993. His detailed knowledge of NASA space missions, close personal relationship with astronauts and scientists, and familiarity with the UFO topic, led to him hearing first-hand UFO reports from NASA astronauts, scientists, and Very Important Persons (VIPs). One of these VIPs was the comedian Jackie Gleason who was a supporter and close personal friend of President Richard Nixon. Gleason met McClelland and was greatly impressed by his intimate knowledge of NASA missions, and especially of what astronauts and scientists had confidentially shared about the UFO topic. The idea of extraterrestrial life fascinated Gleason who reportedly had the largest UFO library in the world at his home.

Gleason confidentially told McClelland all about his 1973 visit to Homestead Air Force Base (AFB) in Florida, where Nixon gave Gleason a guided tour of a classified facility housing the remnants of a crashed UFO and the bodies of dead aliens. The same core story was told by Gleason's second wife, Beverly, in an article she penned in 1983, eight years after their divorce.[20] McClelland's story had a vital additional detail to what Gleason's wife had earlier recounted: the important role played by Nixon's personal assistant in setting up the classified tour – Donald Rumsfeld. In his book, *Space! The Final Frontier*, McClelland wrote:

As they approached Homestead AFB, Florida, he [Nixon] . . . told Gleason they were going there to view alien creatures and their craft, which were stored in a secured area within a hangar at the Air Base. . . . They arrived at a security gate wend were stopped by a young M.P. . . . Gleason then added that a most trusted personal assistant (well known in US politics) of President Nixon stepped forth and greeted both men. Gleason knew the identity of this person and would not disclose the name to me for obvious reasons... This individual had preceded both of them to the base and had already cleared the President into Homestead Air Force Base. The Presidential Assistant was also apparently aware of what was stored there, Gleason said, with certain statements Nixon had made to him.

> Later, McClelland learned through an ONI [Office of
> Naval Intelligence] Naval Aviation Officer, visiting
> ONI at Patrick Air Force Base that this assistant was
> probably Captain Donald H. Rumsfeld, also a former
> Naval Aviator, 1954 -1957. . . . One could assume
> since he was a member of ONI and Rumsfeld
> apparently associated with such officers while
> "bending elbows" together they may have shared
> stories of strange events not heard by friends, family
> members or others.[21]

McClelland went on to describe Rumsfeld's subsequent appointment by Nixon as the 9th US Ambassador to NATO (1973-1974) and him being "in the know" regarding UFO/extraterrestrial events worldwide.[22]

Others have also come forward claiming Rumsfeld has long been associated with highly classified programs involving reverse engineering captured alien or other advanced technologies. Among these is Andrew Basiago, a licensed attorney from Washington State who claims that he participated in a classified (Defense) Advanced Research Projects Agency (aka DARPA) and CIA run project called "Project Pegasus", which involved teleportation and time travel technologies.[23] The alleged technologies not only facilitated viewing past and future events, but also the instantaneous point to point transfers of personnel and equipment in the late 1960s and early 1970s. Basiago claims that Rumsfeld was involved as a Pentagon liaison to Project Pegasus and helping child participants gain eventual entry into prestigious military academies, which could be used as covers for their future covert activities:

> Secretary Rumsfeld was explaining to my father – he
> literally said: "What we plan to do with the kids is in

high school, we're going to admit them to the Naval Academy, as first-year plebes, when they graduate from high school; and we'll use that as a pretext for involving them in future project activities." So there, in 1971/72, they were already planning for what our destiny was going to be in the fall of 1979. And Rumsfeld was aware of what the major plan was.[24]

If Basiago is correct, then Rumsfeld's involvement with Project Pegasus occurred while he was an advisor to President Nixon, which correlates with what McClelland was told by Gleason about Rumsfeld arranging the clandestine visit to Homestead AFB later in 1973. Perhaps even more significant is the idea that Rumsfeld was involved in strategizing how best to strategically place child participants from these classified projects in the Navy or other military services. This raises an intriguing question. Was part of the reason for Rumsfeld's subsequent support in 2000-2001 for the creation of a Space Corps predicated on his knowledge that a clandestine astronaut corps already existed involving participants from highly classified programs dating back to the late 1960s, who had access to or were using reverse engineered alien technologies in one or more secret space programs?

Regardless of the truth behind multiple claims of Rumsfeld's involvement in classified reverse engineering projects and associated secret space programs, there is no doubt over his importance to ensuring the success of the Space Commission's January 2001 recommendations. His vital role was acknowledged by John Tirpak, who wrote in his March 1, 2001 *Air Force Magazine* article:

Over the past decade, military space has generated a stream of reports from blue-ribbon panels. However, the recommendations of this one could carry considerable weight because its chairman, Donald H. Rumsfeld, has become Secretary of Defense. . . . Rumsfeld resigned as chairman of the panel when President Bush tapped him to head the Pentagon, a scant two weeks before the commission published its final Report. However, the Report is said to reflect much of Rumsfeld's thinking on space organization issues and could well serve as a blueprint for reorganization of military space.[25]

There was high confidence among Commission members that legislation for a Space Corps was imminent due to Rumsfeld's appointment as Secretary of Defense, which was scheduled to begin on January 20, 2001. Rumsfeld's role led to General Fogelman publicly stating the creation of a Space Corps was imminent:

The commission's chairman—Donald Rumsfeld—is now the Secretary of Defense, and so military space issues are fresh in his mind, said Fogleman. He added that some sort of restructuring likely will happen soon.

"If I were a betting man, I would bet you that in the [Defense Department] legislative proposal that comes to the Hill this year, this will be in there," Fogleman said. [26]

Rumsfeld's intentions for Congressional legislation that would set up Space Corps and other innovative Pentagon proposals recommended by the Space Commission report were signaled in a major speech he gave on September 10, 2001. Unfortunately, the calamitous events of the next day, completely derailed the bipartisan effort to have Congress move forward with legislation establishing a Space Corps. It would be almost eighteen years before the proposals advocated in the Space Commission report would finally see the light of day in the form of Congressional legislation. The long delay is noteworthy. Was the proposed Space Corps an unfortunate casualty of the September 11 terrorist attack, or was it an intended target? Was there a Deep State operating within the US political system not wanting the Pentagon taking any steps that would jeopardize closely guarded covert space activities, and prevent a future Space Pearl Harbor?

Chapter 2

The Empire Strikes Back - 9/11 Attacks Delay Space Force

The Towers didn't burn up, nor did they slam to the ground. They turned (mostly) to dust in mid air.

— Dr Judy Wood, Where Did the Towers Go?

In the first months of the George W. Bush Presidency, there was bipartisan support for the establishment of a US Space Corps as recommended by the 2001 Space Commission. Donald Rumsfeld's chairmanship of the Commission, his firm advocacy of a Space Corps in Commission discussions, and his subsequent appointment as Secretary of Defense made it all but certain that legislation authorizing the Space Corps' creation would be forthcoming in the new administration. This was confirmed at the time by former USAF Chief of Staff, General Fogelman in an interview he gave to John Tirpak from *Air Force Magazine*.[27] As long as circumstances remained propitious, the Space Commission Report estimated it would take five to ten years to set up the proposed Space Corps.[28] The Commission's warning that a "Space Pearl Harbor" should "not be considered an improbable act" would compel policy makers to take the necessary preventative action by creating the recommended space service.[29] Then something unexpected happened on September 10, one day before the momentous attacks on New York's World Trade Center and the Pentagon. Rumsfeld launched a David and Goliath style battle with the Pentagon bureaucracy over massive funding irregularities.

Rumsfeld gave a press conference where he stated the Pentagon could not account for 2.3 trillion dollars in the fiscal year 1999.[30] This was money that could not be tracked by the Pentagon Inspector General, who had described similar auditing anomalies with the Pentagon budget in 1998 and 2000. [See Figure 1] These auditing anomalies involved sums of money that vastly exceeded the sums being secretly moved through the Pentagon to fund the Intelligence Community. In chapter 7, I will discuss the unique legal authority allowing the CIA and its Director to generate an official "black budget" to fund the Intelligence Community by funneling Congressional appropriations in ways designed to hide the source of funds, and where the funds were going. The intent behind the statutes authorizing this was to allow the Intelligence Community to operate without foreign governments learning anything about the funding of US intelligence agencies and their respective programs.

In his September 10, 2001 speech, Rumsfeld declared war on the Pentagon bureaucracy, and highlighted the legislative reforms he was about to initiate to streamline the way funds were being poorly used for defense purposes, and instead shuffled around the bureaucracy in unaccountable ways. Rumsfeld was effectively taking on the CIA as it laundered money through the Pentagon for funding highly classified projects in addition to its statutory authority for funding the Intelligence Community:

> The topic today is an adversary that poses a threat,
> a serious threat, to the security of the United States
> of America. This adversary is one of the world's last
> bastions of central planning, governs by dictating 5
> year plans. A single capital that it attempts to

impose its command over time zones, continents, oceans, and beyond. With brutal consistency it stifles free thought and crushes new ideas, disrupts the defenses of the United States and places the lives of men and women in uniform at risk. Perhaps this adversary sounds like the Soviet Union, but that enemy is gone. Our foes are more subtle and implacable today.

DOD - Unsupported Accounting Entries 1998-2000

Fiscal Year	Unsupported Entries USD	Inspector General Quotes
2000	1.1 trillion	"department-level accounting entries of $1.1 trillion were unsupported or improper."[i]
1999	2.3 trillion	"department-level accounting entries of $2.3 trillion ... did not follow accounting principles."[ii]
1998	1.7 trillion	"a record $1.7 trillion of unsupported adjustments were made in preparing the statements."[iii]

Figure 1. Inspector General comments on auditing irregularities. Extracted from The Black Budget Report.[31]

You might think I'm describing one of the last decrepit dictators in the world, but their day too is almost past and they cannot match the strength and size of this adversary. The adversary is closer to home, it's the Pentagon bureaucracy. Not the people but the processes, not the civilians but the systems, not the men and women in uniform but the uniformity of thought and action that we too often impose on them. In this building, despite the era of scarce resources, taxed by amounting threats, money disappears into duplicative duties, bloated bureaucracy, not because of greed but gridlock. Innovation is stifled not by ill intent but institutional inertia.[32]

Never before had a Secretary of Defense so pointedly criticized the Pentagon bureaucracy in the way Rumsfeld was doing. His extraordinary speech echoed President Dwight D. Eisenhower's famous January 17, 1961 farewell address where he warned about the power of the Military Industrial Complex. Rumsfeld made clear that in criticizing the Pentagon bureaucracy, he was not attacking the individual military services or the men and women in uniform but the opaque bureaucratic process that stifled innovation and frustrated the implementation of necessary reforms such as the 2001 Space Commission Report. The real target of Rumsfeld's vehement attack was the vast sums of money flowing through the Pentagon, to highly classified reverse engineering and space related projects protected under layers of bureaucracy from Rumsfeld and the chiefs of the different military services:

We know the adversary, we know the threat. And with the same firmness with purpose that any effort against a determined adversary demands, we must get at it and stay at it. Some might ask me how in the world could the Secretary of Defense attack the Pentagon in front of its people. To them, I reply I have no desire to attack the Pentagon, I want to liberate it. We need to save it from itself. The men and women of this department, civilians and military are our allies, not our enemies. They too are fed up with bureaucracy. They too live with frustration, I hear it every day. . . .

We are, as they say, tangled in our anchor chain. Our financial systems are decades old. According to some estimates, we cannot track 2.3 trillion dollars in transactions. We cannot share information from floor to floor in this building because it's stored on dozens of different technological systems that are inaccessible or incompatible. We maintain 20-25 percent more base infrastructure than we need to support our forces. At an annual waste to tax payers of some 3-4 billion dollars. Fully half of our resources go to infrastructure and overhead and in addition to draining resources from war fighting, these costly and outdated systems, procedures, and programs stifle innovation as well. . . .[33]

Critically, Rumsfeld went on to announce legislative initiatives he would undertake with Congress to steer money hidden away in the bureaucracy towards innovative defense projects that would directly assist the different military services to meet 21st century challenges:

To that end, we are announcing today a series of steps the Department of Defense will take to shift our focus and our resources from bureaucracy to battlefield, from tail to tooth. Today's announcements are only the first of many. We will launch others ourselves and we will ask Congress for legislative help as well. [34]

Among the legislative actions being contemplated by Rumsfeld was the creation of a Space Corps that would be essential for meeting future threats such as a Space Pearl Harbor as clearly outlined by the Space Commission report. Unfortunately, what happened the next day on September 11, 2001, led to the effective shelving of a Space Corps for nearly two decades.

Rumsfeld's extraordinary September 10 speech makes clear that he was among a group of Pentagon reformers, or "White Hats," wanting to get control over the vast sums flowing through the Pentagon to fund innovative new defense projects recommended in the 2001 Space Commission Report. Understanding the true intent of Rumsfeld's September 10 speech, the war he was declaring against the Pentagon bureaucracy, his support for innovative Pentagon projects such as Space Corps; and finally, his clandestine involvement in highly classified reverse engineering projects, is vital context when it comes to understanding the full significance of what was happening with the September 11, 2001 attacks. If Rumsfeld's speech was a declaration of war against the "Evil Empire" of the Pentagon bureaucracy, then September 11 represented the Empire striking back.

The September 11 Attacks and the Evil Empire

There is compelling evidence that the September 11 attacks were not solely a result of terrorist actions orchestrated from caves in Afghanistan by Osama Bin Laden and Al Qaeda, but were a "false flag attack" involving significant elements of the US government. There are several compelling facts supporting such a disturbing conclusion. First is that there were two known exercises simulating a terrorist attack scheduled for the morning of September 11, "Vigilant Warrior" and "Vigilant Guardian." This created much confusion for NORAD pilots, as exemplified in the transcript of a conversation between the FAA's Boston Center and a military official due to highly unusual aerial activity that was occurring:

> FAA Boston Center . . . "We need someone to scramble some F-16s or something up there, help us out."
>
> "Is this real world or an exercise?" asked the military liaison officer.
>
> "No, this is not an exercise," responded the FAA official. "Not a test."[35]

Defensive military aviation units such as NORAD stood down for well over an hour believing the attacks were part of a scheduled military exercise.[36]

Second, the 47-story skyscraper, Building 7 (aka WTC 7) of the World Trade Center, collapsed at freefall speed late in the afternoon despite not being hit by any planes and not having any large fires affecting it. It allegedly collapsed due to "ancillary damage" caused by the collapse of the twin towers, despite WTC 7 and the towers being separated by another building (WTC 6) and Vessey Street.[37] Civil engineers have shown through exhaustive analysis that the official explanation from the 9/11 Commission that WTC 7 collapsed due to such ancillary damage was impossible.[38] Analysis of the video evidence shows that the collapse of Building 7 was in fact a controlled demolition. The mysterious collapse of Building 7 is arguably the strongest evidence that the September 11 attacks widely attributed to Islamic terrorists, were false flag events.

Finally, the expected debris of the massive twin towers was largely absent and appeared to undergo a process of "dustification," a process that puzzled civil engineers. Dr. Judy Woods, a former professor of mechanical engineering, conducted a detailed study of the available evidence which she presented in her groundbreaking book, *Where Did the Towers Go? Evidence of Directed Free-energy Technology on 9/11.*[39] In it, she concluded that the dustification of much of the World Trade Center could be not be explained by airplanes loaded with jet fuel or other conventional explanations. She instead concluded that Directed Energy Weapons, likely deployed from space, were used to dustify the twin towers.

These and many other anomalies surrounding the September 11 attacks have led to multiple groups and experts concluding the attacks were in fact a false flag event orchestrated by those with the powerful influence of the US government and military institutions. This takes us to the idea of a Deep State that was behind the September 11 false flag attacks. The basic idea is that the Deep State comprises an 'invisible' or 'shadow government' that manipulates elected officials, the mass media, and the general public through blackmail, coercion and false flag events it orchestrates from behind the scenes. In chapter 11, I will discuss the origins, methods and membership of the *Deep State* and why Space Force poses a threat to its existence.

Given Rumsfeld's leadership role in proposing the creation of a Space Corps, his subsequent second appointment as Secretary of Defense, and his exposure of the missing trillions, a question that can be asked is: Was a key goal of the Deep State in launching the September 11 attack, was to stop the proposed Pentagon reforms, including the creation of a Space Corps designed to stop a future Space Pearl Harbor from happening? If so, then it appears that a Space Pearl Harbor is a contingency anticipated since at least 2001, and the Deep State laid the groundwork for U.S. officials openly acknowledging such a threat, while effectively doing nothing to prevent it. As I will later discuss, predictive programing is an important aspect of how the Deep State operates. Whatever the precise relationship between Rumsfeld, the missing trillions, funding a Space Corps, and the September 11 attacks are, one thing is clear: the subsequent war on terror led to the Pentagon prioritizing funding for expensive military interventions throughout the Middle East and North Africa. Potential funding for the creation of a Space Corps was shelved, until it was resurrected nearly two decades later by members of Congress and President Donald Trump.

Chapter 3

Space Corps Trumped by Space Force

'Maybe we need a new force. We'll call it the Space Force.' And I was not really serious. And then I said, 'What a great idea. Maybe we'll have to do that.'

— President Donald Trump, 3/13/2018.

On June 20, 2017, the Chair of the House of Representatives Armed Services Strategic Forces Subcommittee, Congressman Mike Rogers (R-Alabama), and its ranking minority leader, James Cooper (D-Tennessee), publicly revealed their proposal for the creation of a new military service to be called "Space Corps," which would be formed under the Department of the Air Force. The proposal was included in a bipartisan bill that was incorporated in the House of Representatives version of the National Defense Authorization Act (NDAA) for Fiscal Year 2018. The proposal was passed by the House of Representatives on July 14, 2017, and sent to the US Senate for further action.

Rogers and Cooper's collaboration on the creation of a Space Corps began in 2016, and was an attempt to resurrect the long-forgotten recommendation by the 2001 Space Commission to set up the new military service to prevent a future Space Pearl Harbor. In a December 2019 interview, Cooper brought up the Commission's nightmare scenario of a surprise military attack in space by a major adversary if the US did not take preventive action by setting up a dedicated military space service:

> We got so distracted by the war on terror that we didn't keep an eye on our solar system. . . . We're dangerously close to having slipped behind. We don't know with certainty because these are the most classified programs in the world, but it looks like these other nations have spent billions creating mischief. . . . Within minutes of the start of a new Pearl Harbor attack, we wouldn't feel anything on Earth, and suddenly we'd be deaf, dumb, blind, spastic and impotent."[40]

Unfortunately, the proposal encountered immediate opposition by key figures in the US Air Force and the Trump administration. The most vocal opponents were Heather Wilson, the Secretary of the Air Force, and General David Goldfein, the USAF Chief of Staff, who both addressed the US Senate Defense Appropriations Subcommittee on June 21, 2017, one day after Rogers and Cooper released their proposal. Secretary Wilson said: "The Pentagon is complicated enough . . . This will make it more complex, add more boxes to the organization chart and cost more money. If I had more money, I would put it into lethality, not bureaucracy."[41] General Goldfein echoed Wilson's opposition:

> If you're saying the words 'separate' and 'space' in the same sentence, I would offer, you're moving in the wrong direction. That's why the secretary and I are focused on how we integrate space. . . . Every

mission that we perform in the US military is dependent on space. Now is not the time to build seams and segregate and separate — now's the time to further integrate.[42]

Roughly two weeks later, the Trump White House added its voice to the opposition by releasing a statement saying "the creation of a separate Space Corps . . . is premature at this time."[43] On October 17, 2017, James Mattis, Secretary of Defense, wrote a letter to the US Senate where he joined Wilson and Goldfein in stating their opposition to Roger and Cooper's Space Corps proposal: "Space Corps: I oppose the creation of a new military service and additional organizational layers at a time when we are focused on reducing overhead and integrating joint warfighting efforts."[44] With the chorus of determined opposition from the Pentagon, the Space Corps' proposal failed to gain the necessary support it needed in the US Senate, and did not appear in the Senate version of the 2018 National Defense Authorization Act. It was subsequently dropped from the final version passed by both branches of Congress and signed into law by President Trump on December 12, 2017.

Why was there so much determined opposition to the idea of resuscitating the Space Corps proposal that was asserted back in 2001 to be a necessity in preventing a Space Pearl Harbor by China? One answer is the power of the pro-China lobby that was opposed to making China a national security priority, whether around the globe or in space throughout the first year of the Trump administration. This is confirmed by Brigadier General Robert Spalding (USAF ret.), who worked in the National Security Council (NSC), White House, from May 2017 to January 2018 as the Senior Director for Strategic Planning. He faced considerable pushback to his assertions that China was conducting extensive cyber hacking, corporate espionage, and that its 5G network was a dire national security threat. Spalding recommended elevating China to a higher national security threat status, but his policy advise went unheeded. President Trump was not briefed about Spalding's dire national security warnings despite the increasingly tough stance the former was taking on China's unfair trade policies. The pro-China lobby embedded within Trump's NSC/White House neutralized Spalding and forced him to resign. Frustrated by his White House experience, Spalding subsequently retired from the USAF and wrote a book about what needed to be done to adequately confront the dire threat posed by China across a number of areas.[45]

Less than three months after passage of the 2001 NDAA excluding the Space Corps proposal and Spalding's forced departure from his administration, Trump surprised everyone when he casually declared in a March 13, 2018, speech at the USMC Air Station Miramar, San Diego:

> My new national strategy for space recognizes that space is a war-fighting domain, just like the land, air, and sea. We may even have a Space Force. We have the Air Force. We'll have the Space Force. We have the Army, the Navy. You know, I was saying it the other day — because we're doing a tremendous amount of work in space — I said, 'Maybe we need a new force. We'll call it the Space Force.' And I was not really serious. And then I said, 'What a great idea. Maybe we'll have to do that.'[46]

Trump did not indicate any connection to or knowledge of the failed House proposal for a Space Corps that had been eliminated from the 2018 NDAA. Nor did he suggest any connection to the 2001 Space Commission's recommendations.

Then in May 2018, Trump made another casual reference to creating a Space Force as a new military service at an Army, Navy, Air Force football game:

> "You will be part of the five proud branches of the United States Armed Forces: Army, Navy, Marines, Air Force and the Coast Guard," Trump told the cadets. After a short pause he continued: "And we're actually thinking of a sixth, and that would be the Space Force. Does that make sense?"[47]

Trump was clearly discussing the creation of a Space Force with a small group of policy advisors and members of his administration that were brainstorming how to deal with future national security threats, especially China. This small group very likely included a long-time Pentagon senior consultant, Dr. Michael Pillsbury, who had advised Trump's presidential transition team. Pillsbury is an expert on Chinese history and military strategy, especially the modern-day application of the maxims of Sun Tzu, compiled in the famous book, *The Art of War*. Trump had years earlier shown his fondness for applying Sun Tzu's ideas to business and politics as demonstrated in July 2012, when he tweeted Sun Tzu's famous maxim, "The supreme art of war is to subdue the enemy without fighting."[48] Trump was so captivated by Pillsbury's policy advice that on September 27, 2018, he openly acknowledged Pillsbury as the "leading authority on China."[49]

The title of Pillsbury's best-selling book, *The Hundred Year Marathon China's Secret Strategy to Replace America as the Global Superpower*, encapsulates the policy advise Pillsbury was passing on to Trump.[50] The domination of space was a key part of China's global hegemony plan, so it is no surprise that with the help of Pillsbury and other military strategists, Trump proposed the creation of a Space Force.

SPACE FORCE – OUR STAR TREK FUTURE

For years, military strategists had been constrained from discussing space as a warfighting domain. The prevailing view of space was that it was a benign domain as defined in the 1967 Outer Space Treaty, which banned the placement of weapons of mass destruction in space, and the establishment of military bases on the Moon or other celestial bodies.[51] The dominant view of many US military strategists was that major US adversaries such as China and the Soviet Union only played lip service to the Outer Space Treaty, and were in fact actively planning for future military operations in space.

China's first test of an anti-satellite ballistic missile was in 2007, and has been followed in subsequent years by more secretive and sophisticated tests of antisatellite weapons. This confirmed the suspicions of many US military strategists that China was the developing the capacity for a future Space Pearl Harbor, just as predicted in the 2001 Space Commission Report.[52] China and Russia treated space as a warfighting domain and did not let the Outer Space Treaty restrain their military activities in space. The US was letting itself get overtaken by China and Russia if it maintained the status quo of considering space a benign domain as required by international law. Trump recognized in March 2018 that the US would have to adjust its thinking and consider space a warfighting domain, where the dictums of Sun Tzu would need to be applied.

Consequently, on June 18, 2018, President Trump gave a speech in which he recognized space as a "war-fighting domain" and officially called for the development of a United States Space Force (USSF), which would take over the current space functions of the US Air Force and other military services.[53] The proposed Space Force would become the sixth branch of the US military and would be placed under the administrative control of the Department of the Air Force, which is said to possess approximately 80% of all the US military space assets.[54] At the National Space Council meeting held at the White House on June 18, 2018, Trump said:

38

We must have American dominance in space. . . . I'm hereby directing the Department of Defense and Pentagon to immediately begin the process necessary to establish a Space Force as the sixth branch of the armed forces. . . . We are going to have the Air Force, and we are going to have the Space Force. Separate, but equal. It is going to be something so important.[55]

Trump then instructed General Joseph Dunford, Chairman of the Joint Chiefs of Staff, to "carry that assignment out."[56]

On August 9, 2018, Dunford and the Department of Defense (DoD) released a final report to the Congressional Defense Committees outlining the steps to be taken in implementing Trump's proposal. The "Final Report on Organizational and Management Structure for the National Security Space Components of the Department of Defense" identified two main phases for developing the Space Force through its four constituent components:

Establishing the Space Force will be multi-dimensional and phased. In this first phase, using existing authorities, the Department of Defense will establish several of the component parts of the Space Force. The second phase requires Congress to combine these components into the sixth branch of the Armed Forces. The Department of Defense is immediately pursuing four components:

- Space Development Agency – capabilities development and fielding,
- Space Operations Force – developing space leaders and joint space warfighters,

- Services and Support – leadership and support structures, and
- Space Command – developing Space Force warfighting operations to protect U.S. national interests.[57]

Each of the four components for the first phase subsequently began their implementation process through the Pentagon bureaucracy and did not require Congressional action.

On December 18, 2018, the last of the four components in the first phase of the Pentagon plan laying the foundation for a future Space Force moved forward with a Presidential Memorandum authorizing the creation of a United States Space Command:

> Pursuant to my authority as the Commander in Chief and under section 161 of title 10, United States Code, and in consultation with the Secretary of Defense and the Chairman of the Joint Chiefs of Staff, I direct the establishment, consistent with United States law, of United States Space Command as a functional Unified Combatant Command. I also direct the Secretary of Defense to recommend officers for my nomination and Senate confirmation as Commander and Deputy Commander of the new United States Space Command.[58]

Space Command had previously existed from 1985 to 2002, and was another prominent casualty of the September 11 attacks, where space was deemphasized in the new global war on terror.

Remarkably, two days after US Space Command was again set up as a Combatant Command, a key step in the formation of the proposed Space Force, the Secretary of Defense, General James

Mattis, submitted his resignation. His December 20, 2018, resignation letter cited unreconciled policy differences with President Trump: "Because you have the right to have a Secretary of Defense whose views are better aligned with yours on these and other subjects, I believe it is right for me to step down from my position."[59] Notably absent from the list of accomplishments cited in the letter was any mention of the creation of US Space Command or the setting up of Space Force as a new military service. Mattis was one of the critics for Roger and Cooper's 2017 Space Corps proposal, suggesting that opposition to Space Force was one of the reasons for his unexpected resignation.

On February 19, 2019, President Trump released Space Policy Directive-4, "Establishment of the United States Space Force," which explains the justification for creating a Space Force and formerly requested Congress to pass legislation officially creating the new service.[60] SPD-4 states:

> Section 1. Introduction. Space is integral to our way of life, our national security, and modern warfare. Although United States space systems have historically maintained a technological advantage over those of our potential adversaries, those potential adversaries are now advancing their space capabilities and actively developing ways to deny our use of space in a crisis or conflict. It is imperative that the United States adapt its national security organizations, policies, doctrine, and capabilities to deter aggression and protect our interests. Toward that end, the Department of Defense shall take actions under existing authority to marshal its space resources to deter and counter threats in space, and to develop a legislative proposal to establish a United States Space Force as

41

a sixth branch of the United States Armed Forces within the Department of the Air Force. This is an important step toward a future military department for space. [61]

What is highly significant in SPD-4 is that President Trump was affirming that the creation of Space Force would be a two-step process. First, it would be "initially established within the Department of the Air Force," which was vital for gaining Congressional and Air Force support for the creation of Space Force as a new military service.[62] The second step, the creation of a wholly independent Department of Space Force, would occur some years later. What has been left unsaid in Trump's SPD-4 is that the second step is critical because it is the only way in which the US Navy will agree to hand over authority for its deep space battle groups, which have been operating since the early 1980's, as I will explain in chapter 12. [63]

On March 8, 2019, less than a month after President Trump's SPD-4, Heather Wilson finally resigned as Secretary of the Air Force. Like Mattis before her, Wilson had firmly opposed the creation of a Space Corps when first proposed in 2017 by Congressmen Rogers and Cooper. She had attempted but failed to undercut Trump's efforts to set up a Space Force. According to *Foreign Policy*, her continued opposition led to Trump being on the verge of sacking her:

> Some senior officials know how to disagree with [the president] without being disagreeable to him. Heather Wilson hasn't managed to do that. Her opposition to the Space Force has grated on him and I think he permanently sees her as troublesome and ineffective now.[64]

Not long after Wilson's departure, the Air Force Chief of Staff, the third major Pentagon critic of an independent space service, similarly faced Trump's wrath if he did not come to terms with the creation of Space Force.

In a September 2019 speech, General Goldfein backtracked on his previous dismissal of Congressmen Rogers and Cooper's Congressional proposal for a Space Corps, and now explained that Trump's endorsement of a Space Force freed him to openly advocate for the new service. Goldfein explained that the importance of space as a warfighting domain was a topic he was not permitted to discuss two years earlier when Rogers and Cooper's Congressional Space Corps proposal was first introduced:

> "And it is also our job to bring on this new service"
> — the Space Force. "The president is actually giving us the gift, as the service that's passionate about air and space superiority. Here's the gift. Before his speech, I as chief [of the Air Force] could not stand on the stage and say the words 'space' and 'warfighting' in the same sentence. Forbidden. Prohibited from talking about it. Prohibited from planning about it. When the president stated openly that space is a warfighting domain, and we have to dominate that domain just like we do with every other domain, it opened the aperture for us to talk about what we as a service have been passionate about for years."[65]

Goldfein's speech is a remarkable admission. Why was the Air Force Chief of Staff forbidden to "say the words 'space' and 'warfighting' in the same sentence"? Why was he "prohibited from planning about it"? Who was stopping him and why? His superior in the

Pentagon Hierarchy, Secretary Heather Wilson, according to multiple reports, was the culprit.

Wilson had imposed a service-wide gag order on Air Force officials from talking about an independent Space Force.[66] Despite the gag order, one senior Air Force officer nevertheless decided to risk his career by publicly speaking out about the need for an independent Space Force, in a modern-day repeat of the famous Billy Mitchell incident. Brigadier General Mitchell is regarded by many as the father of the modern US Air Force due to his strident advocacy of an independent Air Force as early as 1925.[67] The Space Force's "Billy Mitchell" was Lt General Steven Kwast, Commander of Air Education and Training Command who spoke at several conferences, and wrote an opinion piece for *The Hill* explaining how the US was quickly losing its edge in space to China.[68] An independent Space Force was necessary to stop this trend according to Kwast who was the only Air Force officer to openly defy the gag order, as explained in *Breaking Defense*:

> The gag order worked – for more than a year, during the most important Air Force debate in a century — the majority of officers have held their tongue. While polls by Air Force Times suggest that a majority of Air Force officers favor a Space Corps, only one of them displayed the moral courage to speak truth to power. His courage opened the floodgates for others to follow, ultimately overturning the false impression of a monolithic Air Force intent on blocking Congress and blocking the Trump Administration. Kwast provides a powerful example of character and moral courage that all officers should emulate.[69]

Notable among the senior Air Force officers who abided by the gag order and did not follow Kwast's lead was General John "Jay" Raymond, Commander of Air Force Space Command. In his speech at the 35th Space Symposium held at Colorado Springs on April 12, 2019, less than two months after President Trump's SPD-4, Raymond did not mention Space Force, nor the need for an independent space service.[70] Indeed, in listening to his speech, one is left with the mistaken impression that Air Force Space Command was more than adequate to meet future space threats.

Kwast was an early favorite to become head of the proposed Space Force rather than Raymond, but Wilson targeted him in one of her final acts as Air Force Secretary in retaliation for violating the gag order. Lt. General Kwast was relieved of his Command halfway through his term and was blacklisted for promotion.[71] Unsuccessful appeals were made to President Trump to intervene:

> Unfortunately, unless President Trump acts quickly, Gen. Kwast will be unwillingly retired from his service because his vision for one of our most urgent national missions – the assured access to and use of outer space – aligned with the Commander-in-Chief's, but not that of the Air Force. The recently departed Secretary of the Air Force, Heather Wilson, made it her personal mission to terminate this highly accomplished general officer's career because he persuasively argued that America's vital interests in space are too important to be subordinated to the priorities of an institution preoccupied with manned aircraft and aerial warfare.[72]

Trump chose not to intervene likely due to his unwillingness to antagonize Pentagon leaders further over his push for Space Force's creation, and Kwast decided to take an early retirement in September 2019.

Lending their support to President Trump and Kwast's advocacy of an independent Space Force, was an influential group of retired USAF generals, Pentagon and State Department officials who in May 2019, wrote an "Open Letter in Support of Establishing the U.S. Space Force." In it they wrote:

> We endorse the position of General John Hyten, USAF, Commander of U.S. Strategic Command, who recently testified, "We're going to have a Space Force someday. I think what the Committee has to decide is when is that going to happen, and I think now is the time...you want to get ahead of the problem, not trail it, not come in response to a catastrophe. Get ahead of the problem." And we applaud the statement of General Joseph Dunford, USMC, Chairman of the Joint Chiefs of Staff, who recently testified, "My best military advice, given the importance of space and the consequences of not doing all we can to optimize the Department to move forward in space, would be to move out now with what might be the 80% solution, refine as we go, and the Committee will have an opportunity to provide oversight to address some of the issues that have been raised." Therefore, we strongly encourage action to establish the U.S. Space Force, to realize the full potential of space power and space capabilities in order to protect and advance U.S. vital national interests.[73]

On August 6, 2019, one of the signatories, Ambassador Henry F. Cooper wrote an article describing the hostility to the creation of Space Force by Secretary Wilson and other Air Force officials.[74] Wilson even continued her opposition from her new position as the President of the University of Texas in El Paso, where she continued to lobby against Space Force or its key components. Her position instead was that the Air Force urgently needed to expand the number of operational squadrons from 312 to 386.[75] A rather curious argument given the diminishing role of air power as space was fast becoming the new strategic high ground, as Chinese military strategists had clearly recognized over a decade earlier. Were Wilson and others acting independently or were they also being influenced by the powerful pro-China lobby that had forced the resignation of General Spalding in early 2018?

It is worth speculating here that the Deep State was opposed to Air Force discussions of space as the new strategic high ground and as a warfighting domain, since this threatened a clandestine long-term plan for China to launch a surprise "Space Pearl Harbor." This would help explain the gag order issued by Wilson on Air Force debates over Space Force, which stifled recognition of its importance in preventing a Space Pearl Harbor despite the clear warning of such an attack in the 2001 Space Commission Report. I will be discussing this possibility further in chapter 11. Nevertheless, the resignations of Secretary Mattis and Secretary Wilson, along with President Trump's SPD-4, cleared the path for General Goldfein to finally start discussing warfighting in space.

In response to Trump's SPD-4, the House of Representatives and the Senate passed two separate bills. The House version used the language and provisions of Rogers and Cooper's Space Corps 2017 legislative proposal. The Senate version used language and provisions provided by the Pentagon and Trump for creation of a Space Force. The final legislation passed by both branches of

Congress largely adopted the Space Force language and provisions in the Senate version. In December 2019, President Trump signed the 2020 National Defense Authorization Act officially creating Space Force as the sixth branch of the US military.

Chapter 4

Official Launch of Space Force

Space is the world's new war-fighting domain. Among grave threats to our national security, American superiority in space is absolutely vital. And we're leading, but we're not leading by enough, and very shortly we'll be leading by a lot.

– Donald J. Trump, at signing ceremony for
NDAA 2020 officially creating Space Force.
12/20/2019

O n December 20, 2019, President Donald Trump signed the Space Force Act into law. It was included in the omnibus 2020 National Defense Authorization Act (NDAA) that authorized funding Pentagon operations for another year, and officially created a sixth branch of the military – US Space Force (USSF), the others being the US Army, Navy, Air Force, Marine Corps and Coast Guard. Even before the new service was officially launched, however, there was controversy over a satirical Netflix show under production that would also be called Space Force.

Netflix's *Space Force* was depicted as the crazy unwanted brainchild of a bungling, ineffectual president that was an unwelcome addition to the Pentagon. The show's premise was a not too subtle dig at President Trump's June 18, 2018 announcement authorizing the Pentagon to take the necessary steps to launch the Space Force.[76] The comedian and lead actor for the new show, Steve Carell, is attributed as its co-creator, along with the series developer, Greg Daniels. Why would Carell, Daniels, and Netflix set out to demean and devalue the new military service only a few months after its official launch? Were the same forces that delayed the creation of Space Corps after the 2001 Space Commission's recommendation also behind setting up the new Netflix series that was released on May 29, 2020?

One explanation for the puzzling series of events that led to Netflix's *Space Force* is that coming less than six months before the 2020 presidential election, the series was setting the foundation for a new democratic president quickly abolishing Trump's creation. Indeed, this is evidenced in great pressure being exerted on the Democratic Party's presidential candidate, Joe Biden, leading up to and after the November 3 election by many Democrats who wanted Biden to cancel many Pentagon programs and abolish Trump's Space Force, as explained by *Politico*:

> Nearly three dozen progressive groups have appealed to President-elect Joe Biden to fold up the new Space Force and cancel major weapons, impose a cap on private contractors, and prohibit lobbyists from filling top Pentagon positions, according to a detailed blueprint sent to the transition team.[77]

Fortunately, the passage of the 2020 NDAA means that Space Force was officially authorized by Congress and is protected by statutory law. Space Force cannot be abolished by a future president without Congress's explicit approval.

In the NDAA, which is nearly 3500 pages long, the agreed-upon language for Space Force appears under Title IX – Department of Defense Organization and Management. Subtitle D discusses how Space Force will be set up and run. It begins with the relevant sections in the NDAA (Title IX, Subtitle D) authorizing Space Force's creation and what the authorizing act will be called in the future:

Subtitle D—United States Space Force

SEC. 951. SHORT TITLE.

This subtitle may be cited as the "United States Space Force Act".

SEC. 952. THE SPACE FORCE.

(a) REDESIGNATION.—The Air Force Space Command is hereby redesignated as the United States Space Force (USSF). [78]

Air Force Space Command had been originally set up in 1982 to develop and deploy Department of Defense satellites. AF Space Command's more secretive purpose, however, was to develop, deploy and monitor antigravity spacecraft, a process I will explain at length in the next chapter. By redesignating "Air Force Space Command" as the "United States Space Force (USSF)," the Space Force Act effectively brings the former to an end. Air Force Space Command was one of the Air Force's ten major commands (now nine). Air Force Space Command was headquartered at Peterson AFB Colorado, with 26,000 personnel located worldwide. These were concentrated at large facilities such as Schriever, Peterson, and Buckley AFBs in Colorado; Los Angeles and Vandenberg AFBs in California; and Patrick AFB in Florida. Most if not all of these Air Force Bases with significant space command units are expected to be renamed "Space Bases" (SB) as a result of the redesignation process.[79] Approximately 16,000 out of the 26,000 civilian and military personnel previously stationed at USAF Space Command facilities have transferred to the new Space Force.[80] Among Air

Force Space Command's primary responsibilities was the operation and protection of the US Global Positioning System (GPS), and the satellite systems used worldwide by the Pentagon for communications and weather forecasting.

Redesignation of Air Force Space Command as Space Force has initiated an 18-month process of transferring personnel and resources over to Space Force, which is scheduled to be completed by May 2021.[81] Like its predecessor, Space Force will be located within the Department of the Air Force as stipulated by the Space Force Act. This mirrors how the US Marine Corps is embedded within the Department of the Navy but remains a separate military branch to the US Navy. It is worth emphasizing that the composition of Space Force, as defined by the 2000 NDAA, is protected under statutory law and cannot be changed by any presidential executive action. Space Force's composition is described as follows:

> (b) COMPOSITION.—The Space Force shall be composed of the following:
>
> (1) The Chief of Space Operations.
>
> (2) The space forces and such assets as may be organic therein. [82]

The appointment and responsibilities of the Chief of Space Operations are explained as follows:

> '§ 9082. Chief of Space Operations
>
> "(a) APPOINTMENT.—(1) There is a Chief of Space Operations, appointed by the President, by and with the advice and consent of the Senate, from the general officers of the Air Force. The Chief serves at the pleasure of the President.

'(2) The Chief shall be appointed for a term of four years. In time of war or during a national emergency declared by Congress, the Chief may be reappointed for a term of not more than four years.

"(b) GRADE.—The Chief, while so serving, has the grade of general without vacating the permanent grade of the officer.

"(c) RELATIONSHIP TO THE SECRETARY OF THE AIR FORCE.—Except as otherwise prescribed by law and subject to section 9013(f) of this title, the Chief performs the duties of such position under the authority, direction, and control of the Secretary of the Air Force and is directly responsible to the Secretary. [83]

The last head of the Air Force Space Command (2016-2019), General John Raymond, became the first Chief of Space Operations (CSO) of Space Force. This enabled him to oversee the smooth transition of Air Force Space Command into the new Space Force. Back on April 14, 2015, General Raymond spoke at an annual Warfighters Lunch at a Space Symposium held at Colorado Springs and told the audience about the danger posed by China's growing antisatellite weapons capabilities: "Soon every satellite in every orbit will be able to be held at risk."[84] Raymond's thinking aligned closely with the 2001 Space Commission Report that warned about a future Space Pearl Harbor, which China and/or other foreign adversary could launch. There is no doubt that his views about space being a warfighting domain played a significant role in the choice by Air Force Chief of Staff, General Goldfein, to nominate him as the first CSO. As mentioned earlier, Goldfein had been constrained from talking about space as a warfighting domain due to a gag order put in place by former Air Force Secretary Heather

Wilson, despite President Trumps Space Policy Directive – 4 being released on February 19, 2019. After Wilson's resignation in May 2019, the gag order came to an end and Goldfein was able to freely speak. Similarly, Raymond was also constrained by the gag order as demonstrated in an April 12, 2019 speech he gave at the 35th Space Symposium at Colorado Springs where he did not mention Space Force nor did he discuss space as a warfighting domain.[85]

Figure 2. General John "Jay" Raymond

As CSO, General Raymond was in control of the administrative aspects of Space Force and would report directly to the Air Force Secretary. Operational control of Space Force would be exercised by the Commander of US Space Command, one of the eleven "Combatant Commands" that oversees all the operational aspects of the US military based in different geographical and functional fields.[86] From August 2019 to August 2020, General Raymond also held the position of Commander of US Space Command, but he relinquished this position to General James Dickenson in order to remain as Chief of Space Operations. At the change of command ceremony, General Dickenson told the audience that he shared similar ideas to Raymond concerning space being a warfighting domain: "Space is a warfighting domain, not because we want it to be, but because our adversaries have seen the advantages that space has provided to our way of life and our way of war and they continue to seek ways to hold our space assets at risk."[87] General Raymond became a statutory member of the Joint Chiefs of Staff on December 20, 2020 and was based at the Pentagon, from which he exercises administrative authority over Space Force, while General Dickenson is in charge of Space Force operations from his Space Command headquarters at Peterson AFB.[88] Put simply, while General Raymond ensures Space Force has all it needs to conduct warfighting operations in space, it

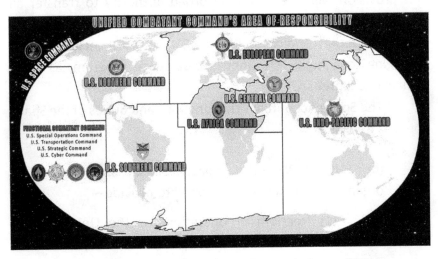

Figure 3. Map of Unified Combatant Commands. Source: DOD.

is General Dickenson that integrates and commands the assets of Space Force and the other military services in space warfighting operations.

The Space Force Act's reference to "assets as may be organic therein" as part of the initial composition of Space Force is left intentionally vague. Here's how Kyle Mizokami explains it in an article for *Popular Mechanics*:

> That's pretty ambiguous language but probably means most of the Air Force's space assets, from satellite launching facilities like Vandenberg Air Force Base in California to spacecraft ground control bases like Schriever Air Force Base in Colorado. It'll also include America's network of GPS satellites, the X-37B spaceplane, and other military space assets. The Space Force will also likely strip away a smaller number of assets and personnel from the U.S. Army and Navy.[89]

This provision will give Raymond broad authority to transfer all assets from the Air Force into Space Force over the 18-month transition period ending in May 2021. This will include assets belonging to a highly classified secret space program, as I will explain in chapter six.

The Space Act outlines the functions and duties of the Space Force as follows:

> (c) FUNCTIONS.—The Space Force shall be organized, trained, and equipped to provide—
>
>> (1) freedom of operation for the United States in, from, and to space; and
>> (2) prompt and sustained space operations.

(d) DUTIES.—It shall be the duty of the Space Force to—

(1) protect the interests of the United States in space;
(2) deter aggression in, from, and to space; and
(3) conduct space operations.[90]

The above functions and duties will give Space Force direct responsibility for protecting the civilian and military satellites that are the backbone of the Global Positioning Satellite (GPS) system that the Pentagon relies upon for its global communications, weather forecasting, and smart weapons systems. Traditionally, this protection was little more than merely monitoring the GPS and repositioning satellites from space debris since space was designated a benign environment.

The US GPS have recently come under direct threat by China which has developed the capacity to destroy all US satellites as exemplified in its 2007 antisatellite missile test. This developing capacity was a major concern of the 2001 Space Commission Report that warned about a future Space Pearl Harbor and China's determination to develop the infrastructure for such an attack. Space Force's first Chief of Space Operations, General Raymond is well aware of China's ability to conduct a surprise space attack as mentioned earlier regarding his 2015 Space Symposium speech warning that all US satellites were now at risk.[91] Raymond was among a growing group of senior Air Force officials that viewed space as a warfighting domain and wanted this to figure more prominently in future policy documents. More recently, in January 2018, a "Top Secret" report by the Pentagon Joint Staff intelligence directorate "revealed that both China and Russia have built anti-satellite missiles and other weapons and will soon be capable of damaging or destroying every US satellite in low earth orbit."[92]

The defense of the US military and civilian satellite infrastructure will be among the most important responsibilities of the Space Force for decades to come. Space Force will have to closely monitor and protect the US GPS, and similar satellite systems of allied nations, from any potential threat by major adversaries who are moving quickly forward in developing and deploying warfighting assets in space. But what space assets will Space Force use to achieve its critical defensive functions and duties as outlined in the Space Force Act?

This is where the Space Force Act's vague reference to "assets as may be organic therein" becomes relevant. This vague reference was intentionally used so the assets belonging to highly classified programs with cutting edge space technologies would be included in the transfer process. Lieutenant General Steven Kwast (USAF ret.) described some of the cutting-edge technologies developed in classified Air Force laboratories in a November 2019 lecture:

> The technology is on the engineering benches today. But most Americans and most members of Congress have not had time to really look deeply at what is going on here. But I've had the benefit of 33 years of studying and becoming friends with these scientists. This technology can be built today with technology that is not developmental to deliver any human being from any place on planet Earth to any other place in less than an hour.[93]

Less than a week before Trump signed the Space Force Act, the Secretary of the Air Force, Barbara Barrett, and Mike Rogers (R-Alabama), one of the two Congressmen who co-sponsored the original House version of the bill for creating a Space Corps, both called for the USAF to declassify the advanced space technologies it has developed. Barrett said: "Declassifying some of what is currently held in secure vaults would be a good idea. . . . You would have to be careful about what we declassify, but there is much more classified than what needs to be."[94] These highly classified space technologies are to be 'organically' incorporated into Space Force by May 2021—the end of the set-up period for Space Force. What do we know of the highly classified technologies that are being gradually transferred over to Space Force? This takes me to historic documents, and claims by multiple insiders, of a military space program with advanced antigravity craft of various designs that has been secretly developed by the US Air Force.

Figure 4. Barbara M. Barrett,
Secretary of the Department of US Air Force (2019-2021).

Chapter 5

USAF Reverse Engineered
Flying Saucers

We now have the technology to take ET home.

— Ben Rich, Lockheed Skunkworks

According to historic documents and multiple insider sources, the US Air Force has been directly involved in the research and development of a secret space program that possesses advanced antigravity propulsion technologies used primarily for intelligence gathering and covert operations worldwide and in space. In the *US Air Force Secret Space Program (2019)*, I presented extensive documentation and testimonies describing the different space assets developed by the Air Force's secret space program.[95] In sum, these include flying saucer shaped craft; triangle shaped craft; and flying rectangle shaped weapons platforms. The first of these advanced aerospace vehicles were reverse-engineered from captured Nazi era flying saucers and crashed extraterrestrial spacecraft first stored at Wright Patterson AFB, and later at the Area 51 facility called S-4. The craft were subsequently built by Lockheed Martin's Skunkworks and other major US aerospace companies at classified facilities such as Plant 42, a joint research and development complex located at Palmdale, California, next to Edwards AFB.

Rather than presenting again the extensive documents and testimonial evidence found in the *US Air Force Secret Space Program*, I have chosen instead to summarize ten undisputed historical facts supporting the existence of a highly classified reverse engineering program involving antigravity (flying saucer) craft, and its main elements. The factual statements will be presented in chronological order followed by a brief comment based on the body of insider testimony, leaked "Majestic" documents, and official Freedom of Information Act documents, which will help the reader appreciate the full significance of what subsequently happened. This should provide a solid overview of the reverse engineering efforts concerning advanced aerospace technologies covertly developed by the USAF.

Fact #1. Nazi Germany's advances in aviation technology were of immense interest to the US Army Air Force and Navy, both of which went to great efforts to acquire Nazi prototypes of craft capable of supersonic flight, and the scientists and engineers involved in their construction.

OFFERS TO BUILD 'FLYING SAUCER' FOR U. S.

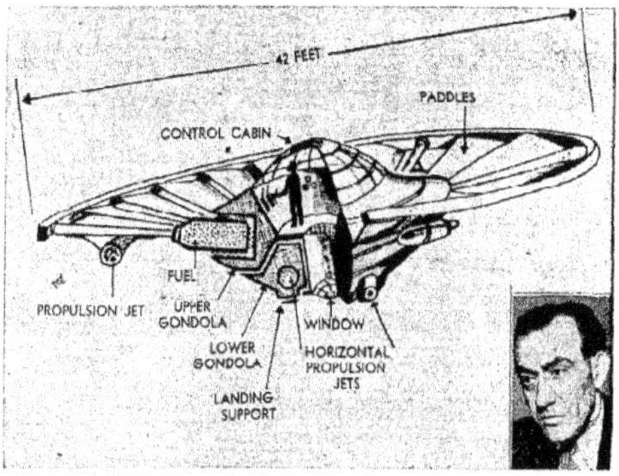

A FORMER LUFTWAFFE captain and aircraft designer, Rudolph Schriever (inset), who says engineers throughout the world experimented in the early 1940s with "flying saucers," is willing to build one for the United States in six to nine months. The 40-year-old Prague university graduate said he made blueprints for such a machine (above), which he calls a "flying top," before Germany's collapse and that the blueprints were stolen from his laboratory. He says the machine would be capable of 2,600 mph with radius of 4,000 miles. Schriever is a U. S. Army driver at Bremerhaven *(International)*

Figure 5. Newspaper Report on Rudolph Schriever's flying saucer prototype

Fact #2. In 1944, the US (Army) Air Force created the Scientific Advisory Group whose chief purpose was to identify future trends in supersonic aerospace technologies and help Air Force scientists develop blueprints for their development.[96] Its successor, the Scientific Advisory Board (1946) played a critical role in studying flying saucer technologies either retrieved from Nazi Germany or from world-wide UFO crash retrieval operations.

Fact #3. In occupied post-war Germany, Nazi aerospace vehicles capable of supersonic flight were brought to the USA under Operation LUSTY (LUftwaffe Secret TechnologY) for research and development at Wright Field/Wright Patterson AFB.[97] Operation LUSTY had separate teams that respectively interrogated captured German scientists, many of whom were brought into the US along with the captured Nazi technologies. According to whistleblower sources, the technologies included four Nazi flying saucers that belonged to the Vril and Haunebu series initially stored at Wright Field in 1945, and then relocated to the newly built S-4 facility at Area 51, soon after its 1955 opening.

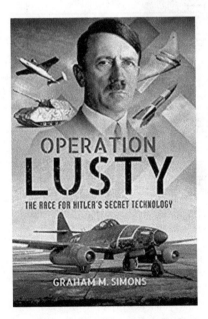

Figure 6. Book describing Operation Lusty.

Fact #4. Several Operation Paperclip German scientists brought into the US, in the immediate post-war era, such as Dr. W.O. Schumann, were experts in advanced propulsion systems using high voltage electrostatics and plasma torsion field physics.[98] Dr. Schumann's involvement in flying saucer research dates back to the 1920s when he worked on the first Vril prototypes according to multiple sources.[99] He was taken to Wright Field to help Army Air Force scientists understand the propulsion systems of the flying saucers being studied there.

W.O. Schumann

Second page of a three page declassified Operation Paperclip Memorandum dated 6 June 1947. This is a list of of German scientists requested by the U.S. Army Air Force for classified research at its Dayton, Ohio facilities. The appearance of Schumann's name is evidence that after his debriefing in post-war Germany, his expertise in aerospace projects was deemed important for the Army Air Force's classified foreign technology research. Source: Richard Sauder, *Hidden in Plain Sight* (2011).

Figure 7. FOIA document confirming W.O. Schumann was part of Operation Paperclip

Fact #5. US Army Air Force reported that a flying saucer had crashed near Roswell, New Mexico, in July 1947, and then retracted this by claiming trained military intelligence officers had misidentified an air balloon when issuing the initial news report.[100] According to leaked documents, the Roswell UFO crash was the catalyst for the creation of the Majestic-12 Group (MJ-12) in September 1947 that organized all aspects of military, national security and scientific efforts concerning UFO crash retrieval operations.[101] After initially reporting directly to Presidents Truman and Eisenhower, MJ-12 went rogue during the latter part of the Eisenhower administration, and was directly implicated in the assassination of President John F. Kennedy.[102]

Figure 8. Initial News Report of Roswell Flying Saucer crash

Fact #6. Developments in antigravity propulsion technologies were discussed favorably in open-source scientific journals during the 1950's, but then mysteriously disappeared from future journal editions despite their revolutionary potential for the aviation industry.[103] This is important circumstantial evidence that antigravity propulsion research had been classified for national security reasons. The US military did not want major adversaries learning that the US was secretly researching and developing antigravity spacecraft. In addition, the open development of electromagnetic propulsion systems directly threatened the oil industry, which was controlled by major US corporations with powerful influence over the federal government and military.

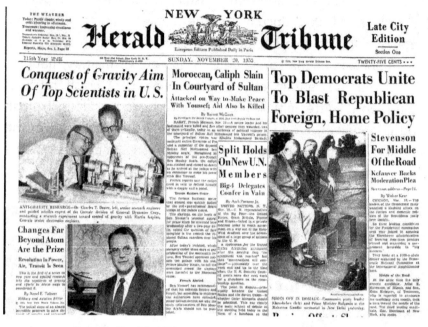

Figure 9. Nov 20, 1955 News report on Antigravity Research

Fact #7. In 1955, the founder of Lockheed Martin's Skunkworks, Kelly Johnson, was involved in establishing Area 51 along with the CIA for the purpose of jointly developing supersonic aerospace vehicles for upper atmospheric and space surveillance.[104] According to insider testimony, the S-4 facility was built in the Papoose Dry Lake region of Area 51, about 12 miles from the more well-known Groom Lake complex where the U-2, SR-71 and Aurora series of reconnaissance aircraft were built. Most, if not all, of the flying saucers stored at Wright Patterson AFB were relocated to S-4 for close study by Lockheed and other aerospace contractors.

Figure 10. Kelly Johnson with an early variant of U-2 at Area 51

Fact #8. In 1989, Robert Lazar publicly revealed that based on a recommendation from Dr. Edward Teller, he began work as a scientist at the S-4 facility on a highly classified reverse engineering program involving nine flying saucers, one of which he was exclusively tasked to study.[105] Lazar confirmed that antigravity propulsion technologies existed, and that exotic elements such as 115 (Moscovium) were used to power the flying saucers. Lazar said the reverse engineering effort suffered from limited personnel and funding, making progress very slow due to the complexity of the advanced technologies. The involvement of Dr. Teller, a member of the MJ-12 Group, raises the possibility that Lazar was an unwitting pawn in a "limited hangout" operation to disclose the reality of reverse engineering efforts of flying saucers, but mischaracterizing overall progress as very slow to non-existent.

Figure 11. Illustration of craft witnessed by Bob Lazar at S4 facility

Fact #9. In 1993, Kelly Johnson's successor as Skunkworks CEO, Ben Rich, concluded a number of public lectures by showing a flying saucer and saying: "We now have the technology to take E.T. home."[106] Two years before his death, Rich was firmly hinting that Skunkworks had been successful in reverse engineering flying saucer craft in contracts first awarded to them more than a decade earlier.

Figure 12. Flying Saucer shown by Ben Rich at end of lectures

Fact #10. Briefings to Congressional and Pentagon officials about the existence of a corporate-run classified reverse engineering program involving "off-world vehicles not made on this earth" were reported in a July 23, 2020, *New York Times* article.[107] The story corroborated decades long claims that reverse engineering of captured UFOs were secretly being conducted by various aerospace military contractors. Importantly, the story covered testimony by a leading astrophysicist, Dr. Eric Davis, who had shared information he had gained from Vice Admiral Thomas Wilson, a former Director of the Defense Intelligence Agency (DIA), about a corporate-run UFO reverse engineering program that he was denied access to in 1997, despite his very senior position.[108]

I will now review the main components of a USAF secret space program (SSP) that dates back to research and development that began in the 1940s with captured flying saucer craft, and led to successful reverse engineering programs over the succeeding decades by major aerospace companies such as Lockheed's Skunkworks.

Reverse Engineered Flying Saucer Shaped Craft

Reports of flying saucer sightings date back to the World War II era, and there are several FBI documents containing reports of workers and soldiers describing the flight performance of saucer shaped craft witnessed near secret Nazi facilities.[109] In my book, the *US Navy's Secret Space Program* (2017), I analyze the testimony of William Tompkins, who was assigned to Naval Air Station San Diego, during World War II. He described his participation in a Navy run espionage program where approximately thirty spies were reporting Nazi progress in developing and weaponizing flying saucer craft for the war effort. He described up to thirty prototypes of flying saucer craft being designed and developed using various propulsion, navigation and weapons systems. In 1950, two credible Italian and German engineers, Giuseppe Belluzzo and Rudolph Schriever, gave interviews published in major newspapers about their wartime experiences in secret Axis power projects to build flying saucers for the war effort.[110]

In my 2018 book, *Antarctica's Hidden History*, a detailed analysis is given reviewing alleged Nazi SS documents that were released at the end of the Cold War by a former member of the Bulgarian Academy of Sciences, Vladimir Terziski.[111] In 1991, Terziski claims he came into the possession of a leaked documentary film from the Nazi SS archives that had been shared among the intelligence agencies of Warsaw Pact countries, which revealed different types of flying saucer craft built in Nazi Germany.[112] The film displayed documents that date from late 1944 and early 1945, with detailed data on four different sized flying saucers that were being flight tested and developed by the Nazi SS in different underground research facilities.

According to an army cryptologist, known as Agent "Kewper" (a pseudonym), who had been recruited by the CIA in 1958 to work on the UFO issue, he personally saw four Nazi German flying saucers that had been brought into the US under Operation Paperclip. Veteran UFO researcher Linda Moulton Howe first interviewed him in 1998. She was convinced that Kewper was a credible eyewitness to the events he disclosed.[113] By 1958, the craft had been moved from Wright Field (later renamed Wright-Patterson AFB in September 1947) to the S-4 facility at Area 51 for storage and further study, which is where he sighted them. In an interview with Howe, Kewper discussed the different types of German craft he witnessed:

> At Area 51, the first two craft we saw looked almost
> identical. They were smaller, not nearly as big as one
> in the back. Col. Jim [USAF; official "tour guide" at

Area 51/S4] mentioned that those two were 'Vril craft.' We asked him what 'Vril' was. The Col. said it was a foreign saucer built in Germany in the 1920s and 1930s. Then he pointed up ahead and said the next three craft were alien (extraterrestrial) craft retrieved from New Mexico. There were three more in the back and they were huge, all sitting on metal sawhorses or stands to keep them off the ground. The disc on the very end was a huge one and Col. Jim said that was a German WWII craft built in 1938 and was jacked up higher on stands because it had a gun emplacement underneath, which he said the Germans called a 'death ray'. It was a different shape than the other craft, was dark in color and had a larger top that stood up probably 10 or 12 feet above the saucer. That one had a diameter of about 50 or 60 feet.[114]

This takes me to an important incident described at length in my book *US Air Force Secret Space Program* (2019), where three different sized flying saucer-shaped craft developed by the USAF were put on display at a highly classified air show in 1988 at Edwards AFB.[115] The location of Edwards AFB for the air show is significant since it is adjacent to Plant 42, the secretive joint research and development facility shared between the USAF and major aerospace companies such as Lockheed Martin's Skunkworks. According to *Global Security*, a number of major aerospace companies operate out of this enormous facility:

Air Force Plant 42 is at Palmdale, CA, north of Pasadena in Los Angeles County. It is operated by Lockheed, Rockwell International, Northrop, and Nero. AFP 42 is located in the northeastern portion of Los Angeles County, California, within the Antelope Valley of the Mojave Desert, approximately 80 miles north of Los Angeles. It has over 6,600 acres (the government owns 85%) and includes approximately 4.2 million square feet of floor space (the government owns 45%). The site includes multiple high bay buildings and airfield access with flyaway capability. The facility also has one of the heaviest load-bearing runways in the world.[116]

The most well-known corporation is Lockheed Martin's famed Skunk Works which "officially" moved to Plant 42 from Burbank, California, in 1989, less than a year after the reported air show. It can be assumed that Skunkworks and/or other major aerospace companies played major roles in building the original flying saucer prototypes, and had subsequently moved to Plant 42 to build the assembly facilities for production models. The craft were called 'Alien Reproduction Vehicles' (ARVs), according to Mark McCandlish, a patent illustrator who first revealed their existence based on the eyewitness report of another patent illustrator, Brad Sorenson.[117] This is what McCandlish had to say about the different sized flying saucer craft seen at the airshow that he illustrated in a drawing:

> [T]here were three vehicles. The first one - the smallest, the one that was partially taken apart, the one that was shown in the video that was running in this hangar November 12, 1988 at . . . [Edwards] Air Force Base – was about 24 feet in diameter at its widest part, right at the base. The next biggest one was 60 feet in diameter at the base . . . the largest of these vehicles was about 130 feet in diameter.[118]

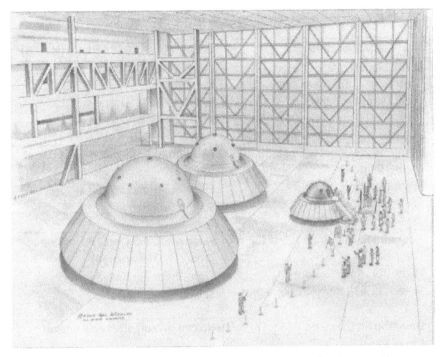

The three flying saucers Sorensen saw at Edwards AFB are comparable in size to three of the four Nazi flying saucers described in the documents extracted from the leaked Nazi SS film described earlier. The similarities are such that it can be asserted the Air Force designs for the ARVs were at least partially a result of them having successfully reverse engineered the Vril and Haunebu series saucers that had been brought into the US after the war by Operation LUSTY. What appears in the following table is a detailed comparison of the flying saucers brought into the US by Operation LUSTY, with the three craft witnessed at Edwards AFB. A detailed comparative analysis of the Nazi Flying Saucers and the Alien Reproduction Vehicles appears in my 2019 book, *The US Air Force Secret Space Program.*[119]

Table 1: **Comparison of Nazi Flying Saucers and US Alien Reproduction Vehicles**

Nazi Germany 1945	US Air Force 1988 (Edwards AFB)
Vril I: Diameter 38 ft (11.5 m) Crew: 2 Flight Duration: 5.5 hours Speed: 7,200 mph (12,000 kmh)	**Small ARV:** Diameter 24 ft (7.3 m) Crew: 4 Flight Duration: Unknown Speed: Superluminal
Haunebu I: Diameter 82 ft (25 m) Crew: Unknown Flight Duration: 18 hours Speed: 10,200 mph (17,000 kmh)	**Medium ARV:** Diameter 60 ft (18 m) Crew: 8-16 (estimated) Flight Duration: Unknown Speed: Superluminal
Haunebu II: Diameter 105 ft (32 m) Crew 20 Flight Duration: 55 hours Speed: 12,620 mph (21,000 kmh)	**Large ARV:** Diameter 130 ft (39 m) Crew 20-40 (estimated) Flight Duration: Unknown Speed: Superluminal
Haunebu III: Diameter 233 ft (71 m) Crew: 32 Flight Duration: 7-8 weeks Speed: 24,855 mph (40,000 kmh)	No comparably sized ARV known

Several conclusions can be drawn from the three flying saucer craft that were witnessed at a classified air show at Edwards AFB in 1988. First, the craft had been successfully reverse engineered from captured Nazi Germany and extraterrestrial flying saucer craft initially stored at Wright Field/Wright Patterson AFB from 1945, and subsequently moved after 1955 to Area 51's S-4 facility.

Second, Skunkworks and/or other major aerospace companies built the first prototype flying saucers (ARVs) that were on display at Edwards AFB, and subsequently built an assembly facility at Plant 42.

Third, the revelations of Robert Lazar and the *New York Times* story focusing on the informal briefings to Congress and the Pentagon by Dr. Eric Davis that government scientists and corporations had failed to reverse engineer a retrieved flying saucer craft, was disinformation. The goal of this decades-long disinformation program that began with Lazar in 1989, was designed to mislead the general public and throw researchers off the trail of successful corporate reverse engineering programs.

Fourth, the craft were ready for operational deployment for different customers. Among the customers would have been Air Force Space Command, Air Force Special Operations Command, the NRO and the CIA, all of whom had valid national security reasons for possessing ARV's such as intelligence gathering, covert operations, and/or military defense.

Consequently, sometime after the May 2021 completion of Space Force's setup phase, it can be expected to take control of any of the reverse engineered flying saucers controlled by its predecessor, Air Force Space Command. More problematic will be whether Space Force will be able to exert authority over ARVs deployed by Air Force Special Operations. This will be an even greater problem with those built for the intelligence community, especially the CIA and NRO. However, the USAF secret space program had more than just reverse engineered flying saucers in its inventory; flying triangles, and flying rectangle shaped antigravity craft have also been built and deployed.

Chapter 6

Integrating the USAF Secret Space Program into Space Force

This first year was all about inventing that service [Space Force]. This next year is all about integrating the Space Force more broadly.

— General Jay Raymond on Space Force
starting its 2nd Year.[120]

The USAF was involved in a highly secret and extensive reverse engineering program involving captured flying saucers that date back to Nazi Germany, and 1940s era UFO crash retrieval operations. The scientific expertise acquired during these efforts concerning different aspects of the propulsion, navigation, communications, and weapons systems of these captured craft, allowed scientists from the Air Force, Navy and major aerospace companies to develop new designs of antigravity craft. Consequently, while the origins of modern-day flying saucers possessed by the USAF and other agencies can be traced back to early reverse engineering efforts, differently shaped antigravity craft have been designed and built by corporations collaborating with Air Force and Navy scientists.

It is important to identify the different space assets used in the USAF secret space program in terms of how these were managed and the nature of the operations they conducted. Ultimately, Space Force will have to integrate the flying saucer and differently shaped spacecraft that were developed, built and deployed in the USAF secret space program, which was run in conjunction with the intelligence community. What complicates such an integration process is the Air Force's historic relationship with the National Reconnaissance Office (NRO), National Security Agency (NSA), and the Central Intelligence Agency (CIA) in building and deploying antigravity spacecraft that were used primarily for space surveillance and covert operations worldwide. While the Air Force historically took the lead in the research and development of antigravity craft that were deployed in the early 1980s, which was a major reason in the creation of USAF Space Command in 1982, the craft were deployed primarily for space surveillance and covert operations. This relegated the Air Force Space Command to playing a subordinate administrative and logistical support role, while the intelligence community, led by the NRO and CIA, took the lead in command and control responsibilities. This meant that Air Force Space Command did not have "need to know" clearance over how reverse engineered spacecraft were being used by the intelligence and covert operations communities running the craft out of Air Force facilities, as I will now show.

TR-3B Flying Triangles and Space Based Surveillance Operations

Among the most credible witness testimonies of the existence of a USAF secret space program is Edgar Fouche whose background and testimony I examined at length in a chapter of the *U.S. Air Force Secret Space Program*.[121] In brief, he served with the US Air Force from 1967 to 1987, before spending another eight years with defense contractors working on a number of classified aviation programs at Area 51 in the Nellis Air Force Range, Nevada. He has supplied documents corroborating his USAF military service and work with defense contractors on various aviation projects. One document showed Fouche was assigned to Nellis AFB during the period from 1976 to 1979, which is when he says he was first assigned to Area 51. Fouche claims he met people there working on what were believed to be the Air Force's most classified aerospace programs.[122]

According to Fouche, there is a triangle shaped supersonic craft called the "TR-3B" which was the most highly classified program at the Groom Lake Area 51 facility he was aware of:

> The TR-3B is Code named Astra. The tactical reconnaissance TR-3B first operational flight was in the early 90's. The triangular shaped nuclear powered aerospace platform was developed under the Top Secret, Aurora Program with SDI and black budget monies. At least three of the billion dollar plus TR-3Bs were flying by 1994. The Aurora is the most classified aerospace development program in existence. The TR-3B is the most exotic vehicle created by the Aurora Program. It is funded and operationally tasked by the National Reconnaissance Office, the NSA, and the CIA. The TR-3B flying triangle is not fiction and was built with technology available in the mid-80's. [123]

A vital point to keep in mind here is Fouche's revelation that the "TR-3B is funded and operationally tasked by the National Reconnaissance Office, the NSA and the CIA," and was built in the mid-1980s with at least three being deployed by 1994. This means

AUG 2 0 1979

NAME U RATE (LAST, FIRST, MIDDLE I... IAL) Fouche, Edgar A		SSAN FR4		ACTIVE DUTY GRADE TSGT

(CHECK APPROPRIATE BLOCK AND COMPLETE AS APPLICABLE)

☐ SUPPLEMENTAL SHEET TO RATING FORM WHICH COVERS THE FOLLOWING PERIOD OF REPORT		☒ LETTER OF EVALUATION COVERING THE FOLLOWING PERIOD OF OBSERVATION	
FROM	THRU	FROM 10 June 79	THRU 14 AUG 79

Precede comments by appropriate data, i.e. section continuation, indorsement continuation, additional indorsement, additional reviewer comments, etc.

FACTS AND SPECIFIC ACHIEVEMENTS: TSgt Fouche is an outstanding NCO and technician. His exceptional performance of all duties, even under adverse conditions, indicates a dedicated interest in his work, and a high degree of professionalism. His wide-ranging knowledge and diverse expertise in diagnostics, and mechanical engineering, coupled with his training in advanced electronics, has helped solve critical mission support problems consistently. His awareness of the big picture for future avionics development and maintenance is an attribute that makes him a valuable asset to TAC. TSgt Fouche is considered one of TACs best R&D team builders in areas of ECM, ATS, and cryptological support. He has proven himself recently in the implementation of the TEWS-TITE bed-down, which was lauded by TAC Hq LGM. STRENGTHS: TSgt Fouche displays excellent capabilities when given greater responsibilities, which was demonstrated in his MAJCOM involvement in cryptological asset training and provisioning. He has high endorsements from his chain of command and is considered an excellent candidate for a command level position. OTHER COMMENTS: This out of cycle report is generated because TSgt Fouche was assigned TDY to the AFFTC-DET 3, Nellis AF Range from 1 June 79 to 14 August 79. His duties and responsibilities for this period have been verified via a separate report. RECOMMENDATION: Promote at the earliest opportunity.

NAME OF EVALUATOR, GRADE, ORGANIZATION, AND LOCATION Brewer, MSgt, USAF 57 CRS, Nellis AFB Nevada	DUTY TITLE NCOIC F-15 AIS		DATE 24 Aug 79
	SSAN (INCLUDE SUFFIX) FR465-	SIGNATURE Brewer	

AF FORM 77a PREVIOUS EDITION WILL BE USED.
&U.S. GOVERNMENT PRINTING OFFICE: 1976-211-391/1105

SUPPLEMENTAL SHEET TO AF FORMS 707, 909, 910, 911 AND 475

1968 - OJT Training (On the Job Training)

This is Ed Fouche's OJT Training (On the Job Training) For his "five level upgrade"

Figure 14. Document confirming Edgar Fouche worked at Nellis AFB adjacent to Area 51

that while USAF personnel may have piloted, crewed or maintained the TR-3B's, overall control was maintained by the NRO/NSA/CIA rather than USAF Space Command since its 1982 inception. In other words, while the USAF Space Command had administrative responsibilities for the TR-3B program such as providing research and development expertise, trained personnel, and logistical support, it was the NRO/NSA/CIA that controlled operations due to the highly specialized nature of space surveillance. This would have greatly impacted who had "need to know" clearance as to how the antigravity craft were actually being used in space operations.

The intelligence gathering responsibilities of the NRO, NSA, and CIA made them the logical choice for managing TR-3B surveillance operations, while USAF Space Command was more suited to providing administrative support. Such an arrangement would work as long as space was perceived as a benign environment from which orbital surveillance could be safely conducted on US adversaries. That arrangement would need to change, however, once space was redefined as a warfighting domain. The role of USAF Space Command/Space Force would shift significantly from administrative support to operational control in order to protect US space assets such as the GPS system from China (or Russia) launching a Space Pearl Harbor.

In a series of questions and answers, Edgar Fouche [EF] provided details about the corporate contractors involved in building the TR-3B, the models built and when test flights began:

1. Who is the primary contractor for the TR-3B?

[EF] Lockheed, Boeing, Northrup, Teledyne Ryan, managed by NRO, NSA and CIA. There were a number of major defense contractors involved to keep different parts of the R&D compartmentalized.[124]

Fouche identified Ben Rich, head of Lockheed's Skunkworks, as the senior project designer in the development of the TR-3B.[125] The involvement of Rich in the development and building of the TR-3B is critical given what we know of his comments about Skunkworks having developed "the technology to take E.T. home."[126]

> 2. What was the date of the first flight of the prototype for the TR-3B?

> [EF] They built a lot of DIFFERENT prototypes from the early 70's on. I believe the first gravity warping vehicle, i.e., Triangle was flown in the early 70's.[127]

It is helpful to know that the first prototypes were built and tested in the early 1970s and involved "gravity warping" (aka antigravity) technologies, which were first discussed in the scientific literature in the 1950s. The early 1970s being the starting date for TR-3B development is also significant given revelations by the USAF/NRO that a secret corps of military astronauts was being trained by NASA in the 1960s for planned Manned Orbiting Laboratory (MOL) Missions.[128] While MOL was ostensibly cancelled in 1969, it is logical to assume that the USAF/NRO astronauts were not just being trained for planned MOL missions, but also for developing skills crucial for flying the first prototype flying triangle vehicles in the early 1970s.

> 3. How many different sizes of the TR-3B were built?

> [EF] Approx. 250 feet (prototype) and three were flying before 1994. The operational model was supposed to be 600 feet. Never saw a large production model. Only saw them over Edwards AFB, AFFTC [Air Force Flight Test Center] and Nevada. [129]

USAF Top Secret Nuclear Powered Flying Triangle - The TR-3B

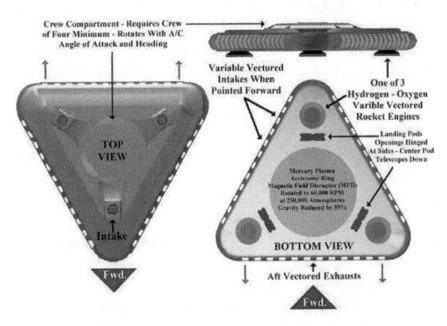

Figure 15. Illustration of TR-3B. Adapted Edgar Fouche Original Version

As far as crew capacity is concerned, the 250 ft prototype could carry a crew of four, indicating that the larger 600 ft version could carry significantly more, and likely had a cargo storage area that could accommodate significant equipment and supplies. Fouche was aware of three of the 250 feet prototypes being built but did not know how many of the larger 600 feet versions were built.

Fouche went on to describe how the TR-3B could be used as a temporary space station:

5. What is the overall mission of the TR-3B?

[EF] Logistics support and transportation for the secret space command used on a planet, moon, or large outpost, you would have a readymade transportable space station. [130]

A trained cadre of USAF/NRO trained by NASA for the aborted MOL program would have been ideal for testing and flying the two differently sized TR-3B craft that could serve as temporary space stations. On June 11, 1985, President Ronald Reagan wrote in his official diary that he had been briefed that "our shuttle capacity is such that we could orbit 300 people."[131] Reagan's admission revealed that a sufficient number of the larger model TR-3B's had been built making it possible to transport and deploy up to 300 astronauts in space. Furthermore, the "secret space command" Fouche mentioned in his answer appears to be different to the USAF Space Command created in 1982, which was redesignated as Space Force in 2019. The former comprised NRO/NSA/CIA officials with operational control over the TR-3B and other classified craft capable of traveling to the Moon and beyond. In contrast, USAF Space Command provided logistical and administrative support to NRO/CIA/NSA surveillance operations using the TR-3B. In the next chapter, I will discuss in detail the collaboration between the NRO and the CIA in setting up a space surveillance program, and the Space Reconnaissance Office set up in 2014, which was staffed by NRO and CIA officials, and private contractors.

Fouche referred to Scotland as one of the locations where an operational TR-3B was based. This is also very significant given flying triangle sightings in both Scotland and Belgium from November 29, 1989, to April 1990. Hundreds of witnesses including police officers saw and photographed these large flying triangles. The sightings were investigated by the Belgium Air Force which resulted in a very well documented incident on March 30, 1990, involving F-16 fighters attempting to intercept the mysterious triangular-shaped craft.[132] Fouche said that based upon his examination of the Belgium photos of the flying triangle and the

TR-3B design schematics he had witnessed, they were the same craft.[133]

Fouche's testimony is vital for understanding the precise relationship between the USAF, NRO, NSA, and CIA in developing, manning, funding and managing the TR-3B program. While the USAF and NRO primarily provided personnel to pilot and crew such missions, the CIA provided the funding and covert operations leadership, while the NSA provided electronic communications and monitoring support. When President Trump asserted the major policy shift that space would be considered a warfighting domain in his 2018 Space Policy Directive 4, this laid the foundation for Space Force eventually establishing operational control over the TR-3B and other covert antigravity craft primarily used in space surveillance or covert operations.

Flying Rectangles and Air Force Special Operations

In the months of September and October 2017, I was sent successive sets of photos showing different shaped UFOs near MacDill AFB by a confidential source, I'll call him JP, who currently serves in the US Army, and has been trained for Special Forces operations.[134] The photos showed three differently shaped UFOs in the vicinity of MacDill AFB, headquarters for two of the Pentagon's eleven unified combatant commands: Special Operations Command and Central Command. Special Operations Command (aka US SOCOM, see *Figure 15*) is responsible for the Pentagon's worldwide covert operations using special forces drawn from Navy Seals (part of Naval Special Warfare Command—NAVSPECWAR), Army Delta Force (part of US Army Special Operations Command—USASOC), Marine Forces Special Operations Command (MARSOC), and other special forces including Air Force Commandos (Air Force Special Operations Command—AFSOC) and Joint Special Operations Command (JSOC). These military special forces use the most advanced military technologies available for ensuring the success of their covert missions. The photos supplied to me by JP are evidence that these covert operations include a small number of antigravity craft controlled by Air Force Commandos working with US Special Operations Command out of MacDill AFB.

Figure 16. US Special Operations Command and subordinate special operations commands

One set of photos sent to me on October 19, 2017, showed two different shaped antigravity craft near MacDill AFB. One of the craft looked like a rectangular platform while the other had a triangular-shaped design similar to the smaller prototype TR-3B described by Fouche. Both craft appeared to use antigravity technology and were interacting with one another. Moments before the October 19 sighting, JP says he received a phone call instructing him exactly when and where the UFO's would appear. He was told to look up into the sky where he saw a black rectangle shaped ship that was followed six seconds later by the triangle shaped craft that interacted with it for nearly a minute and half.[135] JP writes that he has never encountered a rectangular-shaped UFO before, which flew in from the direction of the Gulf of Mexico. In contrast, the flying triangle came in from the direction of MacDill AFB.[136]

A close-up of the first photo in the sequence (*Figure 16*) shows the rectangular-shaped platform UFO taken by JP directly after he received the phone call telling him to look up into the sky.

A close-up of the third photo in the sequence (*Figure 17*) displays the rectangular-shaped platform and the TR-3B-like craft, both appearing to interact with one another while JP watches and hears high pitched sounds.

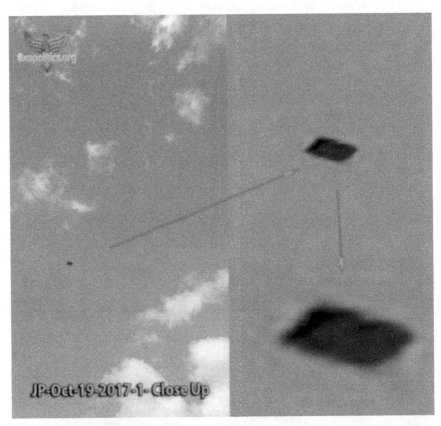

Figure 17. Photo of rectangular-shaped craft (zoom insert added) taken by JP on October 19, 2017.

Based on JP's account of how the photos were taken and their estimated elevation, size, sounds, and maneuvers, they, did not appear to be balloons, drone aircraft, or aircraft using conventional propulsion systems as skeptics may contend. The fact that JP received a phone call to alert him to look into the sky is very significant. It clearly suggests that the UFO's presence was deliberately brought to his attention to display classified technologies for photographing. The phone call he received on October 19, 2017, and the photos themselves are evidence that JP was being used to facilitate a covert disclosure of antigravity craft operating in the vicinity of MacDill AFB. Four days later, JP was to witness the flying rectangle platform again, and this time he claims the encounter became much more personal and involved Air Force Special Operations personnel.

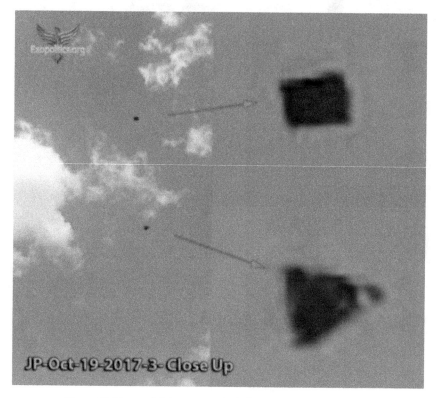

Figure 18. Photo of flying rectangle & flying triangle (zoom insert added) taken by JP on October 19, 2017.

On the morning of October 23, 2017, JP claims he was once again instructed to look up into the sky, this time by two men in a nearby van who pulled up next to him and then quickly sped away. Immediately, he saw a rectangular-shaped platform UFO and used his camera phone to take five photos. He then noticed that he had missing time and when he tried to recall what had happened, he had memory flashes of being inside the flying rectangle he had just photographed.[137] JP estimated that the flying rectangle was about four school buses in length (approx. 40-50 yards), and one and a half school buses in width (approx. 15-20 yards). He specifically recalls being inside of the flying rectangle and walking down a corridor with windows. Outside the windows it was completely black, and he got the impression that the rectangle was flying in space. JP remembers being injected with something, presumably a mind control substance so he would cooperate.

According to JP, the interior of the flying rectangle craft looked and smelled like a military vehicle. Most importantly, he recalled a military patch worn by his abductors which he described as having a red dot and two wings. He first sketched the patch he witnessed and passed on a copy to me. We discussed this further and hours later he found the specific patch online. The patch he identified belongs to Air Force Special Ops. The Air Force patch suggests that the occupants of the craft were part of a squadron of vehicles operating out of MacDill, the headquarters of Special Operations Command which provides the command structure for Air Force Special Operations.

It is rare for an experiencer or abductee to take photos of the craft which has abducted him/her. Often people are incapacitated due to the effects of sedatives or mind control used on them. In the case of JP he was under the influence of the substance injected into him, either prior to boarding or during his time on the flying rectangle. However, after his return to ground, the two operatives soon appeared and instructed him to look at the sky. What this indicates is that the operatives were part of an officially sanctioned covert program run by USAF Special Operations which was encouraging JP to photograph the rectangular-shaped craft, and further, to recall his abduction experience. JP strongly believes that the operatives came from

MacDill AFB, which is very close to where he was living in Tampa, Florida, at the time he took the photos.

Figure 19. Patch used by Air Force Special Operations

On May 24, 2018, JP claims he encountered a human-looking "Nordic" extraterrestrial wearing a USAF uniform who invited him to go for a ride in a landed saucer-shaped craft in a secluded wooded area of Orlando, Florida.[138] JP declined the offer but took photos with his cell phone of the spacecraft as it was departing (see *Figure 5*). His conversation with the Nordic revealed that this group was directly cooperating with the USAF and abiding by the terms of an agreement concerning interactions with the general public. The Nordic wore a uniform that featured the acronym "USAF" with these letters also spelled out in ancient Sumerian. The unique patch enabled the Nordic to walk undisturbed inside USAF bases.

From the information provided by JP and his photos, five important conclusions can be reached. First, the rectangle and triangle shaped vehicles were manned by personnel belonging to Air Force Special Operations located either at its headquarters at Hurlburt Field, Florida, or nearby in underground facilities at MacDill AFB. Two, Air Force Special Operations Command, one of the Air Force's nine Major Commands, possesses a number of antigravity vehicles which it uses for covert operations that are coordinated with the Pentagon's Special Operations Command. Three, Air Force Special Operations was involved in an unofficial UFO disclosure initiative featuring JP. Four, senior officials from Air Force Special Operations were in command of the antigravity vehicles photographed by JP, and knowledgeable about their capabilities, origins and operations. Finally, the USAF has been working with Nordic looking extraterrestrials that operate flying saucer craft out of Air Force bases and collaborate closely with Air Force Special Operations.

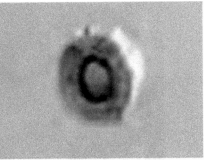

This is the fifth in a sequence of six photos taken by JP on May 24, 2018. The image on the left is the original and the upper right portion shows a close up of the flying saucer craft as it was departing, after having earlier been on the ground where JP met its Nordic extraterrestrial occupant.

Figure 20. Photo courtesy of "JP" (zoom insert added)

Consequently, it comes as no great surprise that on January 30, 2020, US Space Force recruited and promoted a senior officer from Air Force Special Operations Command. Colonel Michael Conley who previously headed the Air Force's 1st Special Operations Wing at Special Operations Command was promoted to Brigadier General for his new position at Space Force.[139] In his new assignment, he is second in charge of Space Operations Command that currently makes up the bulk of the newly created Space Force with nearly 16,000 personnel. The personnel are distributed over five Air Force bases – Vandenberg, Peterson, Patrick, Schriever, and Buckley – which, as earlier mentioned, are being considered to be renamed space bases by the head of Space Force, General Jay Raymond.[140]

Figure 21. Brigadier General Michael Conley

In his previous assignment at Air Forces Special Operations Command (AFSOC), as head of one of the Air Force's eight special operations wings, Conley led special forces personnel known as "Air Commandos" that the AFSOC website describes as follows:

We are America's Air Commandos

We are Air Commandos, quiet professionals, Airmen personally committed to our craft. As the air component of U.S. Special Operations Command, we are capable and ready to conduct special operations anytime, anyplace. We are disciplined professionals dedicated to continuous improvement. Innovative and adaptable, our rigorous and realistic training helps us manage uncertainty and mitigate risk. By training smarter and harder than others, we define our limits, and learn when and where to push them. Inherently joint, we build credibility through habitual relationships that sustain us in the fight. We believe that one person makes a difference. And as our Air Commando heritage demands, we remain culturally bound to get the mission done, or find a way where none exists.[141]

Conley led the 1st Special Operations Wing, from 2018 to 2020 at Hurlburt Field, in Florida. It was during his leadership that a number of triangle and rectangle-shaped antigravity vehicles were photographed near MacDill AFB. Personnel on a rectangle-shaped antigravity vehicle wore patches of Air Force Special Operations according to the witness/photographer JP. These are the same patches worn by the special operations wing led by Conley at Hurlburt Field, which worked closely with MacDill's Special Operations Command in covert operations around the world and in space. This raises the distinct possibility that Conley was involved in the decision to allow antigravity vehicles manned by "Air Commandos" flying near MacDill AFB to be photographed by JP. If so, then Conley was actively part of the covert disclosure initiative by the USAF to reveal its arsenal of antigravity vehicles to the general public, which I described in detail in the book, *US Air Force Secret Space Program*. This possibility gives added significance to Conley's appointment and promotion to Space Force.

Regardless of the question of whether Conley was part of an Air Force initiative to publicly begin acclimating the public to its secret space program in 2018, his new position as deputy commander of Space Force's "Space Operations Command" means that he is in a position to coordinate with Air Force Special Operations Command over the possible transfer of relevant Air Force special operations personnel and space assets over to Space Force. This may include the recruitment/transfer of elements of "Air Commandos" that pilot/crew antigravity craft who presumably will become known in future as "Guardians," the new descriptive term for members of Space Force.[142] Conley may also oversee the transfer of additional covert space assets used by the Air Force's "1st Special Operations Wing" based at Hurlburt Field, over to one of Space Force's newly acquired bases. The most likely candidates are its headquarters at Peterson AFB/SB, or Schriever AFB/SB where a two day space military war games was completed in November 2020.[143] The completion date for these transfers is May 2021, the end of the eighteen month set up period for Space Force.

Conclusion

With the redesignation of Air Force Space Command as Space Force, the question arises over how and when the reverse engineered flying saucers (ARVs), flying triangles, and rectangle-shaped antigravity craft used in collaboration with the NRO, CIA, and NSA, and built by major military contractors, will be transferred over to Space Force. It can be assumed that some of these antigravity craft will be part of the transfer of space assets occurring relatively soon after the end of the 18-month set up period in May 2021. This will most likely begin with the space assets that belonged to Air Force Special Operations involved in some of the events described earlier in this chapter.

However, it is important to understand the previous Air Force cooperation with the NRO and CIA in setting up a secret space program was predicated on the Air Force's subordination to the space surveillance priorities set by the NRO/CIA given the understanding that space was a benign environment. As confirmed by Fouche, the NRO/CIA/NSA were in charge of operations and planning, while Air Force Space Command handled logistics and administration. This dynamic changes significantly with space being redefined as a warfighting domain, thereby shifting priorities away from an exclusive focus on space surveillance—the CIA/NRO/NSA's areas of specialty—to core battlefield tactics such as forward deployment, force multipliers, and regular large scale military exercises. Rather than two or three squadrons of antigravity spacecraft being all that is required for space surveillance and covert operations, Space Force will need closer to 300 squadrons to dominate space as a warfighting domain. This approximates the current 312 operational squadrons deployed by the US Air Force to ensure global air dominance.[144]

Even more important with the strategic shift to space being considered a warfighting domain is that Space Force and US Space Command will have "need to know" how space assets are being deployed by all the military services and the intelligence community. Prior to US Space Command and Space Force's respective creations in August and December 2019, when space was considered a benign environment, Air Force Space Command (1982-2019) and Pentagon leaders could be denied "need to know" access to classified information about NRO/CIA space surveillance operations.

The NRO/CIA is highly likely to resist sharing all its space assets developed for surveillance, despite decades long collaboration with the USAF secret space program, particularly USAF Space Command since 1982. Consequently, this raises the intriguing question, how big a problem is the NRO/CIA space program going to be for Space Force's plans to acquire and integrate space technologies built with the historical cooperation of the USAF?

Chapter 7

Space Force's Challenge with NRO-CIA Secret Space Program

*Let your plans be dark and impenetrable as night,
and when you move, fall like a thunderbolt.*

— Sun Tzu, *The Art of War*

Official government documents confirm the existence of three US space programs that were set up between 1957-1961 with their own unique agendas, capabilities and areas of responsibility. The much-publicized public program was run by the National Aeronautics Space Administration (NASA), a civilian space agency created on October 1, 1958, by Congress and President Dwight Eisenhower. Its unveiling came less than a year after the Soviet Union's launch of the world's first satellite, Sputnik, in December 1957. Another less publicized military space program begun in 1957 and was run by the Pentagon. Through this military program, both the US Air Force and Navy competed in a race to send up their own respective satellite systems for a range of purposes deemed essential for worldwide military operations. The third started soon after, a highly classified joint Pentagon and Intelligence Community program that brought together these two national security groups' mutual interests in space reconnaissance.

An official report by the Center for the Study of National Reconnaissance describes the complex situation created by the three separate US space programs which President John F. Kennedy had to deal with after he assumed power on January 20, 1961:

> Kennedy found in place the highly visible and public, civilian-guided space program directed by NASA, openly funded and widely viewed by the public as a symbol of national greatness dedicated to the peaceful pursuit of new knowledge and accompanying space technology, a military space program that featured communications, early warning, and navigation within the Department of Defense, and yet a third program shared by the Defense Department and the Intelligence Community that focused on space-based reconnaissance, equally a symbol of national greatness, but funded by Congress through secret budgets and wholly unknown to the public in either purpose, size, or scope . . . Each of these three space programs was carried out by separate organizations with their own research and development, acquisition, launch, and operations capabilities.[145]

Kennedy was persuaded that a dedicated government agency focusing exclusively on the task of space-based reconnaissance would have far more success than the separate military services (Navy and Air Force) with their competing priorities and programs cooperating in an ad hoc manner with the intelligence community. Indeed, both the US Navy and Air Force had experienced slow progress and significant setbacks in their respective satellite programs (Vanguard and Weapons Systems 117) in the late 1950s, which led to national embarrassment when the Soviet Union was the first to successfully launch a satellite into Earth orbit. The National Reconnaissance Office (NRO) was subsequently secretly established by President Kennedy on September 6, 1961, and was given the primary responsibility of overseeing the development of America's space-based intelligence surveillance systems.

A unique aspect in the NRO's institutional creation is that it was run jointly by the Pentagon and the CIA. While the Pentagon provided the institutional home for the NRO and the infrastructure it needed for building and launching future satellites, the CIA was responsible for the NRO budget. Operational control and funding of the NRO was shared between the Department of Defense and the CIA according to the 2001 Space Commission Report:

> While the NRO is an agency of the Department of Defense, its budget, the National Reconnaissance Program (NRP), is one part of the National Foreign Intelligence Program (NFIP). The Director of Central Intelligence provides guidance for and approves the NRP and all other elements of the NFIP. The Secretary of Defense ensures implementation of the DCI's resource decisions by DoD elements within the NFIP. As a result, the NRO is a joint venture between these organizations.[146]

A fundamental division of labor had been agreed to between the military services and the NRO when it came to space based surveillance programs. While the military services would be in charge of satellites providing dual use military and civilian services such as GPS, the NRO's space assets would remain highly classified and its data would not be shared with the public. A 1996 Congressional report clarified the division of labor between the

NRO and the Pentagon's Space Command (1985-2002 & 2019-), which integrated the space assets of the different military services:

> Two organizations within the Department of Defense manage space assets: the U.S. Space Command (SPACECOM) is responsible for so-called "white world" satellites (i.e., satellites that are publicly acknowledged) for military programs, and the National Reconnaissance Office (NRO) deals with "black world" (i.e., classified) satellites for intelligence programs. SPACECOM launches and operates satellites for military communication, weather and navigation, which are designed and procured by the military services. NRO designs, acquires, launches, and operates classified reconnaissance satellites.[147]

Up to 1992, when the NRO's existence was publicly disclosed for the first time, its classified operations were largely unknown to most members of the US Congress:

> The U.S. Congress supported the NRO, but only a few selected members were briefed on the history, finances, and operations of the National Reconnaissance Program prior to the 1970s, and then only when it was deemed necessary by the appropriate House or Senate leadership, the Director of Central Intelligence, or the Director of the National Reconnaissance Office. . . .

> The primary function of the legislative branch in relation to the Intelligence Community and the NRO in the early years remained that of providing appropriations. Funding for the NRO, like that for

the Central Intelligence Agency, "was handled by the defense subcommittees of the respective Appropriations Committees of each House of the Congress." These "black" or secret budgets, for security reasons, were buried "in non-descript line items of the defense budgets . . ." and "defense appropriations laws provided an appropriate mechanism for funding intelligence activities."[148]

The extraordinary secrecy and organization of the NRO has been described by aviation writer, Tim Weiner:

> The reconnaissance agency is really a set of secret offices—so secret that they have been shielded from each other, like safes locked within safes. Each office, and each program, had separate management and accounting systems, all "black."

> When these offices and programs were consolidated in the reconnaissance office's new headquarters last year [1995], its top managers found that "no one had a handle on how much money they had," the Senate intelligence committee aide said. There was little or no accountability because of the office's secrecy, he said.[149]

Given the highly classified nature of NRO space operations, its secret existence and the cost of satellite research and development, it developed a unique relationship with the CIA in order to ensure the higher-than-normal funding requirements when compared to other members of the Intelligence Community:

These programs of the National Reconnaissance Office required higher levels of funding provided through a more rapid and less cumbersome mechanism than that which provided funds to the rest of the Federal Government and the defense and national security establishment. From the outset, the NRO "budget process was very 'streamlined' . . . [in that] not many people needed to be consulted to secure budget approval" in Congress or elsewhere. Thus, normal funding and acquisition procedures that applied elsewhere in the Department of Defense and Federal Government were never followed by the NRO.[150]

The NRO absorbed the biggest part of Intelligence Community budget, and this was possible due to its special funding relationship with the CIA. The 1996 Congressional Report emphasized the unique funding relationship the NRO had with the CIA and recommended that Congress maintain this into the foreseeable future:

The Commission endorses efforts by the Secretary of Defense and the DCI [Director of Central Intelligence] to achieve closer coordination and integration of space programs to save costs where possible. However, the Commission believes that the NRO should be preserved as a separate element of the Intelligence Community. Its authority to allocate resources for space activities would be considerably limited if the Commission's recommendations . . . are adopted, but the basic responsibilities of the NRO for the research and development, acquisition, and operation of reconnaissance satellites remain valid. The ability of the NRO to utilize the DCI's special procurement authorities ought also to be preserved.[151]

The reference to the "special procurement authorities" of the Director of Central Intelligence (DCI) is referring to the budgetary power given to the CIA Director by the National Security Act of 1947. From 1947 up to 2005, the CIA Director (aka Director of Central Intelligence) had the exclusive authority to direct funds to members of the "National Foreign Intelligence Program" (renamed National Intelligence Program in 2005), while the Secretary of Defense only had consultative power for the Military Intelligence Program, as outlined in the following statute:

> No funds made available under the National Foreign Intelligence Program may be reprogrammed by any element of the intelligence community without the prior approval of the Director of Central Intelligence except in accordance with procedures issued by the Director. The Secretary of Defense shall consult with the Director of Central Intelligence before reprogramming funds made available under the Joint Military Intelligence Program.[152]

Put simply, the NRO benefited greatly from the funding relationship it had with the CIA. This relationship meant that CIA could direct funds to the NRO with little government oversight or regulation due to the secrecy restrictions. Importantly, the CIA could distribute funds quickly to wherever necessary, which was highly desirable given the expense and unpredictability of space operations. This funding authority historically gave the CIA enormous power to influence and control NRO officials and operations.

The funding situation changed significantly in 2005 with the creation of the position of Director of National Intelligence with the passage of the 2004 Intelligence Reform and Terrorism Prevention Act.[153] The Director of National Intelligence took over from the CIA Director two important historic responsibilities that dated back to the CIA's 1947 formation. First, the position of Director of Central Intelligence was abolished and the responsibility for managing members of the Intelligence Community was handed over to the Director of National Intelligence. Second, it would now be the Director of National Intelligence (DNI), rather than the CIA Director, who would be the president's chief intelligence advisor and deliver the Presidential Daily Briefing.

What was included in the management responsibilities handed over to the DNI was guiding Congressional appropriations through the Department of Defense to the seventeen entities that have made up the Intelligence Community since 2005. These entities were divided into two categories. Department of Defense (DOD) elements were part of the Military Intelligence Program that was created in 2005 out of a merger of two prior military intelligence programs.[154] Non-DOD elements were called the National Intelligence Program (previously called the National Foreign Intelligence Program).[155] Among the eight elements that make up the DOD group (see *Figure 21*) four of these (the NRO, the National Security Agency, the Defense Intelligence Agency, and the National Geospatial Agency) are funded both through the National Intelligence Program and the Military Intelligence Program.

The DNI was now formally in charge of the "official black budget" allocated to the seventeen members of the Intelligence Community, the overall size of which would be announced each year, without identifying how much each member of the Intelligence Community would receive. Put simply, the official 'black budget' is the top-secret slush fund set up by the Department of Defense (DOD), with the approval of the US

Congress, to fund the intelligence community. Each year the DoD lists a number of single line items in its budget that have a program number such as 0605236F, code names like CLASSIC WIZARD or vague description such as "special evaluation program," that do not refer to any weapons system known to the general public, Congressional officials or even defense analysts. These single line items are covers for the official black budget which moves through the DOD in a manner that is coordinated by the formal head of the intelligence community (historically the CIA Director, but since 2005 the DNI) and the Secretary of Defense.

The overall size of the official black budget has been routinely announced since 2005 by the DNI. For the years 2018-2020, the official black budget for the National Intelligence Program (NIP) and the Military Intelligence Program (MIP) were announced to be the following:

> For Fiscal Year (FY) 2018, the aggregate appropriated for the NIP and MIP totaled $81.5B (NIP $59.4B, MIP $22.1B).
>
> For FY2019, the aggregate amount appropriated for the NIP and MIP totaled $81.7B (NIP $60.2B, MIP $21.5B).
>
> For FY2020, the aggregate amount requested for the NIP and MIP totals $85.7B (NIP $62.8B, MIP $22.9B).[156]

The overall size of the intelligence budget as a percentage of the Department of Defense budget averages around 11%.[157] The estimated size of the NRO budget after its existence was officially disclosed in 1992 was somewhere in the range of $5 to $6 billion annually according to Weiner.[158] The actual funding of the NRO by

Statutory IC Elements

DOD Elements:

- Defense Intelligence Agency (DIA)
- National Geospatial-Intelligence Agency (NGA)
- National Reconnaissance Office (NRO)
- National Security Agency (NSA)
- U.S. Air Force Intelligence, Surveillance and Reconnaissance (AF/A2)
- U.S. Army Intelligence (G2)
- U.S. Marine Corps Intelligence, Surveillance and Reconnaissance Enterprise (MCISR-E)
- U.S. Naval Intelligence (N2)

Non-DOD Elements:

- Office of the Director of National Intelligence (ODNI)
- Central Intelligence Agency (CIA)
- Department of Energy (DOE) intelligence component: Office of Intelligence and Counter-Intelligence (I&CI)
- Department of Homeland Security (DHS) intelligence components: Office of Intelligence and Analysis (I&A) and U.S. Coast Guard Intelligence (CG-2)
- Department of Justice (DOJ) intelligence components: the Drug Enforcement Agency's Office of National Security Intelligence (DEA/ONSI) and the Federal Bureau of Investigation's Intelligence Branch (IB)
- Department of State (DOS) intelligence component: Bureau of Intelligence and Research (INR)
- Department of Treasury intelligence component: Office of Intelligence and Analysis (OIA)

Source: 50 *U.S. Code* §3003(4); ODNI

Figure 22. List of US Intelligence Community elements

the CIA, however, is far greater than these estimated figures suggest due to a second black budget created by the CIA.

While the CIA Director had relinquished to the DNI the authority over the distribution of Congressional funds that make up the "official black budget", there was also an "unofficial black budget" that the CIA Director continued to exclusively control. This "unofficial black budget" derives from the budgetary authority given to the CIA Director in the 1949 CIA Act:

> The sums made available to the Agency may be expended without regard to the provisions of law and regulations relating to the expenditure of Government funds; and for objects of a confidential, extraordinary, or emergency nature, such expenditures to be accounted for solely on the certificate of the Director.[159]

As the statute makes clear, the CIA Director could use funds made available to it, acquired through various channels, to be used "without regard to the provisions of law." This means that the CIA Director has enormous power in funding classified programs and disregarding any legal or budgetary restrictions when the Director deemed a project to be of "extraordinary" or "emergence nature." Unlike other agencies, the Director of the CIA is able to prevent the Inspector General of the CIA—an independent official appointed by Congress—from conducting a thorough audit of the CIA's budget acquired through both legal and "extralegal" channels for national security reasons.[160] Importantly, the CIA Director continues to have this unique statutory authority despite relinquishing management of the "official black budget" to the DNI.

In November 2003, I released a detailed study titled "The Black Budget Report," where evidence was presented of the extralegal methods used by the CIA in generating both "official" and "unofficial" black budgets for a large number of classified programs whose scope exceeded the Manhattan Project created during World War II.[161] The "unofficial black budget" involved the CIA siphoning off funds from the congressional appropriations of multiple government agencies, participating in the global drug trade, and involvement in organized crime.[162] The financial proceeds of these extensive extralegal activities, carried out by the CIA's National Clandestine Service (previously the Directorate of Operations), were laundered through the Department of Defense (DoD). This was done in order to stay within the letter of the law as far as the above statutes were concerned, while flagrantly violating their spirit.[163] In my report, I explained that the best evidence for the existence of the CIA's "unofficial black budget" and its scope were auditing irregularities reported by the DOD's Office of Inspector General.

For the years 1998, 1999 and 2000, these were respectively 1.7 trillion, 2.3 trillion, and 1.1 trillion US dollars. [164] The Inspector General reports are important evidence that trillions of dollars were being siphoned through the DOD for the fiscal years 1998-2002 for unknown reasons. Using the Inspector General reports of accounting anomalies, it can be estimated that the CIA "unofficial black budget" is annually in the vicinity of 1.1 trillion dollars—a truly staggering figure when one considers that the entire Pentagon budget for fiscal year 2021 will be approximately 700 billion dollars.[165] Independent researchers such as Catherine Austin Fitts, a former Assistant Secretary of Housing and Urban Development (1989-1990), similarly estimated the CIA's black budget to be in the vicinity of one trillion dollars annually, which she speculated may be used for classified extraterrestrial related projects.[166]

Importantly, the estimated trillion dollar black budget accumulated annually by the CIA for distribution to a vast network of classified programs dealing with advanced technology projects dwarfs the $85 billion "official black budget" that is managed by the Director of National Intelligence (DNI). Consequently, while the 2004 Intelligence Reform and Terrorism Prevention Act appeared to significantly erode the power of the CIA Director by assigning responsibility for managing and funding the Intelligence Community to the DNI, this did nothing to alter the CIA Director's power to direct and fund programs from its "unofficial black budget." Consequently, the close relationship between the NRO and the CIA takes on special significance given the unofficial black budget funds that have been and will continue to be used for classified space reconnaissance and covert operations.

In sum, the CIA possesses an enormous slush fund, the "unofficial black budget," which it uses to fund secret space operations conducted jointly with the NRO. This is entirely separate to NRO programs funded by the DNI's "official black budget." Effectively, there is a two-tiered funding system involving parallel tracks controlled respectively by the DNI and CIA Director, with different levels of classification. While the DNI's funds go to NRO programs known and accounted for by Congress, this does not apply to the CIA's funding of more highly classified programs not known to Congress. These more highly classified NRO programs include manned space stations used for reconnaissance operations.

The NRO's Secret Space Stations

Among the first major tasks assigned to the NRO after its 1961 creation was to cooperate with the US Air Force in a feasibility study of manned satellites that could conduct space reconnaissance. President Kennedy approved the feasibility studies of the proposed manned military space station, which could operate in orbit from between 70 to 400 nautical miles (130-740 km) to conduct surveillance operations.[167] On December 10, 1963, a press release by the Office of the Secretary of Defense provided details about the proposed space station that was officially named the Manned Orbiting Laboratory (MOL):

Secretary of Defense Robert S. McNamara today assigned to the Air Force a new program for the development of a near earth Manned Orbiting Laboratory (MOL).

The MOL program, which will consist of an orbiting pressurized cylinder approximately the size of a small house trailer, will increase the Defense Department effort to determine military usefulness of man in space. . . .

MOL will be designed so that astronauts can move about freely in it without a space suit and conduct observations and experiments in the laboratory over a period of up to a month. The first manned flight of the MOL is expected late in 1967 or early in 1968 . . .[168]

Nearly two years later, President Lyndon Johnson appeared at an August 25, 1965, press conference to publicly authorize the construction and testing of MOL. It was given a budget of $1.5 billion beginning in fiscal year 1965-66. Douglas Aircraft Company was authorized to build the cylindrical laboratory and the modified Gemini capsule for re-entry, while General Electric would build the experimental equipment.[169]

What neither the 1963 Pentagon press release nor Johnson's 1965 press statement revealed is that the military astronauts would be conducting space surveillance operations over designated targets, as a declassified top-secret document to Major General Ben Frank, commander of the USAF Space Systems Division, dated March 10, 1964, confirmed.[170] Another declassified top-secret USAF document dated May 25, 1965, declared: "The initial objective is to develop and demonstrate at the earliest time an operationally useful high resolution manned optical reconnaissance system."[171] A PBS documentary presented interviews with former astronaut participants—dubbed "astrospies"—who pointed out the likely primary targets to be in the former Soviet Union.[172]

What was not known at the time, but was revealed decades later, was that the NRO secretly partnered with the USAF and NASA in the MOL program:

> In order for the MOL program to reach implementation, it required a unique partnership between the Air Force, the National Reconnaissance Office, and NASA. Since the MOL was a manned space flight program, the program required a safe and effective means for taking and returning crew members to and from space. The Air Force turned to NASA to obtain such a space flight capability by securing space capsules developed for NASA's Gemini program. The Gemini capsule was designed to ride atop the larger MOL vehicle, carrying the crew members. Once in space, the MOL crew members would open a hatch on the bottom of the Gemini capsule and travel through a passageway to the laboratory section of the MOL vehicle. They would stay in the laboratory section until returning to the Gemini capsule, with the imagery film, for the reentry through the earth's atmosphere. The Air Force also depended heavily on training procedures and facilities developed for NASA's manned space program.
>
> The NRO contributed the reconnaissance systems that became the primary purpose for developing the MOL. By the time that the MOL program initiated development, the NRO had already developed a

number of camera and signal collection sensors for gaining intelligence from space. The Air Force turned to the NRO to obtain the imagery and sensor systems necessary to use MOL as a reconnaissance platform. The MOL program contracted with Eastman Kodak to develop the camera system that was similar in form to the highly successful KH-7 and KH-8 systems [Keyhole satellites] also developed for the NRO's Gambit photoreconnaissance satellite. These relationships were critical for keeping the MOL program on its proposed schedule and controlling costs of an already complex and expensive program.[173]

The Manned Orbiting Laboratory was conceived as only the first phase of a more ambitious Air Force and NRO military space station. Phase II of the MOL program involved expanding the modular system to allow more diverse operations to be performed in space over longer periods in orbit, as explained by Lt. Col. Mark Erikson (ret. USAF):

> The system itself consisted of a permanently orbiting station module, an earth-based spacecraft comprised of a modified-Gemini capsule for ferry purposes, and a new launch vehicle, probably the Titan III. The crew of four could remain in the 1,700-cubic-foot-station module for 30 days without resupply, while the station itself would remain in orbit for at least a year. The USAF fully expected MODS [Military Orbital Development System] to grow: "Ultimately, as MODS is expanded through modular extension, it will serve as a base from which

experimental military space vehicles can be developed, tested and employed.[174]

Correspondence on October 1963 between the Department of Defense (DOD) and NASA officials, as part of a "DOD-NASA Coordination Agreement," described in more detail what Phase II would entail:

> Phase II (a) is aimed at the selection of major subsystems such as docking system, artificial g system, data handling system, etc., and will incorporate results of the modified Gemini and Apollo Ferry Studies . . . A broad look at subsystem integration is planned utilizing inputs from such current studies as Nuclear Isotope Power . . . and Integrated Life Support System . . . [175]

What this correspondence shows is that the completed space station would have an artificial gravity system, use nuclear power and would be manned. The presence of an artificial gravity system divulges that Phase II would involve a design in which the space station would rotate around a central axis. This suggests a design similar to what Wernher von Braun had proposed back in 1946, which has been dubbed the "Von Braun Station." It incorporated 20-cylindrical sections connected end-to-end:

> The 1946 version used 20 cylindrical sections, each about 3 m in diameter and 8 m long, to make up the toroid. The whole station was about 50 m in diameter and guy wires connecting and positioning the toroid to the 8 m-diameter central power module. This was equipped with a sun-following solar collector dish to heat fluid in a ball-shaped device. The heated fluid would run an electrical

generator. Presumably visiting spacecraft would dock or transfer crew at the base of the power module. Two narrow transfer tubes allowed the crew to move between the living and work quarters in the toroid and the power module.[176]

In the completed Phase II space station, each section would be made up of MOL cylinders sent up separately on a Titan III rocket, and then assembled in space. Given that each MOL cylinder was anticipated to be 56 feet (17 meters) in length (double what von Braun envisaged), the final diameter of the space station would be over 300 feet (91 meters) in diameter.[177]

A declassified document titled "MOL Program Advanced Planning," issued on March 17, 1967, shows that the funding and planning for Phase II were completely separated from the basic MOL program.[178] This made it possible for the basic MOL program to be publicly canceled down the track while the advanced portion (Phase II), involving more complex projects and objectives (i.e., assembling a type of 'Von Braun Station' in space), could continue uninterrupted as a covert program.

In a declassified April 17, 1969, top-secret memorandum by the Secretary of Defense to President Nixon, it was outlined out how the manned version of the MOL program could be canceled, but an unmanned version would secretly continue (out of Vandenberg AFB using Titan IIID rockets).[179] The manned MOL was officially canceled on June 9, 1969, in a memorandum by the Deputy Secretary of Defense to the Secretary of the Air Force which gave instructions for the continuance of the unmanned version with a new contractor competition:

> The Air Force is hereby directed to terminate the MOL Program except for those camera system elements useful for incorporation into an

unmanned satellite system optimized to use the TITAN III D. Directions to MOL contractors should be issued on Tuesday morning, June 10, at which time we will also notify the Congress and make a public statement that MOL is canceled. . . .

All future work on the camera and an unmanned system will be part of the NRP [National Reconnaissance Project]. As a security measure, appropriate elements of the MOL Project Offices and the camera system contracts should be transferred to the Air Force NRP Special Projects Offices at an early date. Overt MOL activities should be phased out in conjunction with closeout of MOL Program activities.[180]

Figure 23. Von Braun Space Station secretly assembled by the NRO

The memorandum meant that Air Force Systems Command, which had been initially in control of building the manned version of MOL, had to transfer primary responsibility over to the NRO, through the rubric of the National Reconnaissance Project (NRP). This meant that the future manned military space stations, the advanced phase of the MOL program, would be controlled by the NRO, rather than the USAF.

Another declassified top-secret memorandum, dated June 7, 1969, two days before the official public cancelation, made clear that the "unmanned MOL program" being covertly continued had been shown in studies to be significantly less efficient than the manned version. Strikingly, it would use the entire "MOL Mission module" originally intended for use in the more costly manned version:

> ALL CONCERNED RECOGNIZE THAT AN UNMANNED SYSTEM USING THE MOL CAMERA WILL HAVE POORER AVERAGE RESOLUTION, BE LESS CAPABLE AND FLEXIBLE, BE LESS RELIABLE, ETC., THAN THE MANNED MOL WOULD HAVE BEEN. . . .

> THE GE [General Electric] AND EK [Eastman Kodak] CONTRACTS ARE TO BE REDUCED IMMEDIATELY TO ONLY THOSE CAMERA SYSTEM EFFORTS APPLICABLE TO A NOT-YET-DEFINED UNMANNED SATELLITE SYSTEM THAT WILL USE THE COMPLETE MOL MISSION MODULE.[181]

This document is critical since it shows that despite the cancellation of the manned MOL program, the "complete mission module" that had been designed and developed by Douglas Aircraft Company would continue to be used for the unmanned version. This only made sense if the real purpose of phase II was to covertly build a manned space station that would be under the control of the NRO rather than the USAF.

Another declassified NRO document, titled "Advanced MOL Planning: Missions and Systems" shows General Electric's plan for reconfiguring MOL so it could hold a space crew of either twelve or forty, depending on how many sections of modules were linked together in the advanced MOL program.[182] The document describes the command module characteristics of MOL and states that by using "three mated cylinders" (each cylinder section is composed of modules), a crew of up to forty could be accommodated. Interestingly, the proposed space station would have self-defense capabilities and be powered either by solar arrays or another power supply which is blacked out in the document's text but is presumably a nuclear generator (see *Figure 3)*.

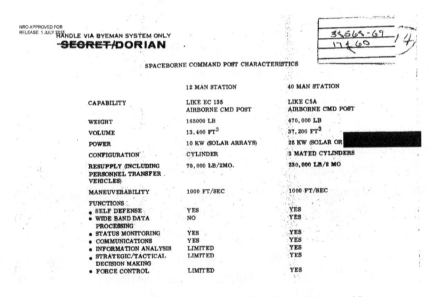

Figure 24. General Electric proposal for Spaceborne Command Posts.

The "Advanced MOL Planning: Missions and Systems" document also illustrates both the configuration of the advanced station and some of its various Earth surveillance activities that General Electric envisaged for the program (see *Figure 4*). Significantly, the proposed space station was designed to monitor threats posed by Intercontinental Ballistic Missiles (ICBMs), submarine-launched ballistic missiles (SLBMs), and aircraft, by relaying real-time surveillance of these to Strategic Air Command. It is possible that the self-defense capability of the space station could eventually enable it to intercept and neutralize such threats.

The declassified "Advanced MOL Planning: Missions and Systems" proposal by General Electric answers a perplexing question raised by the June 11, 1985, entry in the daily presidential diary of Ronald Reagan. In it, he wrote:

> Lunch with 5 top space scientists. It was fascinating. Space truly is the last frontier and some of the developments there in astronomy etc. are like science fiction, except they are real. I learned that our shuttle capacity is such that we could orbit 300 people.[183]

Reagan was not writing about NASA's space shuttle fleet which could accommodate a crew of ten on each of the five shuttles, making a maximum of fifty people put into space if all the shuttles took off simultaneously. However, if the NRO had created two or more secret space stations using MOL modules assembled in space into a configuration similar to the Von Braun Station, then it is easy to fathom the truth behind what Reagan was told in a briefing which he documented in the presidential diary. The training of Air Force and Navy pilots for the advanced MOL program very likely duplicated the same process used in the canceled basic MOL program, in which pilots were covertly recruited for the classified space program although they were led to believe they were being trained to be NASA astronauts.

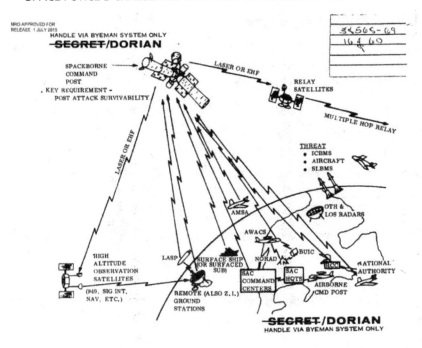

Figure 25. General Electric's illustration of a three section station built with MOL modules that could accommodate forty astronauts.

Of particular interest when examining the developments leading to the different phases of the space station is the role of Fairchild Industries in the canceled manned MOL program and its likely continuation in the same role for the advanced MOL program. Fairchild Industries' role included life support functions for the military astronauts:

> NASA MAY REPEAT MAY PICK UP THE FAIRCHILD-HILLER EFFORT, PART OF THE IBM EFFORT (PRINTERS), THE MOLECULAR SIEVE, AND SOME OF THE LIFE SUPPORT ITEMS, BUT THOSE APPEAR TO BE ABOUT THE ONLY ONES.[184]

The involvement of Fairchild Industries (formerly Fairchild Hiller up until 1971) in running the life support functions for the canceled basic manned MOL program, which in turn could be used in the advanced "unmanned program," is highly significant. After Wernher von Braun officially retired from NASA and the Marshall Space Flight Center in 1972, he immediately moved over to Fairchild Industries located in Germantown, Maryland, and became their vice president.[185] It is worth emphasizing that von Braun had done the most work in conceptualizing a viable space station that began with his 1946 von Braun Station proposal, which was to be built in a modular fashion.

At Fairchild Industries, von Braun led the secret effort to link together in space the MOL modules originally designed by McDonnell Douglas for the manned missions into the required modular sections, just as the Von Braun Station conceptualization had proposed. Lockheed Martin, General Electric and Fairchild Industries were all deeply involved in building the stealth space station(s) for a secret space surveillance program headed by the NRO, funded by the CIA, and made possible through logistical resources provided by the USAF and NASA.

There are many conclusions to be drawn from the MOL space station program. The public had been deceived into believing that MOL had been canceled in 1969. In fact, only the basic MOL program was terminated, not the more ambitious and advanced "unmanned" MOL program using complete MOL modules which were secretly launched into space from Vandenberg AFB. Throughout the 1970's and 1980's, these unmanned MOL modules were initially assembled into the three-section configuration proposed by General Electric, and eventually, into larger configurations such as the 20-section Von Braun Station. It is also important to keep in mind that the modules offered life support systems and were fully capable of supporting a crew.

Corey Goode, who claims to have served in a secret space program from 1987 to 2007, says he saw electronically archived classified documents of the assembled NRO space station. He described it as having nine modular cylindrical sections joined together into a circular arrangement—a nonagon—similar in overall shape to the Von Braun Station, but with less than half the sections. Using General Electric's crew estimates for a three-section configuration capable of housing forty crew, a nine-section configuration would hold approximately 120 crew. Goode said that there are currently two or three of these space stations in operation which have been outfitted with advanced stealth technologies.[186] What corroborates the documentary evidence and Goode's claims that manned space stations have been secretly built and deployed in Earth's orbits by the 1980s is a critical admission by President Ronald Reagan in his Presidential Diaries about America's ability to deploy 300 people in orbit.[187]

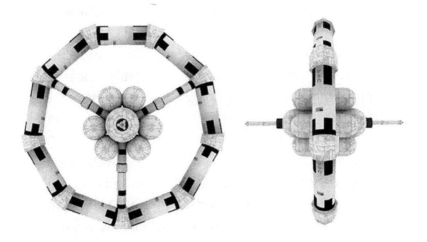

Figure 26. NRO Space Station comprised of nine cylindrical sections.
Credit: Sphere Being Alliance

Reagan's comments are critical since they confirm the existence of manned NRO space stations used for orbital surveillance, which were funded by the CIA's unofficial black budget and consequently used for unknown CIA-led covert space operations.

The Space Reconnaissance Office & Section 31

In 2000, a Commission was convened to discuss the future of the NRO given the close Congressional scrutiny it had received since its 1992 public unveiling, and criticisms by members of Congress over its continued culture of secrecy and perennial budget overruns.[188] In order to adapt to the new public climate, the NRO Commission recommended a two tiered approach where the bulk of NRO projects would be subjected to continued Congressional budgetary scrutiny, while its more sensitive programs would be absorbed by a new even more secretive organization that would be immune to such Congressional scrutiny.

> Foremost, the [NRO] commission recommended creating a "special projects office," an Office of Space Reconnaissance, within the NRO, dedicated to developing new satellite capabilities using the most advanced technologies available, cloaked entirely in secrecy, and fully exempt from the many funding rules required for U.S. Government procurement programs. Thus configured, the NRO could hastily, secretly, and aggressively field necessary satellite systems. The proposed Office of Space Reconnaissance, led by the NRO director, would "take its marching orders directly from a panel composed of the U.S. President, Secretary of Defense and Director of Central Intelligence." "A small cadre of experienced CIA and military personnel" operating "under a separate 'security compartment'," would man the office, relying "heavily upon the creativity of the contractor community for its work." Such an office was necessary, Senator Kerrey claimed, because "some

effort needed to be made to make certain that the NRO continues to do what it has done over the last 40 years, which is to produce one-of-a-kind technology."[189]

The proposal for the creation of an Office of Space Reconnaissance buried deep within the NRO that would escape Congressional scrutiny and budgetary oversight predictably led to widespread criticism from those knowledgeable about the NRO Commission's deliberations:

> Space policy analysts and Defense Department officials, for example, reacted warily to proposals that might lead to a super-secret office within an already highly-secret NRO, an office that would be exempt from public scrutiny, normal procurement and funding rules, and, perhaps, Congressional oversight. One observer claimed that the NRO already operated, and had always operated, with significant secrecy and a streamlined acquisition process, often to the chagrin of NRO critics in Congress, the media, and elsewhere. Now, ironically, the NRO Commission was calling for the pendulum to swing back toward deeper secrecy.[190]

Despite such concerns the NRO Commission Report went ahead and recommended the creation of the Space Reconnaissance Office:

> The Secretary of Defense and the Director of Central Intelligence should establish a new Office of Space Reconnaissance under the direction of the Director of the NRO. The Office should have special acquisition authorities, be staffed by experienced

military and CIA personnel, have a budget separate from other agencies and activities within the National Foreign Intelligence Program, be protected by a special security compartment, and operate under the personal direction of the President, Secretary of Defense and Director of Central Intelligence.[191]

The NRO Commission went on to describe how the Space Reconnaissance Office would have complete autonomy within the NRO and operate with budgetary funds supplied by the CIA's black budget.

> This would require that the Secretary of Defense grant this Office special exemptions from standard DoD acquisition regulations. It would rely heavily upon the DCI's special statutory authorities for procurement. It would be under the direction of the NRO Director, but would operate in secure facilities separated from NRO activities. It would create and defend a separate budget element within the National Foreign Intelligence Program and have its own security compartment. It would have a small CIA and military staff and senior and experienced program managers, and would also rely heavily upon the creativity of the contractor community for its work. It would respond, through a special Executive Committee, to direction from the President, the Secretary of Defense and the DCI. The new Office would attack the most difficult intelligence problems by providing advanced technology that will lead to frequent, assured,

global access to protect U.S. national security interests.[192]

The NRO Commission's recommendation was clear that the Space Reconnaissance Office would have its own separate funding, leadership and rely heavily on corporate contractors. The latter would ensure a greater degree of secrecy and protection from troublesome Freedom of Information Act requests.

The initial intent of the NRO Commission was to fund the Space Reconnaissance Office through the official black budget controlled at the time by the CIA Director in his/her dual hat capacity as Director of Central Intelligence (DCI). The DCI would sit on the proposed Special Executive Committee that included representatives from the Office of the President and the Secretary of Defense. The situation changed significantly in 2004 with the passage of the Intelligence Reform and Terrorism Prevention Act, wherein the "official black budget" was transferred to the Director of National Intelligence (DNI) and the position of DCI was abolished.

This would have meant that the CIA Director, who controlled the much larger "unofficial black budget," would not have had a position on the Executive Committee that would run the proposed Space Reconnaissance Office. Also, creating the Space Reconnaissance Office within the NRO would have led to the unwelcome involvement of the DNI in space activities that the Director of the CIA wanted to hide. Consequently, the decision was made to launch the proposed Space Reconnaissance Office, not within the NRO as recommended by the Commission, but within the CIA instead.

This is precisely what occurred as evidenced in a Central Intelligence Agency Executive Director Memorandum dated September 11, 2014, titled: "(U) Concurrence to Create the Office of Space Reconnaissance."[193] The Office of Space Reconnaissance was established under the CIA's Science and Technology

Directorate as explained by Douglas Pasternak in an article with *U.S. News*:

> Last year, *U.S. News* has learned, Defense Secretary Donald Rumsfeld and CIA Director George Tenet created a new top-secret office to develop cutting-edge spy satellite technologies. The office is an arm of the CIA's Directorate of Science and Technology. The new office maintains bogus commercial "cover" facilities outside the agency's headquarters in Langley, Va., and CIA officials are talking to defense contractors about developing new satellites. "Tenet formed the office," says a former senior Pentagon official, "because he wanted exquisite intelligence collection capabilities." According to several former Pentagon and CIA officials with close ties to U.S. intelligence, the office was created, in part, because of the NRO's declining performance. The CIA denies this but won't discuss the new satellite operation.[194]

It is important to keep in mind Pasternak's observation that the Langley commercial facilities created for the Space Reconnaissance Office are a cover, the real work was being done elsewhere—that would almost certainly include the NRO's Chantilly, Virginia, headquarters.

Frank Calvelli, the Deputy Director of the NRO at the time, confirmed the creation of the Space Reconnaissance Office within the CIA's Directorate of Science and Technology (DS&T) at a Congressional Hearing held on March 15, 2016: "the CIA's DS&T Office of Space Reconnaissance (OSR) was formally established in 2014 to provide CIA officers a career path focused on space and space-related acquisitions."[195] In an official Press Release, the DNI James Clapper, revealed the close relationship between the CIA's newly created Office of Space Reconnaissance and the NRO, which would be run by the director of the NRO, Dr. Raymond "Ray" Cook, just as recommended in the NRO Commission Report:

> Ray is currently the director for the Office of Space Reconnaissance within CIA's Directorate of Science and Technology where he is leading their efforts to integrate NRO's fulfillment of its IC mission. Ray is concurrently the NRO director of Mission Operations. Before joining the NRO, Ray led multi-agency IT infrastructure, data sharing and compliance within CIA. [196]

The creation of the Office of Space Reconnaissance that would be run by the NRO Director who would be "dual hatted" as a senior CIA official within its Science and Technology Directorate. This would ensure that the CIA Director would effectively run space reconnaissance activities using personnel and technical resources from the NRO. In short, while the Office of Space Reconnaissance was nominally run by the CIA out of its Langley headquarters, the real work was being done out of NRO facilities with dual hatted administrators, whose programs were being funded by the CIA's massive unofficial black budget. In this way, the most highly classified NRO space reconnaissance programs could be moved entirely over to the authority of the Office of Space Reconnaissance, while the programs themselves remained in NRO facilities, thereby removing the DNI, Secretary of Defense, and Office of the President, from any administrative oversight, or budgetary scrutiny. Effectively, this turns the Office of Space Reconnaissance into a rogue operation run by the CIA outside of the normal chain of military command. Neither the President nor Secretary of Defense has any knowledge of or direct authority over the Office of Space Reconnaissance.

The existence of the Office of Space Reconnaissance creates a major problem for the US Space Force. The CIA and the NRO effectively run an officially sanctioned space reconnaissance program with virtually unlimited funding to purchase spacecraft constructed from multiple corporate contractors, and to hire personnel from private contractors or military services. None of these space assets and operations are monitored by Congress or the Department of Defense given the CIA's authority over the Office of Space Reconnaissance, and its operations out of one or more NRO facilities. If Space Force is likened to Gene Rodenberry's fictional Starfleet, as I will discuss in chapter nine, then the Office of Space Reconnaissance can be likened to Section 31!

Chapter 8

Space Force Priorities: US Dominance, International Law & Preventing a Space Pearl Harbor

The eyes of the world now look into space, to the Moon and to the planets beyond, and we have vowed that we shall not see it governed by a hostile flag of conquest, but by a banner of freedom and peace.

— President John F. Kennedy.[197]

After the 2019 creation of Space Force, two foundational documents were released by its first Chief of Space Operations, General John "Jay" Raymond, in an attempt to define the new military service's core identity, mission priorities and overall guidelines. The first is a 40-page document released in June 2020, with the title "Space Capstone Publication: Spacepower Doctrine for Space Forces" that presents the "service's first articulation of an independent theory of spacepower."[198] Remember, prior to the creation of Space Force, space had always been deemed a benign environment. Today, however, it is considered a warfighting domain. Therefore, a doctrine of space power needed to be developed, which is what the Space Capstone Publication presents.

The Space Capstone Publication was followed on November 9, 2020, by a 12-page document titled, "Chief of Space Operations Planning Guidance," which presents "foundational direction for the Space Force to advance National and Department of Defense (DoD) strategic objectives."[199] Essentially, this second document defines how Space Force is going to integrate with the other military services to achieve its objectives. While the first document provides the broad doctrinal framework for the key concepts that define Space Force's identity and operations, the second provides a practical set of guidelines for how the Spacepower Doctrine is to be put into practice.

Within the first document, the primary purpose of the Space Capstone Publication is described as follows:

> The Space Capstone Publication is the inaugural doctrine manual for the United States Space Force, providing a basis for training and education, and informs decision-making, mission analysis, objectives, and the development of military space strategy in support of national security, national defense, and national military strategies.[200]

This encompasses how Space Force plans to project its military power into space. It goes on to explain how Space Force's overall mission is vital to long term US national interest:

> Access to space is essential to U.S. prosperity and security — it is a national imperative. The many benefits our Nation derives from space include mass communications, financial and economic information networks, public safety, weather monitoring, and military technology. Like any source of national power, the United States must cultivate,

develop, and protect these benefits in order to secure continued prosperity.[201]

There is no better example of the importance of space to US "prosperity and security" than the Global Positioning Satellite (GPS) system, which is used worldwide for communications and commerce, and for pinpoint targeting by the US military. If anything were to happen to the US GPS system, which currently comprises thirty-three satellites, this would not only blind the US military, but it would severely impact the national economy.

Additionally, Space is considered to be vital for future economic growth and entrepreneurial activity, which ranks high among Space Force's core goals according to the Space Capstone Publication:

> Today, the entirety of economic and military space activities is confined to the geocentric regime; however, commercial investments and new technologies have the potential to expand the reach of vital National space interests to the cislunar regime [area between Moon and Earth] and beyond in the near future. As technology marches forward, U.S. military spacepower must harmonize with the other instruments of power to protect, defend, and maintain the Nation's strategic interests in space.[202]

The potential economic value of space as more aerospace technologies become available, allowing entrepreneurs to go cheaply into space to establish multiple commercial services, is vast. Space tourism, mining and communications are likely to be the driving forces for a vast economic boom, especially in the cislunar region which comprises the area between the Earth and Moon orbits. According to the US Chamber of Commerce the "space economy is expected to turn into a trillion-dollar industry over the coming years."[203]

The Space Capstone Publication describes how space has dramatically changed from a domain involving peaceful cooperation and scientific exploration by the international community:

> Space was once a sanctuary from attack, but the emergence, advanced development, and proliferation of a wide range of demonstrated counterspace weapons by potential adversaries has reversed this paradigm. Today, space, like all other domains, is realized to be contested due to the increasing threat to orbiting assets by adversary weapons systems. There is no forward edge of the battle area behind which military spacecraft can reconstitute and recover. Spacecraft remain in orbit through peace and war where they are potentially at risk from adversary counterspace capabilities and the hostile space environment. [204]

Similarly, General Raymond begins his Planning Guidance document by explaining how space has shifted from a benign security environment to one where warfare can be expected in the near future:

> **The Space Force has a mandate in national strategy, policy, and law to be both pathfinder and protector of America's interests as a space-faring nation.** The convergence of proliferating technology and competitive interests has forever re-defined space from a benign domain to one in which we anticipate all aspects of human endeavor – including

warfare. The return of peer, great power competitors has dramatically changed the global security environment and space is central to that change.[205]

According to the 1967 Outer Space Treaty, space was considered to be a peaceful environment for scientific exploration. No country was allowed to station military forces or weapons in space, the Moon, or other celestial objects in order to maintain space as a "benign domain." General Raymond is here asserting that recent military developments by "great power competitors" mean that space is no longer a benign environment and that preventative military measures need to be taken. More specifically, Raymond is referring to China and Russia's development of sophisticated anti-satellite technologies capable of disrupting or destroying the US satellite grid. Such a possibility was first outlined in the January 11, 2001, Space Commission Report, which I discussed in chapter one, warning about a "Space Pearl Harbor" and the need for a new military service to prevent it.[206] China's successful first test of an anti-satellite weapon in 2007 set off alarm bells in the Pentagon about the future plans of China's Communist Party leaders. Many national security analysts began warning that Communist China had made space a priority for its climb to global hegemony before 2049—the one hundred year anniversary of the Communist Revolution.[207]

The Space Capstone Publication goes on to explain how Space Force plans to integrate other nations sharing common interests in a way similar to how the NATO Alliance was formed around the US as the driving force to prevent aggression from the Warsaw Pact:

Military space forces are the warfighters who protect, defend, and project spacepower. They provide support, security, stability, and strategic effects by employing spacepower in, from, and to the space domain. This necessitates close collaboration and cooperation with the U.S. Government, Allies, and partners and in accordance with domestic and international law. [208]

Space Force recognizes that the best way to thwart Communist China's plans to become the dominant space power is to ensure widespread collaboration between democratic nations to defend space assets from future Chinese aggression. This is a similar strategy to how the US is partnering with regional allies to prevent China establishing dominance over the South China sea.

When it comes to international space law, the Outer Space Treaty is clear that deployment of "nuclear weapons or any other kinds of weapons of mass destruction" are not permitted, there are to be no military bases on celestial bodies, but it allows the deployment of military equipment or personnel in space for "peaceful purposes:"

The use of military personnel for scientific research or for any other peaceful purposes shall not be prohibited. The use of any equipment or facility necessary for peaceful exploration of the Moon and other celestial bodies shall also not be prohibited. [209]

Consequently, deploying defensive weapons systems and manned facilities such as space stations designed to protect the GPS system, space mining, space tourism, etc., are permitted under international law. As long as Space Force deploys military forces for strictly defensive purposes, and avoids sending weapons of mass destruction into space, then it is in compliance with international treaty obligations.

Space Force, however, plans to be far more than merely the core of a multinational military operation:

> Spacepower requires explorers, diplomats, entrepreneurs, scientists, developers, and warfighters. Military space forces — *protectors of America's space interests* — are first and foremost the warfighters who protect, defend, and project U.S. spacepower. These professionals must simultaneously commit themselves to two demanding professions: warfighting and the mastery of space.[210]

The intent here is to develop a multidisciplinary force that can transplant American culture and values into deep space. It is not enough for the US to establish military dominance in space, but to ensure the spread of democratic and republican values.

General Raymond explains in his Planning Guidance document how the Space Force can prepare for future warfare in space that is defensive in nature:

> The United States Space Force is called to organize, train, equip, and present forces capable of *preserving America's freedom of action in space; enabling Joint Force lethality and effectiveness;* and *providing independent options — in, from, and to space.* . . . While we will extend and defend America's competitive advantage in peacetime, **the ultimate measure of our readiness is the ability to prevail should war initiate in, or extend to space.**[211]

Deterring major adversaries from launching military hostilities is explained as a key priority in order not to lose US space dominance in the Planning Guidance document:

America needs a Space Force able to deter conflict, and if deterrence fails, prevail should war initiate in or extend to space. Space capabilities enhance the potency of all other military forces. Our National leadership requires resilient and assured military space capabilities for sustained advantage in peaceful competition, or decisive advantage in conflict or war. . . .

The change in the geo-strategic and operating environment that compelled the creation of the Space Force means that many of our legacy space capabilities must be reevaluated for ongoing relevance. **Let me be clear – if we do not adapt to outpace aggressive competitors, we will likely lose our peacetime and warfighting advantage in space.**[212]

China and Russia are both viewed as the primary adversaries capable of militarily destroying the US satellite grid in a future war or in a surprise attack; a Space Pearl Harbor:

Chinese and Russian military doctrines indicate they view space as essential to modern warfare, and view counterspace capabilities as potent means to reduce U.S. and allied military effectiveness. Modern Chinese and Russian space surveillance networks are capable of finding, tracking, and characterizing satellites in all earth orbits. Both Russia and China are developing systems using the electro-magnetic spectrum, cyberspace, directed energy, on-orbit capabilities, and ground-based antisatellite missiles to destroy space-based assets.[213]

China in particular has been undergoing rapid military modernization with the staggering growth in its economy. Measured in Purchasing Power Parity, China's economy has already overtaken the US, and it is steadily increasing its military expenditures, especially in space which it considers to be the strategic high ground and the US military's Achilles Heel.[214]

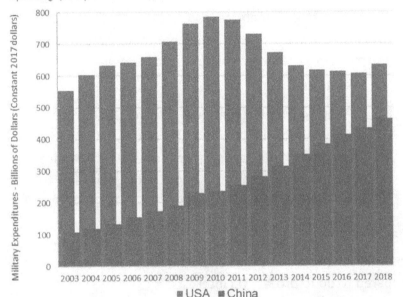

Figure 27. Comparison of US and China Military Spending in PPP terms

The possibility of China launching a "Space Pearl Harbor" is something that began to concern US military strategists as far back as the 2001 Space Commission Report. Space Force's immediate goal will be to protect the US GPS and other satellite grids from a surprise Chinese attack, which would otherwise incapacitate the US military all over the planet. From the perspective of China's

Communist Party leadership, however, as I explain in *Rise of the Red Dragon* (2020), China is merely catching up to what the United States (and Russia) had already secretly developed and deployed in space decades earlier.

As far as future military conflict in space is concerned and fulfilling the obligations of international law, this is what the Space Capstone Publication has to say:

> Military spacepower is inextricably linked to war. Military space forces must operate in this new warfighting domain to contribute to winning our Nation's wars. Thus, war's enduring nature and modern character shape and define military spacepower. . . .

> In keeping with international law, the United States acknowledges that the use of space is for peaceful purposes, while preparing for the reality that space must be defended from those who will seek to undermine our goals in space.[215]

The Capstone document provides an expansive view of potential enemies in space, and what Space Force needs to be prepared to do to protect US interests:

> Space warfare targets the mind of an adversary and seeks to neutralize their capability and will to resist. Military space forces compete against thinking actors who threaten our Nation's prosperity, security, or political aims. Thus, military space forces must prepare to outwit, outmaneuver, and dominate thinking, competent, and lethal aggressors who are attempting to thwart U.S. actions. . . .

Military spacepower cannot unilaterally win wars, but like landpower, seapower, airpower, or cyberpower, its success, absence, or failure could prove catastrophically decisive in war. Because military spacepower has the potential to be the difference between victory and defeat, it must be viewed with equal importance as military power in any other domain. This observation is the strategic imperative for creating the United States Space Force as an independent military Service capable of maximizing military spacepower as a distinct and vital formulation of military power. [216]

It is worth remembering that only a year earlier, General Raymond was among those that were bound by the gag order imposed by Air Force Secretary Heather Wilson on any discussion of Space as a warfighting domain. The Space Power Doctrine reveals the extent to which General Raymond and other senior Air Force officers, aside from Lt. General Steven Kwast, had been constrained in expressing their views of the importance of space as a warfighting domain.

Not surprisingly, General Raymond emphasizes developing breakthrough space technologies in dealing with potential military conflict in his Planning Guidance document:

Space Force will use strategic investments to cultivate a strong, diverse and competitive American space industrial base. Civil and commercial developments that pave the way for exploration and commercialization beyond near-Earth orbit will both generate technology that benefits the USSF and require an order of magnitude expansion of our ability to sense, communicate and act to protect and defend American interests in cis-lunar space and beyond.[217]

General Raymond is here suggesting major aerospace defense contractors such as Lockheed Martin, Northrop Grumman, General Dynamics, Boeing, etc., will play vital roles in developing breakthrough space technologies that can be used to deter adversaries in space. While development of breakthrough space technologies is framed as a future need, the reality is that such technologies have already been secretly developed by major aerospace companies. The produced technologies have been subsequently sold off to different "customers" such as US military commands, intelligence agencies, DARPA, and major allies for decades.

As previously explained, there is extensive testimonial and documentary evidence showing how the US Air Force, the Navy, CIA, and NRO developed separate secret space programs in response to earlier developments in Nazi Germany that carried over into the post-war era. As a result of decades-long cooperation with major corporations in reverse engineering captured Nazi and alien spacecraft, advanced anti-gravity spacecraft and electromagnetic weapons systems were developed and deployed by different entities within the US national security establishment. Among the major challenges facing Space Force today is how it deals with the advanced space program secretly developed and deployed by the CIA and NRO controlled by the Space Reconnaissance Office.

The critical requirement for gaining access to breakthrough aerospace technologies by a US military service, combatant command, or intelligence agency is to demonstrate a clear need for such advanced technologies for completing space-related missions. When space was considered a benign environment, this favored the acquisition of reverse-engineered technologies by intelligence services or special operations groups that used space for intelligence gathering or small-scale covert operations. The bulk of breakthrough aerospace technologies consequently went to intelligence entities such as the NRO, CIA, DIA, NSA, and the Pentagon's elite covert operations organizations such as Air Force Special Operations and Special Operations Command.

Even US Space Command (1985-2002) and Air Force Space Command (1982-2019) were then limited in how much access they had to such breakthrough "black world" technologies as acknowledged by Edgar Fouche's revelations about the TR-3B. He explained that such technology was under the operational control of the CIA and NRO, while the Air Force itself provided administrative and logistical support. The Air Force's Space Command therefore assisted the CIA and NRO to conduct space surveillance operations. In addition, Air Force Special Operations used such space technologies for covert operations around the planet as explained earlier. The Pentagon's Joint Chiefs of Staff and the unified combatant commanders, with the notable exceptions of Special Operations Command and (Air Force) Space Command, were largely denied access. This was because major military space operations were deemed unnecessary due to space being considered a benign environment.

All that changes with General Raymond's Planning Guidance document and the Space Capstone Publication, both of which expand upon President Donald Trump's earlier Space Policy Directive-4, which made space a warfighting domain requiring defense of America's space assets.[218] Space is now considered a warfighting domain where large scale military operations may be necessary to protect the US satellite grid. This means that breakthrough corporate technologies that previously were denied to the different military services due to their high-level security classification and international space law constraints, are now permitted either through Space Force (which incorporates the former USAF Space Command) or US Space Command, both of which were respectively created or reconstituted in 2019.

General Raymond emphasizes the haste with which these advanced technologies should now be incorporated into Space Force and for immediate action to be taken to protect the US satellite grid:

> The strategic environment demands we act boldly now to build a Service designed to act with speed and decisiveness to ensure the United States maintains its advantage in the domain. . . . This CPG [Chief of Space Operations Planning Guidance] identifies those characteristics and capabilities within the force that must evolve. We do not have the luxury of delay for further analysis. [219]

Raymond is here referring to Space Force becoming an effective deterrent against a future Space Pearl Harbor attack knocking out America's GPS and other satellite systems. This requires Space Force developing and deploying breakthrough technologies, many of which are currently in the process of being transferred to Space Force.

Raymond's strategic priorities are supported by the Secretary of the US Air Force, Barbara Barret, who has called for declassifying many space technologies kept hidden from the general public and even from different elements of the Air Force itself. On December 7, 2019, she declared:

> Declassifying some of what is currently held in secure vaults would be a good idea. . . . You would have to be careful about what we declassify, but there is much more classified than what needs to be.[220]

In conclusion, redefining space as a warfighting domain means that formerly highly classified technologies developed by corporations and military laboratories for exclusive use in space by the intelligence and special operations communities will be eventually acquired by Space Force. This is most likely going to occur soon after the 18-month set up period for Space Force ends in May 2021. These advanced space technologies will be made available for large scale deployment in future space combat operations and maintaining US space dominance. The most immediate goal in establishing and maintaining US Space dominance is controlling the cislunar region, the Moon and Mars. In the short term, this means Space Force will compete with the rival aerospace forces established by China and Russia for space superiority. In the long term, Space Force is destined to clash with secret space programs run by a shadowy consortium of transnational corporations, and an even more elusive "Dark Fleet" that I will discuss in chapter 11. Establishing space cooperation between major democratic nations is vital to achieving an optimal future for the US. Consequently, it is no great surprise that such an optimal future has been envisaged by USAF Space Command/Space Force officials to be similar to the fictional Star Trek series.

Chapter 9

Space Force & Ensuring a Star Trek Future

They used to say that if Man was meant to fly, he'd have wings. But he did fly. He discovered he had to.

— James T. Kirk, "Return to Tomorrow"

O n September 5, 2019, the US Air Force Space Command (now Space Force) hosted a Space Futures Workshop to explore the evolving conditions in space up to the year 2060 as a result of a decision by the Trump Administration in February 2019 to redefine Space as a "warfighting domain."[221] Approximately sixty officials and experts from the Department of Defense, NASA, NATO, private industry and academia gathered to discuss the most likely developments in space over the next forty years, and how these could be responded to in a way that ensured US space leadership. The Workshop determined that the long-term trend was that the US would experience a relative economic decline compared to China and India, and this would significantly impact military budgets each devoted to space as a warfighting domain. Consequently, the main strategy of US policy makers would be to develop a multinational space coalition thereby ensuring continued US dominance and the most optimal future, despite future economic trends and Communist China's growing military assertiveness.

There were eight future space scenarios that were discussed and analyzed by Workshop participants who used three main variables to separate each as humanity increasingly traveled into space: civil, commercial, and military. 'Civil' related to the values, laws and the size of the population in space. 'Commercial' related to amount of economic activity in space generated through mining, exploration, trade, and other activities. 'Military' related to the extent a leading nation and its allies was able to dominate space as a warfighting domain.

The most optimistic scenario was a "Star Trek" future as explained in the *Space Futures Workshop Report* where all three variables were optimized in space from a US perspective:

> **Star Trek**: *Most optimistic and expansive*
>
> The U.S. coalition retains leadership over the space domain and has introduced free-world laws and processes that have led to significant global civil, commercial, and military expansion in space and resulted in large revenue streams. Thousands of humans live or work in space at a variety of habitats across cislunar space, the Moon, and Mars.[222]

The US coalition would mainly comprise Western nations that held similar values of democracy, individual liberty, rule of law and government transparency. Most importantly, the Star Trek scenario would require the declassification/development of many energy and propulsion technologies that would be necessary for the human presence to expand beyond the cislunar region. Electromagnetic propulsion systems, warp drives, nuclear fusion reactors, stargates, photonic healing, and other futuristic technologies necessary for deep space travel, would have to be declassified and released into the public arena. As discussed earlier, the CIA, the NRO, and major corporations have classified such technologies, even from senior Air Force officials and despite the Secretary of the Air Force calling for greater declassification.[223] Alternatively, national security orders placed on over 5900 patent applications could be released through sweeping presidential executive orders.[224] This would enable the current generation of scientists and engineers to reinvent the wheel, so to speak, thereby bypassing any roadblocks imposed by the CIA/NRO and the Deep State in not sharing such technologies.

The next most optimistic scenario was "Garden Earth" where two of the three variables were optimized:

Garden Earth: *Optimistic and expansive*

The U.S. coalition retains leadership over the space domain and has introduced free-world laws and processes that have led to significant global civil, commercial, and military expansion in space and resulted in large revenue streams. However, human presence is limited and most processes are controlled remotely or robotically.[225]

The Garden Earth scenario is largely predicated on the idea that current rocket fuel propulsion systems will continue to be widely used for space exploration with major innovations that make them affordable for commercial and military activity in deep space. Elon Musk's Space X has led the way in introducing major innovations with existing rocket propulsion systems with the successful development of reusable rockets. Nevertheless, the major rocket propulsion systems employed by Space X continue to use combustible fuels such as kerosene for the Falcon 9 rockets and methane for the Starship rockets. Kerosene rocket propulsion systems were first used by Nazi Germany in the 1940s for its V2 rockets. This scenario would emerge if advanced spacecraft propulsion technologies continue to be highly classified and withheld from public release.

The third optimistic scenario was Elysium where again two of three variables were optimized:

Elysium: *Optimistic and expansive*

The U.S. coalition retains leadership over the space domain and has introduced free-world laws and processes that have led to significant global civil, commercial, and military expansion in space. Thousands of humans live or work in space at a variety of habitats across cislunar space, the Moon, and Mars. However, large revenue streams have yet to materialize. Commercial activity is focused in LEO [Low Earth Orbit] to GEO [Geosynchronous Earth Orbit] terrestrial communications, information, PNT [Pointing, Navigation, and Timing], and to provide key parts of the civil and commercial infrastructure required for the continued expansion of human presence in space.[226]

This scenario would arise if space was deemed by the international community to be common heritage of humanity, as envisaged in the 1967 Outer Space Treaty.[227] The international proscription of private property in space would be a major disincentive for corporations to heavily invest in space mining and other commercial ventures. Another disincentive would be the creation of an international regulatory commission similar to "The Enterprise" envisaged in the Law of the Sea Convention that would be in charge of levying licenses and taxes on commercial space activities.[228]

The fourth and final optimistic scenario, "Space Today" involves only one variable being optimized, the military:

Space Today (Space as a Warfighting Domain):
Positive

The U.S. coalition is the leading military space power, though space is a highly contested warfighting domain and an essential element in integrated, cross-domain warfare. Commercial and civil space activities are limited to LEO to GEO systems with minor levels of tourism. Military space systems are highly resilient, maneuverable, robotically refuelable, self-healing to attack, highly integrated, artificial intelligence driven, highly autonomous, and reconstitution ability is enhanced. The U.S. coalition holds the advantage in using civil and commercial capabilities to support military capabilities.[229]

The "Space Today" scenario would arise if futuristic space technologies, electromagnetic propulsion, nuclear fusion, etc., were not declassified or not allowed to be developed by private industry for national security reasons. This would mean that Space Force and the aerospace forces from other countries would continue to monopolize the most advanced space technologies exclusively for covert military and surveillance purposes.

The common variable for all four optimistic scenarios is that a US military coalition is dominant in space affairs. The report describes this space coalition as follows:

The U.S. coalition is the lead military space power. Other space faring nations continuously challenge that lead through expansion of their own capabilities or through alliances with other space faring nations. The U.S. coalition has the range of military capabilities necessary to:

- Protect the critical elements of their extensive civil, commercial, and human presence across cislunar space from conventional and cyber threats.

- Protect the combined commercial, civil, and military command, control, communications, computer, intelligence, surveillance, and reconnaissance (C4ISR) infrastructure to monitor and control space operations and provide information services in, through, and from the cislunar environment during peace and conflict.

- Project military power throughout the cislunar environment to exercise selected space superiority in time and place as needed for conflicts within space and as part of larger, cross-domain conflicts.

- Preempt any other nations monopolizing key logistics points (lunar poles, Lagrangian points, *etc.*) or key assets (asteroids, lunar water, *etc.*) for military uses.[230]

The US led multinational space coalition, with Space Force at its core, has many of the characteristics of the fictional Starfleet in the *Star Trek* series. Indeed, the official logo of Space Force has a striking resemblance to the fictional logo of Starfleet. Given that the most optimistic scenario is described as the "Star Trek" future, then it would not be inconsistent to describe this multinational coalition developing a future Starfleet. In the final chapter, I will discuss the possibility that the multinational space coalition proposed in the Space Futures Report and its resemblance to Starfleet is not an accident of history but was deliberately seeded into the collective consciousness of humanity in the mid- 1960s.

Figure 28. Starfleet and Space Force Logos

Three out of the four negative scenarios discussed in the Space Futures Workshop report involve another nation or bloc of nations being the dominant military space power:

> These three future scenarios posit a major growth in the importance of space and share the characteristic of an alternate to a U.S. coalition as the leader across the civil, commercial, and military elements of space power. They further posit a significant power advantage of this lead space power over the U.S. and its allies. While who might develop to be this leading space power is uncertain, we have chosen names with a Chinese reference since China is presently the most likely candidate. In these futures, the alternate lead space power views the U.S. coalition as a rival at best and a potential adversary at worst.[231]

Given that China is the most likely dominant space power for these negative scenarios, and it currently is a one-party totalitarian Communist state, then the implications are most worrisome. If China continues to be run by the Communist Party, then what is being anticipated over the next forty years is a Cold War era-esque rivalry between two blocs of nations run respectively by the leading democratic and communist nations. This would largely be a repeat the Cold War rivalry between the US and the Soviet Union from 1945 to 1991, but one where both sides possess military space fleets seeking to expand their strategic dominance over the cislunar region, the Moon, Mars, asteroids and deep space.

The report goes on to describe how pessimistic each future scenario is when measured in terms of the three variables discussed in the workshop: civil, commercial, and military. The most pessimistic scenario is "Zhang He" since the social and commercial variables are contextualized by the military dominance of another space power, most likely China:

Zhang He: *Expansive but most pessimistic*

An alternate nation [China] exercises leadership over the space domain and has introduced laws and processes that promote their interests or limit the actions of rivals. Leveraging their growing technological edge and by using non-competitive practices, they attract a growing, disproportionate share of global space revenue streams. Thousands of humans live in space to maintain lunar and Mars bases to promote national prestige, further patterns of dependency, and support the technology and infrastructure for commercial and military space leadership.[232]

Such a scenario could arise by a number of factors that may overlap or occur sequentially. First, the US could become a failed state due to civil war conditions manufactured by the Deep State as a result of prolonged unrest caused by the contested 2020 elections. Second, China could launch a Space Pearl Harbor knocking out the US GPS system (and perhaps the European Union's Galileo Satellite

System), thereby making the US (and Europe) dependent on China's BeiDou Navigation Satellite System. Third, the US military could be absorbed into a global military force nominally administered by the United Nations, but in fact controlled by the Deep State. Finally, China could succeed in developing artificial intelligence and 5G/6G technologies to the extent that it becomes the dominant technological power on Earth and in space, and it releases previously suppressed aerospace technologies.

Another pessimistic scenario is Xi's Dream, named after China's current paramount leader:

Xi's Dream: *Expansive but pessimistic*

An alternate nation is the lead space power, though the importance of space is driven by the increased human presence in space for exploration, tourism, and to support and maintain commercial space capabilities. Large revenue streams have yet to materialize. Commercial activity is focused in LEO to GEO terrestrial communications, information, PNT, and to provide key parts of the civil and commercial infrastructure required for the continued expansion of human presence in space.[233]

Again, a scenario may emerge where corporations are not incentivized to establish space mining or other commercial activities. This may be due to private property laws not being extended into space, which is considered the common heritage of humanity, and/or a space regulatory agency being created that issues onerous licenses or taxes for commercial space ventures.

Another pessimistic scenario where an alternative nation [China] and its allies exerts military dominance over space is called "Dark Skies." It is similar to the "Space Today" optimistic scenario described earlier in terms of space being a highly contested warfighting domain except that China and its allies, rather than the US, are the dominant space power. This would be the scenario emerging in a post-Space Pearl Harbor environment where the US GPS system has been destroyed, perhaps along with the European Union's Galileo. China's BeiDou GPS system would become the default satellite service used by nations all over the planet.

The final pessimistic scenario is one where neither the US nor China are the dominant space power, but there is flourishing economic activity in space where corporations make enormous profits. Predictably it is called the Wild Frontier:

> No clear space power exercises leadership over the space domain. However, the growth in space capabilities of national and private entities has resulted in global civil, commercial, and military expansion in space and led to large revenue streams. However, human presence is limited, driven primarily by national prestige, exploration, and tourism.[234]

This scenario would arise if corporations become the dominant space power by utilizing the advanced aerospace craft they have reverse engineered on behalf of the US military and intelligence services. Using hundreds of thousands of highly trained special forces operatives drawn from every nation who would fly fleets of advanced aerospace vehicles, a transnational corporate consortium may ultimately become the dominant space power. Aided and abetted by the Deep State, the consortium can ensure that national militaries remain Earth-bound in order to comply with an overly broad interpretation of the Outer Space Treaty's proscription against "nuclear weapons or any other kinds of weapons of mass destruction" in space.[235] In such a scenario,

Space Force would be fated to become a second-rate military power compared to what corporations are able to deploy in space.

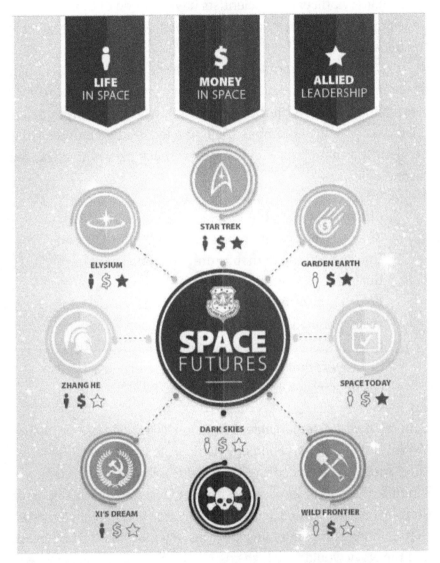

Figure 29. Eight space future scenarios: Space Futures Workshop Report.

The Workshop report did not describe contemporary developments in China which suggest it is well advanced in its efforts to develop a Space Navy that could establish over the next forty years the military space dominance described in the "Zhang He," "Xi's Dream," and "Dark Skies" scenarios. Nevertheless, senior USAF military officers and scientists have warned of China's secret development of a space navy and warned of what this entailed in the decades ahead.

The most authoritative source on the secret construction of a Chinese Space Navy comes from Steven Kwast, a former Lieutenant General with the US Air Force who retired from active military service in September 2019. In a lecture two months later, he disclosed that China is developing a space navy with advanced technologies:

> China is our competition. Russia is our competition. They see the power of the economy of space . . . and they are rushing to that future. . . . China has already built the organization, and has the strategy, the doctrine and the technology, and the builders for their guardian force in space. They are building a navy in space with the equivalent of battleships and destroyers that will be able to maneuver and kill and communicate with dominance.[236]

General Kwast's remarkable admission is echoed by Dr. James Sheehy, the Chief Technology Officer for the Naval Aviation Enterprise. In a letter to the US Patents and Trademark Office in support of a patent application for a Hybrid Aerospace Undersea Craft by another Navy Scientist, Dr. Salvator Pais, Sheehy asserted that China was currently investing heavily in similar technologies, and the Navy would face high costs if the patent was not granted:

> 2. . . . . Dr. Pais is currently funded by NAWCAD [Naval Air War Center Aircraft Division] to design a test article instrumentation to demonstrate the

experimental feasibility of achieving high electromagnetic (EM) field-energy and flux values. . . . He is currently one year into the project and has already begun a series of experiments to design and demonstrate advanced High Energy Density / High Power propulsion systems.

3. . . . If successful the realization of this result demonstrates that this patent documents the future state of the possible and moves propulsion technology beyond gas dynamic systems to field-induced propulsion based hybrid aerospace-undersea craft . . .

5. Based on these initial findings I would assert this will become a reality. China is already investing significantly in this area and I would prefer we hold the patent as opposed to paying forever more to use this revolutionary technology.[237]

More evidence that China is developing a secret space navy based on advanced technologies acquired from the US and other foreign sources is presented in *Rise of the Red Dragon: The Origins and Threat of China's Secret Space Program* (2020). The negative scenarios described in the Space Futures Workshop are well founded and highly credible, thereby requiring urgent preemptive action by the US as outlined in the Workshop Report.

Space Futures Workshop Report Conclusion and Recommendations

The Workshop Report featured important conclusions about the eight future scenarios discussed in the Workshop, and the need to prioritize space affairs if the US is to remain the dominant space power for the next forty years:

> A failure to remain the leading space power will place U.S. national power at risk. The U.S. and its allies must promote and optimize the combined civil, military, and commercial exploitation of space that best serves the nation's interests.
>
> Maximizing the strength, range, and diversity of U.S. government and commercial space activities is essential to ensure the U.S. leads across a broad range of national capabilities. A commensurately strong space industrial base is essential.[238]

Consequently, the Space Futures Workshop made a number of important recommendations:

> 1. The US must develop a long-term, national space strategy to ensure continued leadership. This strategy should be developed across government, industry, and academia to ensure synergy of efforts to optimize and promote overall U.S. national space power and grand strategy. . . .
>
> 4. Essential capabilities and technologies to enable positive future outcomes must be developed by the whole of government. An investment, policy, and regulatory strategy must be pursued to ensure those capabilities.[239]

The most significant step that needed to be taken in support of the Star Trek future was to establish a multinational space coalition that would work with US Space Command/Space Force in taking necessary military action to protect the alliance's vital interests in space. A monumental move towards ensuring a Star Trek future was the signing of the Artemis Accords.

Chapter 10

Artemis Accords as First Step to Space NATO & Future Star Fleet

We are at a point in history where a proper attention to space, and especially near space, may be absolutely crucial in bringing the world together.

— Margaret Mead

On December 11, 2017, President Donald Trump issued Space Policy Directive-1 which called for the return of humans to the Moon, commercial exploitation of space, and human missions to Mars and beyond. The Directive called for "an innovative and sustainable program of exploration with commercial and international partners to enable human expansion across the solar system and to bring back to Earth new knowledge and opportunities."[240] On May 13, 2019, NASA administrator Jim Bridenstine announced that the commercial and multinational partnership to return to the Moon by 2024 would be called Artemis – named after the Goddess of the Moon and the twin sister of Apollo in Greek mythology.[241] The Artemis Program involves nine planned Moon missions spanning from November 2021 to 2029 using a variety of launch, orbital and landing vehicles provided by different nations and companies.

The multinational cooperation and corporate involvement envisaged in the Artemis program was a catalyst for a comprehensive agreement being proposed between participating countries that would be consistent with international space law. On May 15, 2020, Bridenstine released details of the proposed international treaty that would be called the Artemis Accords. The Accord's primary goal was to establish a multinational coalition that in addition to supporting NASA's Artemis missions to the Moon, also envisages joint missions to comets and asteroids, and eventually a human mission to Mars. The Artemis Accords would provide the legal underpinning for human expansion into, and resource extraction throughout, the solar system.[242]

Significantly, Mike Gold, NASA's Associate Administrator for International Relations, explicitly made a connection between the proposed Artemis Accords and the *Star Trek* future described in the 2019 *Space Futures Report*: "Via the Artemis Accords, we hope that the future will look a lot more like "*Star Trek*," and a lot less like "*Star Wars*" by getting ahead of these issues."[243] In response to a letter by Ryan Britt from the news site *Inverse* asking Gold about how much *Star Trek* influenced the proposed Artemis Accords, he replied:

> *Star Trek* has always been an inspiration for many of us in the space field," Gold told *Inverse*. "Although it never flew into space, the first shuttle was named after the Starship Enterprise, and Nichelle Nichols helped recruit NASA's first African American and female astronauts. It's also fair to say that the principles described in the Artemis Accords were developed to create the peaceful future filled with awe, wonder, and adventure that is depicted in *Star Trek*. *Star Trek* is the dream that the Artemis

program and the Artemis Accords can transform into reality.[244]

Consequently, on October 13, 2020, the first set of bilateral agreements making up the Artemis Accords were signed between the United States and seven countries with national space programs: Australia, Canada, Italy, Japan, Luxembourg, United Arab Emirates and the United Kingdom.[245] It is expected that the Accords will soon be expanded as more nations participating in the International Space Station program sign on. These include Belgium, Denmark, France, Germany, Netherlands, Norway, Spain, Sweden, and Switzerland.

It was initially hoped Russia would join as explained in an article by Canadian journalist, Matthew Ehret titled: "Can NASA's Artemis Accords Spark a U.S.-Russia Alliance,"[246] despite initial public opposition to the signing of the Artemis Accords by the chief of Russia's Space Agency (Roscosmos), Dmitry Rogozin, in an interview with TASS.[247] The March 10, 2021, signing of an agreement between China and Russia to build a research station on the Moon crushed these early hopes, and significantly increased chances of a future arms race in space between competing blocs of nations.[248]

The Artemis Accords begin by affirming the importance of complying with four multilateral space treaties signed and ratified by United Nations member states:

> AFFIRMING the importance of compliance with the Treaty on Principles Governing the Activities of States in the Exploration and Use of Outer Space, Including the Moon and Other Celestial Bodies, opened for signature on January 27, 1967 ("Outer Space Treaty") as well as the Agreement on the Rescue of Astronauts, the Return of Astronauts and

the Return of Objects Launched into Outer Space, opened for signature on April 22, 1968 ("Rescue and Return Agreement"), the Convention on International Liability for Damage Caused by Space Objects, opened for signature on March 29, 1972 ("Liability Convention"), and the Convention on Registration of Objects Launched into Outer Space, opened for signature on January 14, 1975 ("Registration Convention"); as well as the benefits of coordination via multilateral forums, such as the United Nations Committee on the Peaceful Uses of Outer Space ("COPUOS"), to further efforts toward a global consensus on critical issues regarding space exploration and use . . .[249]

The first and most important of these multilateral agreements is the Outer Space Treaty that establishes a framework for the peaceful exploration of space by encouraging scientific cooperation, banning weapons of mass destruction being deployed in space, and preventing the creation of military bases on the Moon. In addition, the Outer Space Treaty declares space to be the common property of humanity, and that all space activities, including commercial, should be conducted for the benefit of all countries.

A notable exception in the list of space treaties affirmed by the Artemis Accords is the absence of the "Agreement Governing the Activities of States on the Moon and Other Celestial Bodies" (aka Moon Treaty which I will shortly discuss). Thus far none of the major spacefaring nations, USA, Russia, China, Japan and the European Space Agency have ratified the Moon Treaty. Out of the eight signatories to the Artemis Accords, only Australia has signed the Moon Treaty. The Moon Treaty is the fifth of the international treaties that make up what the United Nations Office for Outer

Space Affairs considers "international space law".[250] In practice, however, the Moon Treaty is widely regarded as a failure since only eighteen out of 193 member states of the United Nations have ratified it. At best, the Moon Treaty is considered a "shadow of customary international law" though that can quickly change if any of the major spacefaring nations ratify it.[251] That looks very unlikely, however, given President Donald Trump's explicit rejection of the Moon Treaty as part of customary international law in an April 6, 2020 Executive Order:

> The United States is not a party to the Moon Agreement. Further, the United States does not consider the Moon Agreement to be an effective or necessary instrument to guide nation states regarding the promotion of commercial participation in the long-term exploration, scientific discovery, and use of the Moon, Mars, or other celestial bodies. Accordingly, the Secretary of State shall object to any attempt by any other state or international organization to treat the Moon Agreement as reflecting or otherwise expressing customary international law.[252]

The Artemis Accords go on to explain how they are intended to implement the provisions of four earlier treaties (minus the Moon Treaty) thereby remaining in full compliance with "international space law."

> DESIRING to implement the provisions of the Outer Space Treaty and other relevant international instruments and thereby establish a political understanding regarding mutually beneficial practices for the future exploration and use of outer

space, with a focus on activities conducted in support of the Artemis Program . . . [253]

Section 1 of the Accords outline the purpose and scope of the planned joint space missions:

> The purpose of these Accords is to establish a common vision via a practical set of principles, guidelines, and best practices to enhance the governance of the civil exploration and use of outer space with the intention of advancing the Artemis Program. Adherence to a practical set of principles, guidelines, and best practices in carrying out activities in outer space is intended to increase the safety of operations, reduce uncertainty, and promote the sustainable and beneficial use of space for all humankind. The Accords represent a political commitment to the principles described herein, many of which provide for operational implementation of important obligations contained in the Outer Space Treaty and other instruments.[254]

Section 1 of the Artemis Accords makes clear that signatories believe they are providing for "operational implementation of important obligations contained in the Outer Space Treaty." In short, while the Outer Space Treaty is vague on how obligations expected of its signatories will be operationalized, the Artemis Accords attempts to spell these obligations out in great detail for the practical exploration and exploitation of space resources. The Artemis Accords has additional sections dealing respectively with: 2 – Implementation; 3 – Peaceful Purposes; 4 – Transparency; 5 – Interoperability; 6 – Emergency Assistance; 7 – Registration of Space Objects; 8 – Release of Scientific Data; and 9

– Preserving Outer Space Heritage. All of these do not deviate from the spirit and intent of the obligations of the Outer Space Treaty and the other treaties making up international space law.

Extraction of Space Resources for the Benefit of Humanity

It is Section 10, Space Resources, where the Artemis Accords first deviates from the spirit and intent of the Outer Space Treaty. The Accords state:

1. The Signatories note that the utilization of space resources can benefit humankind by providing critical support for safe and sustainable operations.

2. The Signatories emphasize that the extraction and utilization of space resources, including any recovery from the surface or subsurface of the Moon, Mars, comets, or asteroids, should be executed in a manner that complies with the Outer Space Treaty and in support of safe and sustainable space activities. The Signatories affirm that the extraction of space resources does not inherently constitute national appropriation under Article II of the Outer Space Treaty, and that contracts and other legal instruments relating to space resources should be consistent with that Treaty.

3. The Signatories commit to informing the Secretary-General of the United Nations as well as the public and the international scientific community of their space resource extraction activities in accordance with the Outer Space Treaty.[255]

The key idea being proposed is "that the extraction of space resources does not inherently constitute national appropriation," thereby making it possible for corporations, countries or other entities to begin mining operations. Effectively, the Artemis Accords are saying that resource extraction can be done without ownership being required or asserted over the areas being mined.

When it comes to space resource extraction, this is what the Outer Space Treaty had to say:

Article 1

The exploration and use of outer space, including the Moon and other celestial bodies, shall be carried out for the benefit and in the interests of all countries, irrespective of their degree of economic or scientific development, and shall be the province of all mankind.

Outer space, including the Moon and other celestial bodies, shall be free for exploration and use by all States without discrimination of any kind, on a basis of equality and in accordance with international law, and there shall be free access to all areas of celestial bodies.

The Outer Space Treaty makes it clear that resource extraction is "for the benefit and in the interests of all countries" even if their lack of economic and scientific development makes it impossible for them to participate in space exploration. The underlying spirit and intent here is that nations and/or other organizations, e.g., aerospace corporations, exploiting space resources would set up an international trust, or some other mechanism, which would disseminate the benefits of space resource extraction operations to all countries—not just those with space programs. This is made explicit in the Moon Treaty, which describes how resources are to be shared equitably among world nations, including developing countries without space programs:

> [Article 11.7] (d) An equitable sharing by all States Parties in the benefits derived from those resources, whereby the interests and needs of the developing countries, as well as the efforts of those countries which have contributed either directly or indirectly to the exploration of the Moon, shall be given special consideration.

In order to achieve this goal, the Moon Treaty calls for the establishment of "an international regime" to oversee the distribution of the profits accruing from space mining:

> [Article 11] 5. States Parties to this Agreement hereby undertake to establish an international regime, including appropriate procedures, to govern the exploitation of the natural resources of the Moon as such exploitation is about to become feasible.

The "international regime" would be analogous to "The Enterprise" established in the Law of the Sea Convention, as explained by Michael Lister, writing for *The Space Review*:

> The form of the international regime introduced in the Moon Treaty has yet to be fleshed out, but it is probable that it would be similar in form to the international regime called "The Enterprise", which was proposed in Part XI of the 1994 Agreement of the Law of the Sea Convention to oversee the mining of mineral resources in the world's oceans, including poly-metallic nodules. The nature of the

Enterprise was envisioned to oversee developed nations and private companies operating under their jurisdiction and would have required a portion of the mineral wealth mined from the ocean floor to be allocated to the Enterprise for distribution among the developing countries. More worrisome for countries such as the United States was that the Enterprise as envisioned also required that developed nations transfer technology to the Enterprise so the non-developed could also participate in the extraction of resources from the ocean floor.

If the international regime envisioned by the Moon Treaty takes a form similar to that of the Enterprise, developed nations would be required to relinquish a portion of the resources extracted from the Moon and other celestial bodies. They would also be required to surrender technology developed by private industries under their jurisdiction for extracting extraterrestrial resources so that developing nations could participate in the activity of acquiring those resources as well. This implies that the Moon Treaty's common heritage view applies not only to extraterrestrial real property and resources but to intellectual property rights as well.[256]

In contrast to the intent of the Outer Space Treaty that was outlined in the unsuccessful Moon Treaty, Section 10 of the Artemis Accords merely states that the "utilization of space resources can benefit humankind by providing critical support for safe and sustainable operations." This makes the benefit to all nations from space resource extraction an indirect one since these are "safe and sustainable," rather than something that directly benefits and meets the interests of other nations. Nor does Section 10 mention anything about an "international regime" designed to distribute the benefits of commercial space activities to all countries. Instead, the Artemis Accords are designed to protect the interests, activities and profits of those directly conducting economic activities in Space, the Moon, asteroids and comets. This is in accord with an Executive Order issued by President Trump on April 6, 2020:

> Americans should have the right to engage in commercial exploration, recovery, and use of resources in outer space, consistent with applicable law. Outer space is a legally and physically unique domain of human activity, and the United States does not view it as a global commons. Accordingly, it shall be the policy of the United States to encourage international support for the public and private recovery and use of resources in outer space, consistent with applicable law.[257]

This means that major aerospace corporations and Artemis Accords signatory nations conducting space operations with commercial goals would be under no obligation to share their profits with the rest of humanity, let alone countries without space programs as expressed in the Outer Space Treaty and the Moon Treaty. This is why Russia's Roscosmos chief, Dmitry Rogozin, said he believed the Artemis Accords' support for privatizing space "runs counter to international law."[258] Another area of tension between the Artemis Accords and international space law concerns the demilitarization of space.

Outer Space Treaty & The Demilitarization of Space

Before discussing what the Artemis Accords have to say about the use of military force in space, it's worth reviewing what major space powers have done in terms of the development and deployment of space weapons, and what the Outer Space Treaty had to say about demilitarizing space. This is what the Outer Space Treaty said about deployment of weapons of mass destruction in space:

Article IV

States Parties to the Treaty undertake not to place in orbit around the Earth any objects carrying nuclear weapons or any other kinds of weapons of mass destruction, install such weapons on celestial bodies, or station such weapons in outer space in any other manner.

The Moon and other celestial bodies shall be used by all States Parties to the Treaty exclusively for peaceful purposes. The establishment of military bases, installations and fortifications, the testing of any type of weapons and the conduct of military maneuvers on celestial bodies shall be forbidden.[259]

In short, space would not be used for deploying nuclear weapons or other weapons of mass destruction capable of being used in offensive military operations, and the Moon and other celestial bodies would be demilitarized. However, the Outer Space Treaty does not proscribe the deployment of defensive military weapons in space that are designed to protect space assets from any kind of attack. The planned deployment of space weapons that are claimed to be purely defensive in nature date back to the Reagan administration.

In March 1983, President Ronald Reagan announced his Strategic Defense Initiative:

> Let me share with you a vision of the future which offers hope. It is that we embark on a program to counter the awesome Soviet missile threat with measures that are defensive. Let us turn to the very strengths in technology that spawned our great industrial base and that have given us the quality of life we enjoy today.
>
> What if free people could live secure in the knowledge that their security did not rest upon the threat of instant U.S. retaliation to deter a Soviet attack, that we could intercept and destroy strategic ballistic missiles before they reached our own soil or that of our allies?[260]

Some of the new antiballistic missile weapons Reagan was referring to were space based:

> A research-and-development effort that emerged from SDI was Brilliant Pebbles, which was focused on technology that would enable basing interceptors in space. . . . The weapons required included space- and ground-based nuclear X-ray lasers, subatomic particle beams, and computer-guided projectiles fired by electromagnetic rail guns—all under the central control of a supercomputer system. By using these systems, the United States planned to intercept intercontinental ballistic missiles while they still flew high above the Earth, minimizing their effects.[261]

Publicly, Reagan's Strategic Defense Initiative failed to gain Congressional support and never took off. However, there are many reasons to believe it was covertly developed and deployed in a highly classified operation funded by the CIA's unofficial black budget described in chapter seven. However, rather than Reagan's Strategic Defense Initiative being the first space weapons program that was covertly deployed, there is credible evidence that the Soviet Union had developed and deployed such weapons nearly a decade earlier.

In 1961, Dr. Peter Beter was appointed by President John F. Kennedy as the General Counsel for the US Export-Import Bank and served in that position until 1967 under President Lyndon B. Johnson. As might be expected from his high-level position, Dr. Beter had impeccable connections to other top level sources within the Military Industrial Complex who shared with him much information about the classified space activities of both the Soviet Union and the US. In a series of audio-letters, which would be considered podcasts today, Dr. Beter claims that the US and USSR were in a race to develop space-based weapons in the 1970s.

Dr Beter described how in the 1960s and 1970s, the US and USSR were fiercely competing both in a race to the Moon and in the development of particle beam weapons that could operate across the distance between the Moon and Earth. It was clear that whoever first developed a particle beam weapon that could operate from the Moon would possess an overwhelming strategic military advantage on Earth. According to Beter, while the US was forging ahead in the race to the Moon, the Soviets were ahead in developing particle beam weapons. In his Audio Letter 26, released on September 30, 1977, Beter wrote:

> By 1972, these experiments still were a long way from a suitable weapon for deployment on the moon. But ominous developments in the Soviet

Union led to the decision to cut off the Apollo program prematurely so that the construction of the secret moon base could be rushed ahead.[262]

According to Beter, Diego Garcia was used as a spaceport for sending the multiple missions necessary for the US military to build a moon base:

> Early in 1973, soon after the supposed end of the American moon program, we began hearing about a place called Diego Garcia in the Indian Ocean. Supposedly we were merely building a communications installation there, yet the drastic step was taken of relocating all the 20,000 or so natives of this little island to other areas. More recently, we have heard about Diego Garcia as the site of a new American naval base; but, my friends, you still haven't been told the whole story. Diego Garcia, my friends, is the new space-port from which secret missions to the moon have been launched during the building of the moon base. [263]

The process of removing all the inhabitants of Diego Garcia began with a 1966 agreement between the British and US governments that called for the US to be given an unpopulated island for a planned military base on the British territory.[264] The transfer of the Chagossian inhabitants of Diego Garcia was completed on April 27, 1973, thereby making possible the remote spaceport revealed by Dr. Beter. Diego Garcia was the ideal location for a space launching pad according to Beter:

> Unlike Cape Canaveral, where Saturn rocket launches are impossible to hide, Diego Garcia is remote and isolated, and even the natives are no

longer there to watch what goes on. What's more, Diego Garcia is practically the perfect moon-port, located as it is almost on the earth's equator, and a space vehicle launched eastward into orbit from Diego Garcia passes over a nearly unbroken expanse of water for more than half the circumference of the earth. The only means of monitoring the early flight of a space craft launched from Diego Garcia, therefore, is from ships.[265]

In his 1977 newsletter, Beter wrote about the information he had received from his sources about the US moon base:

> I was first alerted to the existence of a secret base on the moon last November 1976 – but it has been one of the best kept of all Rockefeller secrets, and it was only a few weeks ago that I was able to confirm its existence and learn the complete story; and since that time, events have moved with lightning speed.[266]

Beter went on to give details about the deadly race to develop particle beam weapons as it played out in 1977:

> Throughout this year an unseen but deadly race has been underway to see who would get an operational Particle Beam first: the Rockefellers, at their secret moon base; or the Soviet Union, in earth orbit. By late spring, a Salyut manned space craft was launched that carried out preliminary tests of beam-weapon techniques, using lasers in order to simulate the Particle Beam. [267]

Beter next gave details about the race between the USSR and US to develop particle beam weapons for deployment in space and on the Moon. The Soviets succeeded in developing the first operational particle beam weapons in Earth orbit, and destroyed the newly built US moon base:

> By the 26th of September, American personnel at the secret Rockefeller moon base nestled in Copernicus Crater were almost ready. Their Particle Beam was almost operational—but they were too late. By late that day, the Soviet Union began bombarding the moon base with a Neutron Particle Beam. Through the night, and all day on September 27 the moon base was bombarded without mercy with neutron radiation just like that produced by a neutron bomb; and by that evening as Americans looked up at the peaceful full moon overhead known as the Harvest Moon, the last few Americans on the moon were dying of neutron radiation. America had lost the Battle of the Harvest Moon.[268]

Circumstantial evidence in support of Dr. Beter's remarkable claims is that the Soviet Union was the first to deploy manned military space stations back in the 1970s. The Soviet's Salyut space station program began in 1971 with Salyut 1, and ended in 1986. Hidden within the Salyut program was a highly classified military space station program called Almaz, which was not publicly known at the time. Salyut 2, 3 and 5 were in fact part of Almaz program, and were officially claimed to be crewed military surveillance missions. Salyut 5 was launched on June 22, 1976 and fell back to Earth on August 8, 1977. This is consistent with the timeframe given by Dr. Beter that the Soviets had deployed a particle beam weapon in Earth orbit to destroy a secret US military Moon base.

Additional support for Beter's claims comes from a US State Department document referring to the Soviet destruction of a US Moon base sometime in the 1970s. It was part of a cache of diplomatic cables released by Wikileaks in 2010/2011. The document is dated January 24, 1979, and is titled "Report that UR Destroyed Secret US Base on Moon."[269] It was correspondence involving one or more officials from the U.S. State Department to Samuel L. Devine, a Republican member of the US Congress. The document has tags "Operations–General | UR – Soviet Union (USSR)" which reveals that "UR" stands for the USSR. The document was marked unclassified, which suggests that the content of the correspondence involved open source material publicly available at the time. The public source was almost certainly Dr. Beter's audio letters. I lodged a Freedom of Information Act request to the State Department on July 29, 2019, to clarify what was discussed in the 1979 document. The State Department has yet to acknowledge or reply to my request. The facts are that US State Department officials were discussing Beter's claims back in 1979; this was never publicly revealed until Wikileaks released the former's diplomatic cable dump; and the State Department has not responded to a FOIA request for clarification, all add credence to Dr. Beter's revelations.

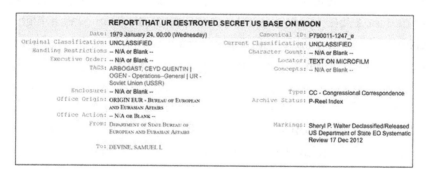

Figure 30. Leaked Wikileaks State Department document

If it is accepted that the Soviet Union successfully deployed particle beam weapons through the Almaz military program in 1977, and these were used to destroy a secret US military Moon base, it is easy to understand why this would have been a catalyst for Reagan's 1983 Strategic Defense Initiative. Reagan was playing catch up to the Soviet weaponization of space, and was marshaling US resources to match and surpass what the Soviets had secretly achieved.

The above historic developments make clear that space was secretly weaponized by the two Cold War superpowers. Does this mean the USSR and US violated the 1967 Outer Space Treaty's (and the Moon Treaty's) clear prohibitions against deploying weapons of mass destruction in space? If a particle beam weapon in Earth orbit can be used to destroy a Moon Base almost 240,000 miles (400,000 km) away, then it would surely qualify as a weapon of mass destruction that is proscribed by International Space Law. The events described by Dr. Beter makes clear the difficulty in separating offensive and defensive weapons systems for the purpose of staying in compliance with International Space Law. Particle beam weapons can be used for both defensive or offensive purposes, the latter taking it perilously close to being a weapon of mass destruction. It is not surprising that while lip service is given to space treaties' prohibitions against the placement of weapons of mass destruction in space, the two superpowers ignored these while seeking to gain a strategic military advantage in space.

Consequently, it is not unexpected that one of the major concerns of the 2001 US Space Commission report recommending the creation of a Space Corps in 2001 was intelligence data indicating Russia and China were developing, or even possessed ground and space based anti-satellite weapons capable of launching a devastating "Space Pearl Harbor." It can be safely assumed that in December 1991, the newly formed Russian Federation inherited most if not all of the space-based weapons developed by the Soviet Union. However, the chaotic beginning of the Russian Federation and the collapse of its economy left it scant financial resources to maintain technological parity with the US when it came to space weapons. This led to China strategically realigning itself with Russia, and furiously beginning the task of bridging the space weapons gap between itself and the US.

Technology exchange agreements, industrial espionage and cyber hacking have all been used by China to gain the blueprints of US and Russian advanced technology secrets including space weapons. Books such as Robert Spalding's *Stealth War* and Michael Pillsbury's *The Hundred Year Marathon* explain the wide range of mechanisms used by China to get such technology secrets, and begin reverse engineering them.[270] The Pentagon's 2020 Annual Report to Congress on China's military and security developments confirmed the scale of the industrial espionage that was occurring by citing a 2018 hacking case involving two Chinese nationals with links to China's national security complex:

> In December 2018, the U.S. Department of Justice indicted two PRC nationals associated with a hacking group operating in China, known as Advanced Persistent Threat 10 (APT10), for conspiracy to commit computer intrusions, conspiracy to commit wire fraud, and aggravated identity theft. They worked for a Chinese company in association with the PRC Ministry of State Security (MSS) to conduct computer intrusions, resulting in the theft of hundreds of gigabytes of sensitive data involving aviation, space and satellite technology, manufacturing technology, pharmaceutical technology, oil and gas exploration and production technology, communications technology, computer processor technology, and maritime technology.[271]

China's rapid economic growth in the early 1990s, and the military modernization program subsequently undertaken by the People's Liberation Army have made it a military force to be reckoned with. Today, China's conventional Navy is larger than the US Navy as confirmed for the first time in the Pentagon's 2020 Annual Report to Congress:

> Shipbuilding: The PRC has the largest navy in the world, with an overall battle force of approximately 350 ships and submarines including over 130 major surface combatants. In comparison, the U.S. Navy's battle force is approximately 293 ships as of early 2020.[272]

Despite China's strident public claims in support of the demilitarization of outer space, it has for several decades been secretly developing a space navy and sophisticated weapons system to be used for the projection of its military forces deep into space.[273] According to the Pentagon's 2020 Annual Report to Congress:

> **The PRC's Space Enterprise.** The PRC's space enterprise continues to mature rapidly.

> Beijing has devoted significant resources to growing all aspects of its space program, from military space applications to civil applications such as profit-generating launches, scientific endeavors, and space exploration.

> The PLA has historically managed the PRC's space program. The SSF [Strategic Support Force] Space Systems Department is responsible for nearly all PLA space operations.

181

In 2019, the PRC described space as a "critical domain in international strategic competition" and stated the security of space provided strategic assurance to the country's national and social development.[274]

In *Rise of the Red Dragon* (2020), I explain in detail the historic evolution of China's secret space program and how it was made possible by Deep State support that went back as far as 1950.

China is fast approaching the day when it will be capable of launching a Space Pearl Harbor on the US Global Positioning System (GPS) grid comprising between twenty-four to thirty-two satellites that has been fully operational since 1995.[275] A critical milestone was reached with China's successful completion in June 2020 of its own GPS alternative, BeiDou (Big Dipper), with the deployment of the last in its grid of thirty satellites.[276] China is no longer reliant on the US GPS system, which was transferred over to the control of the US Space Force in early 2020. The defense of the US GPS is now one of Space Force's primary responsibilities. This is not surprising as the main justification in the initial proposal for a Space (Corps) Force in the 2001 Space Commission report was to prevent a potential Space Pearl Harbor attack.

The Artemis Accords provide a foundation for joint military action by Space Force and the military forces of allied nations to protect not only the US GPS system, but also the European Union's Galileo GPS system comprising a total of thirty satellites that went live in 2016. More significantly, the Artemis Accords have a number of provisions describing how signatories plan to cooperate in order to protect their personnel, equipment and space operations from "harmful interference."

Protecting Space Safe Zones from Harmful Interference

Article IX of the Outer Space Treaty describes two scenarios where "harmful interference" may arise, and in both cases recommends international consultation to remedy the situation. The first scenario involves a state party to the treaty or its citizens' planning or conducting activities that may lead to "harmful interference" in another party's space missions. The second scenario is where a state party experiences harmful interference from another party to the treaty:

> A State Party to the Treaty which has reason to believe that an activity or experiment planned by another State Party in outer space, including the Moon and other celestial bodies, would cause potentially harmful interference with activities in the peaceful exploration and use of outer space, including the Moon and other celestial bodies, may request consultation concerning the activity or experiment.[277]

Taking consultative action to deal with "harmful interference" is therefore recognized by signatories to the Outer Space Treaty as the only legal conflict resolution mechanism available to resolve disputes in space. The Artemis Accords provides additional means for resolving space disputes either between its signatories or with non-signatory nations.

The Artemis Accords has a section titled "Deconfliction of Space Activities" where it presents recommended methods for resolving space disputes. The Artemis Accords begin by acknowledging the validity of the consultative process recommended in the Outer Space Treaty:

[Section 11] 3. Consistent with Article IX of the Outer Space Treaty, a Signatory authorizing an activity under these Accords commits to respect the principle of due regard. A Signatory to these Accords with reason to believe that it may suffer, or has suffered, harmful interference, may request consultations with a Signatory or any other Party to the Outer Space Treaty authorizing the activity.[278]

The Artemis Accords then goes on to introduce the idea of a "safety zone" as a practical means of dealing with harmful interference:

[Section 11] 6. The Signatories intend to use their experience under the Accords to contribute to multilateral efforts to further develop international practices, criteria, and rules applicable to the definition and determination of safety zones and harmful interference.[279]

Importantly, the Artemis Accords is here recommending a multilateral process where signatories presumably play a critical if not dominant role in developing rules and practices for determining safety zones.

The next section in the Accords elaborates further on the idea of a safety zone and how it can be used in dealing with harmful interference:

[Section 11] 7. In order to implement their obligations under the Outer Space Treaty, the Signatories intend to provide notification of their activities and commit to coordinating with any relevant actor to avoid harmful interference. The area wherein this notification and coordination will be implemented to avoid harmful interference is referred to as a 'safety zone'. A safety zone should be the area in which nominal operations of a relevant activity or an anomalous event could reasonably cause harmful interference.[280]

So far, the Accords have discussed consultations, notifications, coordination, rules, practices, and the idea of safety zones to deal with harmful interference. These are all consistent with the banning of weapons of mass destruction established by the Outer Space Treaty. It is the following section, however, that introduces a major military element in how space conflicts are to be resolved:

> [Section 11] 9. The Signatory establishing, maintaining, or ending a safety zone should do so in a manner that **protects** public and private personnel, equipment, and operations from harmful interference. The Signatories should, as appropriate, make relevant information regarding such safety zones, including the extent and general nature of operations taking place within them, available to the public as soon as practicable and feasible, while taking into account **appropriate protections** for proprietary and export-controlled information [emphases added]. [281]

The above section outlines that "appropriate protections" are necessary for "personnel, equipment, and operations from harmful interference." It is hard to imagine how such "appropriate protection" can be achieved in space by anything other than a well-trained and equipped military entity such as the US Space Force, which is expanded to include similar forces from other Artemis Accords signatory nations. Any doubt that the US Space Force is prepared to use military force to protect the assets of the US and its Artemis Accord allies from "harmful interference" is laid to rest in the National Space Policy document released by President Trump in December 2020. It states:

> All nations have the right to explore and to use space for peaceful purposes and for the benefit of all humanity, in accordance with applicable law. Consistent with that principle, the United States will continue to use space for national security activities, including for the exercise of the inherent right of self-defense. Unfettered access and freedom to operate in space is a vital national interest.
>
> The United States considers the space systems of all nations to have the right to pass through and conduct operations in space without interference. Purposeful interference with space systems, including supporting infrastructure, will be considered an infringement of a nation's rights. Consistent with the defense of those rights, the United States will seek to deter, counter, and defeat threats in the space domain that are hostile to the national interests of the United States and its allies. Any purposeful interference with or an attack upon the space systems of the United States or its allies that directly affects national rights will be met with a deliberate response at a time, place, manner, and domain of our choosing.[282]

Consequently, the creation of a multilateral military space force is the most reasonable outcome of Artemis Accords provisions to provide "appropriate protections" and to establish "safety zones" designed to prevent "harmful interference" in the commercial and exploratory activities of member states. None of the economic benefits of which—it needs to be emphasized—is required to be distributed for the "benefit of all humanity" as stipulated in the Outer Space Treaty, but is not required in the Artemis Accords.

In conclusion, Section 11 of the Artemis Accords ostensibly dealing with "Deconfliction of Space Activities" implicitly contains mutual defense provisions to protect signatory nations and their corporate contractors from experiencing harmful interference in their exploration and resource extraction missions involving the Moon, Mars, asteroids and comets. This is a bold step towards something similar to the North Atlantic Treaty Organization (NATO) being established in space.

Consequently, it should not come as a big surprise that on October 22, 2020, NATO's Secretary General Jens Stoltenberg announced that a Space Center is being established at Ramstein Air Base in Germany:

> NATO is determined to keep our cutting edge in all domains. Land, sea, air, cyber, and space. Last year, we declared space as an operational domain for NATO. And today we took another important step.
>
> Ministers agreed to establish a new NATO Space Centre at Allied Air Command in Ramstein, Germany.
>
> - It will help to coordinate Allied space activities;
>
> - Support NATO missions and operations from space, including with communications and satellite imagery;
>
> - And protect Allied space systems by sharing information about potential threats.[283]

Stoltenberg's announcement does more than merely extend NATO operations into space alongside the newly established US Space

Force and Space Command. It is a major step towards the establishment of a future Space NATO emerging out of the Artemis Accords, where the US Space Force provides the core of a multinational military space alliance to protect the GPS systems of the US and European Union, and to protect safety zones established under the Artemis Accords. Such a Space NATO, as long as it did not involve deploying weapons of mass destruction in space, and establishing military bases on the Moon or other celestial bodies, would be consistent with International Space Law. Recalling what NASA's Mike Gold had to earlier say about the Artemis Accords creating a Star Trek future, it is reasonable to conclude that the establishment of a multinational Space NATO is a precursor to a future Starfleet that protects the Earth, GPS systems, off-world colonies, and deep space operations. While NASA officials and many devoted Star Trek fans heartily embrace a Star Trek future, it terrifies the Deep State.

Chapter 11

Why Space Force Terrifies the Deep State

Those who deny freedom to others, deserve it not for themselves.

— Abraham Lincoln

In chapter seven, I examined three space programs that are known to officially exist in the US: a civilian program run by NASA; a Pentagon satellite program involving both the USAF and Navy; and a surveillance program run by the National Reconnaissance Office (NRO). The NRO program is jointly run by the Pentagon and the CIA, and it is the most highly classified among the three known space programs. These three space programs all involve rocket propulsion technologies for launching satellites, space craft and space stations that continue to operate to the present day.

As discussed in chapter five, however, captured German and extraterrestrial flying saucer craft were successfully reverse engineered and built by major aerospace companies for different customers: NRO, CIA, USAF Special Operations, USAF Space Command, DARPA, etc. In addition, the scientific breakthroughs in reverse engineering captured flying saucer craft led to a new physics involving electrogravitics, torsion fields, tachyons, antimatter, etc., that collectively make up the different propulsion systems of fleets of antigravity spacecraft capable of tremendous speeds without limitations imposed by the law of inertia. The subsequent triangle-shaped and rectangle-shaped craft were built and incorporated into multiple Secret Space Programs (SSPs) that evolved behind the scenes. These SSPs are hidden behind the official space programs involving satellites, space probes, landing craft, space stations etc., sent up with conventional rockets by NASA, USAF/Navy and the NRO/CIA.

While the three known space programs are all funded through congressional appropriations that can be tracked, the SSPs are all funded by the CIA's unofficial black budget that is not trackable. The unofficial black budget funds are still routed through the Pentagon since this is necessary to keep the entire funding process within the letter of the law as found in the 1949 CIA Act. Consequently, over the decades of secret reverse engineering and construction of antigravity craft incorporated into the various SSPs, there are many thousands of space activities that have occurred with zero transparency and accountability. These are run by various control groups, some of which lie entirely outside of the military chain of command. These control groups work through the CIA, which plays an inordinate role in command and control of SSPs through the "unofficial black budget."

Thus far, I have discussed the secret space programs run by the NRO/CIA, and the USAF's Special Operations and Space Command that have been used largely for space surveillance missions and covert operations around the planet for national security purposes. Space Force is in the process of absorbing some of the personnel and spacecraft used in these operations but will be challenged by the NRO/CIA which for decades has had operational control, and predictably will not relinquish all of their assets that have been managed by the Office of Space

190

Reconnaissance since 2014. Keep in mind that Space Force's hand in this bureaucratic turf war is strengthened by the redefinition of space as a warfighting domain. However, it can be predicted that the NRO/CIA will relinquish little of the operational control of the antigravity spacecraft they have accumulated over the decades for space surveillance missions conducted in collaboration with USAF Space Command. As far as the antigravity spacecraft assets controlled by USAF Special Operations, it can be assumed that only a limited number of these will be absorbed into Space Force and US Space Command for operational reasons given the ongoing needs of Special Operations Command, which is also one of the eleven combatant commands in the Pentagon.

What is known about the SSPs in terms of technologies, capabilities and operations come from multiple "insiders" that have come forward to reveal their participation in various aspects of these programs. These insiders sometimes have excellent credentials as in the cases of William Tompkins, Clark McClelland, Edgar Fouche and Emery Smith, who have all provided documents substantiating their work with either major aerospace corporations, military services, or "official" space programs.[284] Other insiders such as "Kewper," "JP" and Corey Goode are more controversial since they have chosen to remain anonymous or lack background documentation to directly support their testimonies.[285] Nevertheless, the testimonies of the latter group are sincere, consistent and backed by leaked documents and circumstantial evidence. I have covered the testimonies and backgrounds of these and other insiders in the five preceding volumes of my Secret Space Programs book series.

In December 2020, a new insider came forward with powerful corroborating testimony about the existence of SSPs: Professor Haim Eshed the former head of Israel's spy satellite program. From 1981 to 2011, Prof. Eshed was a Professor at the Technion Space Research Institute and also the first Director of

Israel's Challenge Program in the Defense Ministry's Administration for Research, Development of Weapons and Technological Infrastructure (MAPAT). MAPAT was the body that directed Israel's spy satellite projects and therefore worked closely with its US equivalents: the NRO and Air Force Space Command. During his tenure, Prof. Eshed commanded the launch of 20 Israeli satellites, and was awarded Israel's prestigious Security Award three times.[286] On December 5, 2020, major newspapers around the world began publishing stories about an interview he gave and his new book that revealed details about a US SSP that Israel has covertly assisted. Even more startling was his claim that the Trump administration was in contact with a "Galactic Federation" that was advising against revealing the existence of extraterrestrial life:

> The UFOs have asked not to publish that they are here, humanity is not ready yet. Trump was on the verge of revealing, but the aliens in the Galactic Federation are saying: Wait, let people calm down first. They don't want to start mass hysteria. They want to first make us sane and understanding. They have been waiting for humanity to evolve and reach a stage where we will generally understand what space and spaceships are.[287]

Overall, the testimonies of Professor Eshed and other insiders, along with supporting documentation and circumstantial evidence, provide a rare big-picture perspective of what is happening in and beyond Earth's orbit. If these insider testimonies are accurate, then this has powerful implications for Space Force in the years ahead as it sets out to fulfill its core mission, as described in foundational documents such as "Spacepower Doctrine" and General Raymond's "Chief of Space Operations Planning Guidance" covered in chapter eight.

What I am about to describe will be another quantum leap for readers in terms of what has been discussed in previous chapters, which generally focused on the reverse engineering and construction of a variety of antigravity spacecraft for the different space programs discussed so far. What I will now be focusing on in this chapter are the alleged operations of SSPs that extend far beyond space-based reconnaissance, and why Space Force represents a major threat to the continuance of such operations. Some readers may find it difficult to accept the reality of what is about to be presented and dismiss it as merely the product of overly imaginative minds or officially sanctioned disinformation. However, the information needs to be considered if we are to develop a big-picture overview of what may be happening in outer space, and what Space Force will have to contend with if it is to fulfill its core mission.

According to multiple insiders, for decades outer space has been used by rogue SSPs and their hidden control groups to manipulate humanity through multiple egregious practices that have escaped public awareness and scrutiny. These practices include genetic experiments conducted with captive humans, false flag operations, off world bases using forced labor to build advanced technologies for an interstellar trade, and, most controversial of all, a galactic slave trade. In addition, secret agreements have been reached with a breakaway German-led space program that was first established in Antarctica, but later established bases on Mars, Ceres and elsewhere in our solar system, and even conducts missions far outside of our Solar System. These agreements have allegedly led to extensive collaboration with a German "Dark Fleet" (aka Nacht Waffen) that uses tens of thousands of highly trained US military personnel and scientists for extensive periods for nefarious missions.

Finally, there are agreements with extraterrestrial civilizations that have long monitored humanity's progression as a planetary civilization and regularly intervened in human affairs through genetic experiments and historic cataclysmic events. This has led to jointly run genetic experiments between extraterrestrials and the control groups in charge of secret space programs. In this regard, Professor Eshed's December 2020 revelations provides powerful corroboration for what other insiders have been claiming for decades:

> There's an agreement between the US government and the aliens. They signed a contract with us to do experiments here. They, too, are researching and trying to understand the whole fabric of the universe, and they want us as helpers. There's an underground base in the depths of Mars, where their representatives are, and also our American astronauts.[288]

Many of the egregious SSP practices just described have been secretly funded through the CIA's massive trillion dollar "unofficial black budget" and close collaboration with other nations such as Israel. The 2019 creation of the US Space Force threatens to expose, confront, and even bring to an end many of these egregious practices. Critically, the Space Force will eventually have to confront the enormous power the CIA has welded behind the scenes through its unofficial black budget. Consequently, I need to first explain the nature of the control groups running the SSPs, and the connection to the CIA, before presenting details of abusive space practices that systematically violate universal human rights.

Understanding the Deep State and Control Groups Running SSPs

There have been many historical references to a shadow government, an invisible government or a Deep State that pull the levers of political power from behind the scenes. Among the earliest references to such an entity was former President Theodore Roosevelt who said in a 1912 speech:

> Behind the ostensible government sits enthroned an invisible government owing no allegiance and acknowledging no responsibility to the people. To destroy this invisible government, to befoul the unholy alliance between corrupt business and corrupt politics is the first task of the statesmanship of the day.[289]

Only a year later, President Woodrow Wilson echoed Roosevelt's sentiments when he stated:

> The government, which was designed for the people, has got into the hands of the bosses and their employers, the special interests. An invisible empire has been set up above the forms of democracy. . . . Some of the biggest names in the US in the field of commerce and manufacturing are afraid of somebody, of something. They know that there is a power somewhere so organized, so subtle, so watchful, so interlocked, so pervasive that they had better not speak above their breath when they speak in condemnation of it.[290]

What Roosevelt, Wilson and other political leaders have repeatedly pointed out is that behind the representative

195

government that ostensibly governs the US, there is a powerful group that is truly in charge of the nation's future. This is nicely summarized in *Deep State: Pulling Strings from Behind the Scenes*:

> In a nutshell, the Deep State is a state within a state — a shadow government that manipulates and shapes the policies of the visible government, without regard to the best interests of the country, the U.S. Constitution, the laws enacted by Congress, and the public policies of the president, who heads the executive branch.[291]

What is important to keep in mind here is that Roosevelt and Wilson had confirmed the existence of a Deep State decades before World War II and the Roswell UFO incident. This means that when the advanced technologies of extraterrestrial visitors found their way to Earth, the Deep State was already long in charge, and prepared to exploit these technologies for their own purposes.

As to who created the Deep State, there have been historical references to the descendants of extraterrestrial visitors that arrived on Earth and directly ruled over humanity millennia ago. Both Manetho's *History of Egypt* and the Sumerian King's List described historical epochs that witnessed a transition from direct rule by the gods (extraterrestrials), to direct rule by the sons of gods (human extraterrestrial hybrids); and finally to human rulers who claimed direct ancestral connection to these ancient extraterrestrial rulers (divine right of kings).[292] The Roman historian, Eusebius, summarized Manetho's *History of Egypt* as follows:

> From the Egyptian History of Manetho, who composed his account in three books. These deal with the Gods, the Demigods, the Spirits of the

Dead, and the mortal kings who ruled Egypt down to Darius, king of the Persians . . . After the Gods, Demigods reigned for 1255 years, and again another line of kings held sway for 1817 years; then came thirty more kings of Memphis, reigning for 1790 years; and then again ten kings of This, reigning for 350 years. . . . [293]

This intervention by the gods (extraterrestrials) in human affairs is echoed in the Book of Enoch, that refer to 200 Fallen Angels that arrived on Earth, and quickly dominated humanity:

6.1 And it came to pass, when the sons of men had increased, that in those days there were born to them fair and beautiful daughters.

6.2 And the Angels, the sons of Heaven, saw them and desired them. And they said to one another: "Come, let us choose for ourselves wives, from the children of men, and let us beget, for ourselves, children. . . ."

6.6 And they were, in all, two hundred and they came down on Ardis, which is the summit of Mount Hermon. And they called the mountain Hermon because on it they swore and bound one another with curses.[294]

These ancient extraterrestrial visitors and their hybrid offshoots used advanced technologies and superior psychic abilities to control and corrupt humanity. The names of these fallen angels/gods/extraterrestrials are often denoted in ancient religious texts as demons.

Fast forward to the modern era, where there are numerous references by occult researchers to thirteen ruling bloodline families that revere their ancestral connections to ancient extraterrestrial visitors. These bloodline families have a power hierarchy, the apex of which is headed by Satan. This is discussed at length in books such as Jim Marrs' *Rule By Secrecy*,[295] William Bramley's *Gods of Eden*,[296] and David Icke's *The Biggest Secret*.[297] The basic idea is that a select group of families with distinct bloodlines have accumulated power and pass this on from one generation to another. While the thirteen ruling families compete against one another for power and influence, they are all headed by one supreme temporal ruler: Satan. Here is what Fritz Springmeir had to say about the thirteen ruling bloodline families (aka Deep State):

> In short the Illuminati are generational Satanic bloodlines which have gained the most power. A generational Satanist described the Illuminati as "Satan's elite. . . ." In mockery and imitation of God's 12 tribes, Satan blessed 12 bloodlines. . . . The 13th Satanic bloodline was instilled with the direct seed of Satan so that they would not only carry Christ's blood—but also the blood of his "brother" Lucifer.[298]

In October 2008, a self-described Illuminati/Deep State insider, who used the pseudonym, "Hidden Hand," came forward to answer questions from members of the Above Top Secret Forum.[299] The responses are consistent with other authoritative occult books such as *The Law of One,* and illustrate an extraterrestrial element in the thirteen ruling bloodline families:

I am a generational member of a Ruling Bloodline Family, our Lineage can be traced back beyond antiquity. From the earliest times of your recorded "history", and beyond, our Family has been 'directing' the 'play' from behind the scenes, in one way or another... There are 13 'base' or 'core' original bloodlines. Yet there are many many [sic] other lines that spring from these, as do rivers from the oceans.[300]

Of the thirteen base bloodlines, the Hidden Hand says that only three are indigenous to Earth. The rest have off-world origins, the "Fallen Angels" as described in the Book of Enoch/Genesis. The Hidden Hand clearly identifies where the most power is found among the thirteen bloodlines:

I want to be clear on this Bloodline issue. The ones you know, they are of earthly lineage. Yes, they have their place in the Family, but the Real Power lines, do not originate from this planet.[301]

This is an important clue into the nature of the Deep State—participants believe themselves to be descended from off planet civilizations. Further clarifying the identity of the most powerful bloodlines, the Hidden Hand says they derive from the "group soul" or entity known as Lucifer:

Our Creator, is the one you refer to as 'Lucifer', "The Light Bearer" and "Bright and Morning Star". Our Creator is not "The Devil" as he has been spuriously portrayed in your bible. Lucifer is what you would call a "Group Soul" or "Social Memory Complex", which has evolved to the level of the Sixth Density. . . . In appearance, were you to gaze upon Lucifer's

199

fullest expression of our Being, the appearance would be that of a Sun or a "Bright Star". Or, when stepping down into a 3rd Density vibration, we would appear as what you may term an 'Angel' or 'Light Being'.[302]

While "the Family" is led by ten extraterrestrial bloodlines, all thirteen bloodlines see themselves as physical manifestations of Lucifer—a highly evolved spiritual being who has taken on the assignment of creating a negative polarity which gives humanity the opportunity to evolve by making better moral choices. So while Satan occupies the position of temporal ruler, a custodian of sorts, Lucifer is considered to be the more remote spiritual ruler over the thirteen bloodline families. If we use a corporate metaphor for the thirteen bloodline families, each of which controls different fiefdoms, Satan would be the CEO, while Lucifer is the Chairman of the Board of Directors.

This is vitally important background information for appreciating the situation on Earth during the interwar period just prior to World War II, when human looking "Nordic" extraterrestrial visitors accelerated their contacts with humanity due to rapid technological advances. I describe these historical events in detail in *Antarctica's Hidden History: Corporate Foundations of Secret Space Programs* (2018). To briefly summarize, as a result of the initial extraterrestrial contacts that began in Germany during the 1920s, reverse engineered extraterrestrial spacecraft began to appear with the first Vril flying saucers built in the early 1930s, just prior to Hitler becoming the leader of Nazi Germany. These initial flying saucer prototypes were followed by the more advanced Haunebu series that were made possible through formal agreements reached between Nazi Germany and a Reptilian group of extraterrestrials called the Draconians. The German secret society that was behind the Vril spacecraft, the Thule Society, was controlled by one of the thirteen ruling bloodline families—the Krupp Family, which Springmeier has described at length in *Bloodlines of the Illuminati*.

Consequently, through trickery, persuasion and false promises, Hitler was manipulated into giving enormous resources to the construction of a hidden redoubt in Antarctica for constructing flying saucer technologies and other superweapons that could be used for the war effort, or the fortress could be used as a sanctuary if needed. When Nazi Germany began to collapse during the latter stages of World War II, the promised superweapons that would save Hitler's Third Reich failed to materialize. Instead, the breakaway German Antarctica Space Program continued developing its superweapons, and flying saucers that would be equipped with LASER cannons, and other types of directed energy weapons without interruption during and immediately after World War II.

By late 1946, when the US Navy had launched a punitive naval mission to Antarctica, the German Fourth Reich was ready. The Truman Administration's Operation Highjump arrived in early 1947 and was given a bloody nose by the Fourth Reich's flying saucers that easily destroyed all that the US Naval task force could throw at the Antarctic Germans. This disastrous military defeat suffered by the US Navy was followed soon after with German flying saucer flights over the US mainland beginning in June 1947, which led to similar humiliating losses by the US (Army) Air Force.[303] The creation of the Majestic 12 group in September 1947 was designed to give policy advice to the president about how to deal with the overall situation created by both extraterrestrial visitors and the existence of a German SSP flying over US territory with impunity. The Fourth Reich continued to conduct overflights over the next five years, and in an unprecedented show of power, had their flying saucer squadrons fly over Washington D.C., on successive weekends in July 1952.[304]

The Majestic 12 Group (aka MJ-12) along with key figures within the administration of the newly elected President Eisenhower began secret negotiations with Fourth Reich representatives, many of whom were prominent scientists brought into the US under Operation Paperclip. Key US political leaders such as Allen Dulles (CIA Director), John Foster Dulles (Secretary of State), and Nelson Rockefeller (National Security Advisor) played major roles in the ensuing negotiations, and the eventual agreement was reached in 1955. Rockefeller was a scion of one of the thirteen bloodline families identified by Springmeier, and the Dulles brothers both answered to the Rockefellers. The Rockefellers in turn were closely associated with, or subordinate to, another of the thirteen bloodline families: the Rothschilds. Soon after his appointment as CIA Director in 1953, Allen Dulles became the formal head of MJ-12 as revealed in a Majestic 12 document called the "Burned Memo."[305] Dulles used his wartime experience of negotiating deals between Nazi elites and the US government to perform a similar role in reaching agreements with the Antarctica Germans. The 1955 deal involved the Fourth Reich receiving major infusions of personnel and resources in return for scientific expertise in the research and development of recovered extraterrestrial spacecraft, and captured Nazi flying saucers.

Consequently, in the 1960's, the Apollo Program was secretly run by the Fourth Reich which used the manned moon landing missions propelled by Saturn V rockets as a cover for providing massive funding and resources to developing fleets of electromagnetically propelled antigravity spacecraft that made up the Antarctic German space program—the Dark Fleet.[306] While the Apollo Program got Americans to the Moon, it got Germans to Mars, Alpha Centauri and beyond! Over time, the Antarctic German base was handed over to a consortium of international aerospace corporations that built large numbers of differently sized and shaped antigravity spacecraft for the Dark Fleet. According to Corey

Goode, this international consortium is called the Interplanetary Corporate Conglomerate, and it has built its own fleets of antigravity spacecraft that operate independently in space.[307]

Today there are two secret space programs that are the direct offshoots of the German redoubt established in Antarctica, which built the first fleets of 'modern' human-made flying saucer craft. One is the Dark Fleet controlled by the Fourth Reich, which has reestablished its base of operations on Mars, and another is a transnational consortium that continues to operate out of Antarctica. Both of these SSPs are controlled by at least three of the thirteen ruling bloodline families that make up the Deep State (Krupp, Rockefellers and Rothschilds). Both SSPs operate fleets of antigravity craft conducting a number of covert operations that consolidate or expand their operations on Earth and in outer space. Importantly, these Deep State controlled antigravity fleets have received funding or other forms of logistical support from the CIA as a result of agreements dating back to 1955.

Historically, the CIA and NRO collaborated closely with MJ-12 and the Deep State in a variety of covert space operations. These involved false flag events and multiple unacknowledged special access programs all of which were funded through the CIA's black budget. Today, it is the NRO and the CIA's Office of Space Reconnaissance that works closely with the Deep State in space operations and collaborates with the SSPs of both the Fourth Reich and International Consortium. The creation of the US Space Force represents a powerful threat to future covert operations conducted by these SSPs. Understanding the threat posed by Space Force requires a brief overview of covert space activities that have been historically conducted by the Deep State, the end of which would be a prospect that terrifies the Deep State.

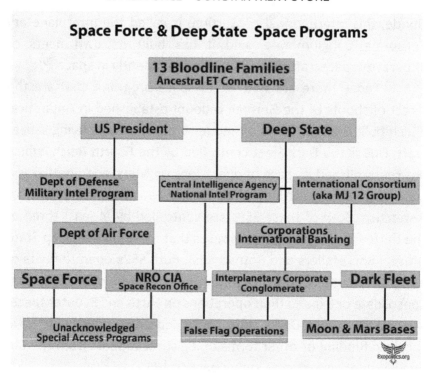

Figure 31. Space Force within Deep State Power Structure

Ending False Flag Events from Space

Among the psychological warfare tools used by the Deep State to manipulate humanity in order to achieve its agenda is the creation of false flag events. It has long been recognized that national sentiment could be easily manipulated by manufacturing tragic events which, when fanned by a complicit media, lead to strident public support for a military response.[308] The sinking of the USS Maine in Havana (1898), the sinking of the HMS Lusitania (1915), the Reichstag fire (1933), and the Gulf of Tonkin incident (1964) are all examples of worldwide false flag events contrived by the Deep State to inflame the prospect of war or militant crackdowns in one country or another. With the advent of space-based technologies, the Deep State received another powerful tool that could be used to manipulate humanity. In addition to placing highly classified reconnaissance satellites into orbit whose existence is unknown, the NRO-CIA has also placed directed energy weapons in space for use in CIA led covert operations.

Along with the space assets made available by the International Consortium, false flag events orchestrated from satellites and antigravity spacecraft in Earth orbit have occurred. There is much evidence that the September 11, 2001, attacks involved the use of Directed Energy Weapons from Space, as documented by Dr. Judy Woods in *Where Did the Towers Go?*[309] Any doubts over the existence of such space-based weapons were laid to rest on September 16, 2020, when Mark Esper, the Secretary of Defense at the time, admitted that US adversaries had deployed such technologies:

> Meanwhile, in space, Moscow and Beijing have turned a once-peaceful arena into warfighting domain. They have weaponized space through killer satellites, directed energy weapons, and more, in an effort to exploit our systems and chip away at our military advantage.[310]

There is also evidence that hurricanes have been purposely steered to specific locations using microwave MASER satellites from Earth orbit. In the case of Hurricane Irma (September 2018), I explained in a previous book how it was purposefully directed towards MacDill AFB in retribution for the USAF Special Operations covertly disclosing some of its antigravity spacecraft by allowing them to be photographed.[311] Similarly, forest fires have been sparked using earth orbiting satellites or SSP craft equipped with Directed Energy Weapons as best evidenced by live satellite feeds of fires being started in Oregon and California during the summer of 2020.[312]

False flag events orchestrated from space were made possible by the command and control responsibilities assigned to the NRO-CIA due to space being considered a benign environment, which only permitted surveillance operations under international law. That has changed with space now being considered a warfighting domain, thereby elevating Space Force to a position of authority when it comes to command and control of US space assets. This directly impacts the NRO-CIA since its historic ability to launch false flag events has been dependent on having command and control of space operations out of their jointly run facilities, which since 2014 has been located in the Office of Space Reconnaissance. Space Force is therefore a direct threat to the NRO-CIA and Deep State since it takes away one of the major tools used to manipulate humanity—false flag events orchestrated from space.

Forced Labor and International Space Law

Another way that Space Force impacts the Deep State involves humans who have been tricked into signing contracts to serve limited periods in off-planet locations, such as Mars, and then made to work as forced labor for the rest of their lives. Such recruitment programs are run by the CIA in collaboration with the International Consortium and the Dark Fleet according to witnesses. Laura Eisenhower, the Great Granddaughter of President Dwight D. Eisenhower, has emerged as a credible witness testifying that she and a former friend were subjected to an intense recruitment effort to such a program.[313] Similarly, Corey Goode has described how many thousands of people are recruited annually in this way, and live miserable lives on Mars or other Deep State space facilities.[314] The scenario of a Mars corporate dictator systematically abusing the rights of workers was actually a topic of discussion in a June 2015 workshop hosted by Britain's interplanetary Society with the provocative title: "How to Overthrow a Martian Dictatorship."[315]

Space Force threatens this exploitative practice since under both domestic and international law, US citizens made to work as forced labor, whether systematically abused by host nations or corporations, have a right to legal protection and repatriation.[316] They can even be declared to be hostages, and therefore subject to rescue by US Special Forces, which regularly perform hostage rescues around the world, as permitted by international law.[317] Article I of the Outer Space Treaty declares international law to extend into outer space and celestial bodies:

> Outer space, including the Moon and other celestial
> bodies, shall be free for exploration and use by all
> States without discrimination of any kind, on a basis
> of equality and in accordance with international law,
> and there shall be free access to all areas of celestial
> bodies.[318]

This means that Mars is subject to international law. If the German and/or corporate authorities on Mars declare that they are a sovereign entity entitled to pass their own laws regulating the territory they control, this would not be recognized since it violates Article II of the Outer Space Treaty which states:

> Outer space, including the Moon and other celestial
> bodies, is not subject to national appropriation by
> claim of sovereignty, by means of use or occupation,
> or by any other means.[319]

Article II clearly proscribes the appropriation of Mars or other celestial bodies such as Ceres by any sovereign entity asserting "national appropriation." If a corporate entity wants to establish exclusive control or sovereignty over a celestial body, then at best it could appeal to the Artemis Accords which recognizes the right of corporations to establish facilities in outer space or celestial bodies for commercial purposes. However, any facilities on Mars that violates the sovereign rights of US citizens or those of the nations that are party to the Artemis Accords, would be targets of Space Force and its multinational space alliance. The German and Corporate Space programs operating on Mars and elsewhere in our solar system will be faced with either significantly improving the quality of life of workers or having them repatriated by Space Force, which would significantly impact their profits and influence.

Ending the Galactic Slave Trade

According to the testimony of secret space program whistleblower, Corey Goode, a galactic human slave trade exists where millions of captured humans are taken off planet to distant colonies on other worlds to be bartered or abused. In a Q&A session I did with Goode on May 29/30, 2015, he explained just how extensive the galactic human slave trade has been, the principal parties involved, and the egregious mistreatment of those unfortunate enough to have been taken captive:

> It starts out with in some cases with [sic] your run of the mill organized crime groups who are into the sex and slave trade which is very much alive in the 20th and 21st centuries. Many of these crime groups or gangs have specialists who work from lists of desired people to be obtained (many others are victims of

opportunity). These specialists often are kind elderly looking people or professional people (including Medical, Law Enforcement and Education to name a few) that no one would consider a threat, come in contact with a lot of people and are generally trusted. These people operate in just about any country you can think of. Often people are grabbed who live on the streets, in third world countries . . . or from inattentive parents. This level of human trafficking brings in many hundreds of thousands of people per year into the slave trade. These people do not know or care what happens to the people they obtain and hand off to handlers in exchange for money.

Then there are the special operator groups who have a specific shopping list and will go through a great deal of trouble and personal risk to obtain certain types of individuals that are on their lists. People at this level know that their victims are going into something bigger than just the global human trafficking systems and they deal directly with Cabal/Illuminati types. These Cabal/Illuminati types then funnel abducted people into their processing centers where the people are cataloged and it is decided if they will be sent below ground for various uses by allied ET's or will be used as a commodity in off world trade.[320]

Goode has identified the important role played by the Deep State in identifying and rounding people up for the Galactic Slave Trade. Therefore, Deep State officials possess enormous power over others which they are able to wield in a capricious manner.

Goode explained that in space there is no universal currency system and that barter is widely used. Slaves are therefore used to barter for advanced technologies or other goods:

> There is no currency or financial system that is used between space faring civilizations so everything is based on bartering. Some ET's are interested in some of the Earth's Art (again some of our most famous missing historical art pieces are in off world collections), Luxury Items like Spices/Chocolate (strangely enough), Animal and Plant Life, while many others are interested in trading their technology and biological specimens they have obtained elsewhere for Human Beings. These Humans are used for many purposes including manual slave labor, sex trade, engineering/manufacturing (we are well known for the abilities some of us have with certain technical skill sets). There are some of the ET's that use Humans as food resources in various ways (of which I will not go into detail). [*sic*][321]

Goode went on to assert that the Galactic Slave trade has been a historic phenomenon, thus elites saw an opportunity to piggy-back on its coattails and profit from it:

> The Secret Earth Governments and their Syndicates discovered that a large amount of humans were being taken off the planet by various ET's anyway so they decided to find a way to profit from it and have control over which people were being taken. In prior arrangements they were made promises of receiving technologies and biological specimens for

allowing groups to abduct humans but the ET's rarely delivered on their promises. Once they had developed the advanced infrastructure (ICC) in our Sol System along with advanced technologies (that some of the thousands of ET groups traveling through our system were now interested in obtaining) and now had the ability to deter most unwelcome guests from entering Earth's airspace the Cabal/ICC then decided to use human trafficking as one of their resources in interstellar bartering.[322]

Goode's description of the role played by the Deep State in identifying, capturing and selling people for the galactic slave trade is well illustrated in the case of Tony Rodrigues, who first publicly revealed his experiences in an interview released on ExoNews TV on September 24, 2016.[323] According to Rodrigues, he was forcibly taken to serve for twenty years as a slave for the Deep State because he humiliated a fellow student in Middle School, who happened to be the son of a Deep State/Illuminati figure. As a capricious punishment, the child's father arranged for Rodrigues to serve as a slave for twenty years, before being age regressed, having his memories wiped, and returned back in time to live out his life as though nothing had happened. Rodrigues was transformed from a bright precocious A grade student, into a deeply traumatized pre-teen who struggled with school.

Rodrigues says that he spent the first six years of his servitude being exposed to Satanic Ritual Abuse ceremonies, and later was exploited as a drug courier and sex slave in Peru and Seattle, Washington. Rodrigues says that the subsequent fourteen years of his punishment involved many months of training and evaluation on the Moon, and then Mars, before being transferred to the planetoid Ceres to work as a slave for the German-run secret space program, the Dark Fleet. He claims that Ceres is occupied and controlled by the Dark Fleet, which is where he was physically based most of the time.

Rodrigues has been able to identify some of the individuals that exploited him in Seattle, and the locations where he was forcibly held before being taken into space. In email correspondence with me [MS] on August 16, 2015, he [TR] identified unique aspects of Seres' geology such as the bright white spots photographed by NASA's Dawn flyby only a few months earlier (March 2015) as water geysers:

> [MS] What do you know of the strange lights on Ceres that NASA has been releasing to the public?

> [TR] I believe there's a geyser there - the crater looks exactly like one we flew over later in my career - the geyser shoots water and some other chemicals high into the sky there like 10-20 miles it only goes off every 7 years or something like that, and we flew right next to it one time - the crew was allowed to leave stations and go to a wall to look out - the ship had the transparent walls that could be turned on and off as well as view ports that were located along the little stations we had to take breaks at - there were food replicators there and water as well as first aid and a head and a small refrigerator which I never used once.

> It was white and looked like the inside of an airplane - only in that area. The geyser was one of the most beautiful things I saw in that entire time. There were other occasions that we passed over geysers around other moons but I never looked at them as I stayed at my post.[324]

Rodrigues also claimed that Seres has abundant interior water reserves that supply a large underground base. It was only in October 2018, when Dawn did another, much closer, flyby of Ceres that more detailed photographs of the white spots were taken. After exhaustive analysis, the spots were finally identified by NASA scientists as salt deposits caused by brine water percolating up from Ceres' interior, as discussed in a 2020 article published in *EarthSky* by science journalist, Deborah Byrd:

> Dawn scientists now say that the salty liquid on Ceres' surface came from a reservoir of brine, or salt-enriched water, deep in Ceres' interior. Scientists say this brine reservoir is about 25 miles (40 km) deep and hundreds of miles wide. Ceres itself is less than 600 miles across (1,000 km) across. So, in other words, Ceres is now understood to have a relatively vast interior reservoir of briny water.[325]

This directly supports Rodrigues claim that the white spots are associated with water geysers that erupt every seven years or so from a vast underground ocean that supplies the Dark Fleet's underground base. Importantly, his information predated the official NASA explanation by five years. This is remarkable corroboration for Rodrigues' testimony and his authenticity as a witness for the existence of a galactic slave trade.

What gives further credence to Goode and Rodrigues' incredible testimonies is a first-hand witness report by William Pawelec who was a computer operations and programming expert with the USAF. Pawelec started his own electronics security company, and worked for high profile US defense contractors such as SAIC (Science Applications International Corporation) and EG&G (now URS Corporation). He received high level security clearances and had access to many classified projects. Prior to 2001, Pawelec decided to reveal what he knew about deep black projects, which he believed were hiding advanced technologies from the US public. He conducted a recorded video interview with Dr. Steven Greer, and gave the strict instruction that it would only be published after his death. He died on May 22, 2007 and the video was published posthumously on December 14, 2010.[326]

Among his many revelations is information concerning the development of the first electronic RFID tracking chips that were developed as early as 1979 according to Pawelec. He explained the history of their development, and the role his Denver-based company played in setting up meetings with government agencies, which were interested in using the chips for security purposes. In his video interview, Pawelec said:

> At the time in the security industry, a lot of us had a lot of concerns about tracking and locating people that had been kidnapped. Particularly what was going on in Europe at the time where we were having NATO officers, even the Prime Minister of Italy, kidnapped . . . These people were drained [of information] or they were brutalized or both... One of the goals of the industry was to develop technology that would allow us to track these people or locate them quickly.[327]

He explained that the tracking chips, which were very small and shaped like a pill, had multiple functions:

> Now this particular pill shaped device, very minute, had a lot of flexibility in its capabilities. It was basically almost a transponder. You could send a frequency to it and it would respond back with its unique number which could not be changed once

the chip was made. Yet there were a lot of capabilities that could be added to this chip such as monitoring temperature, blood pressure, pulse, and even wave forms out of the brain.[328]

Pawelec said that soon after demonstrating an even more sophisticated lithium niobate chip in 1984, which could be tracked from a distance of 120 kilometers in space, he discovered a small Silicon Valley company had been set up to manufacture billions of them. He learned that "after they had made billions and billions of these little chips" the factory was shut down a year later, and all information about the chips disappeared.[329] Pawelec said that the small company responsible for making the billions of tiny chips "was a division of a rather major European electronics firm that had the plant - Siemens."[330]

Pawelec's testimony suggests that the Siemens corporation had acquired the rights and control over the tracking chip technology, built billions of them in less than a year using a US subsidiary, and then arranged for the local manufacturing plant to close with all information about the tracking chips now gone. These chips were very likely used to monitor a galactic slave trade, and the use of forced labor on secret colonies on Mars and elsewhere in our solar system, just as claimed by Goode and Rodrigues. If a galactic slave trade does exist, then what does the creation of Space Force mean for the future of such an illicit trade with humans embedded with RFID tracking chips?

In the short term, it is certain that the increased presence of Space Force in monitoring and tracking all space traffic will eventually expose the existence of such an illicit trade. Once this happens, it can be predicted with great confidence that the public reaction will be overwhelmingly negative. Space Force will be authorized to take steps to intercept spacecraft involved in the galactic slave trade, and eventually bring an end to such a horrific practice. Therefore, we are destined to repeat human history as in after the abolition of slavery in the United Kingdom in 1807, the Royal Navy soon after began intercepting slave trading ships on the high seas, freeing the captive slaves, and destroying slave trading facilities through their celebrated West Africa Squadron [1808-1860].[331] Space Force is fated to repeat such a sequence of events and bring this egregious chapter in human affairs to an end. Consequently, Space Force threatens the massive revenue earned by Deep State linked SSPs from the galactic slave trade, the loss of which would be a tremendous setback to their future operations and power.

Preventing a Space Pearl Harbor

The chief mission of Space Force is to protect the US satellite system and prevent a Space Pearl Harbor attack, which was first predicted as far back as 2001. Not surprisingly, one of the first actions of Space Force was to take over the operation of the US GPS system from the USAF. Today, Space Force personnel are maintaining the US GPS and other satellites belonging to the different military services in order to protect them from possible foreign interference such as cyberwarfare, hacking, electronic interference, or kinetic action.

Once Space Force acquires antigravity craft of its own, it will be much better equipped to defend the US satellite grid from any possible military attack, thus making a repeat of the 1941 Pearl Harbor surprise attack very unlikely. Unfortunately, the time it will take Space Force to acquire such technologies may prove costly. It is highly unlikely that the NRO/CIA will share any of the antigravity spacecraft developed for classified space surveillance missions, despite these having been set up with the administrative and logistical support of Space Force's predecessor, US Space Command (1982-2019).

Also, it is unclear how and to what extent Air Force Special Operations will relinquish command and control over antigravity craft used for covert operations worldwide. Transfers of such craft may be minimal since Air Force Special Operations is part of a different command structure to Space Force and Space Command. This means that Space Force will most likely have to acquire the bulk of its future squadrons of antigravity craft directly from Lockheed's Skunkworks and other major aerospace companies. This will be both time consuming and very costly, and will require the US Congress agreeing to a significant increase in the budget of Space Force. It is hard to see how this will happen in the current partisan political climate where the real national security threat posed by China is being ignored by the general public, mass media and Congress.

In the meantime, China is moving forward rapidly with its military modernization programs, which involve the construction of 5th generation aircraft, hypersonic missiles, modern naval ships, and electromagnetically propelled antigravity spacecraft. This led to great concern over whether the US Space Force will be able to keep up with the rapid construction and deployment of China's Space Navy. As mentioned in chapter eight, China is secretly building a modern-day Space Navy with the equivalent of destroyers and cruisers in space.[332] It will eventually become a formidable force in deep space operations, eclipsing the number of similar craft built by multiple US military and intelligence units. China's antigravity spacecraft are being built in remote facilities such as Dingxin Test and Training Base in the remote Gobi Desert region of Gansu province, as discussed in *Rise of the Red Dragon*.[333] One can get an idea of the secret construction rate of China's space navy by examining the rapid construction of China's conventional navy.

In September 2020, the Department of Defense released its "2020 China Military Power Report" and revealed that China now "has the largest navy" and is "the top ship-producing nation in the world by tonnage."[334] China's People's Liberation Army Navy (PLAN) now has 350 surface warships and submarines compared to the US Navy's 293 according to the Pentagon report. According to Matthew Funaiole, a China military expert, "China can produce ships very fast. There is absolutely no doubt about that."[335] The gap in overall ship numbers will only continue to grow since China's ship building construction rate is much faster than the US due to lax labor laws, minimal government regulations, and virtually unlimited funding from the Communist Party. There is no reason to think that China's secret space navy is not experiencing similar rapid construction rates. This is especially the case since multiple PLA strategists have identified space as the new strategic high ground and the Achilles heel of the US military, which must be exploited in China's Assassins Mace strategy. Writing for the *Epoch Times*, Joshua Philipp summarizes the war strategy of the Chinese Communist Party (CCP):

> The CCP's military strategy for a war with the United States would rely heavily on weapons like this, under its so-called "Assassin's Mace" or "Trump Card" program. This would include the use of anti-satellite weapons and other key technologies to destroy the systems that enable core technologies of the U.S. military.
>
> "These modern Trump Card and Assassin's Mace weapons will permit China's low-technology forces to prevail over U.S. high-technology forces in a localized conflict," states a 2011 report from the National Ground Intelligence Center.[336]

Space Force, however, is taking necessary action by working with European and international partners in setting up a multinational military space alliance. It is only through the creation of such an alliance that Space Force has a real long-term chance of stopping what China is secretly building and deploying in space. Such a space alliance constitutes a major threat to Deep State plans to turn the US into a failed state through a devastating Space Pearl Harbor and to make China the new global hegemon.

In conclusion, in addition to ending egregious space practices such as false flag events, forced off-word labor, a galactic slave trade, and a planned Space Pearl Harbor, what truly terrifies the Deep State is a multinational space alliance led by the US Space Force that can bring about the optimal Star Trek Future discussed in chapter nine—the rise of a modern-day Starfleet!

Chapter 12

The Rise of Starfleet

For all its nods to political correctness over the years, *Star Trek* is about one thing and one thing only: the militarization of space.

— Christopher Knowles[337]

I n the highly influential September 5, 2019, Space Futures Workshop report, top US space policy experts, NASA and Space Force's predecessor, USAF Space Command, decided that future space policy needed to be oriented toward optimizing a Star Trek Future. This required the creation of a multinational military space alliance to protect "global civil, commercial, and military expansion in space."[338] Major steps towards that goal were the signing of the Artemis Accords on October 13, 2020,[339] and the creation just over a week later of a Space Center at NATO's Ramstein Air Base in Germany.[340] The proposed Space Center will work closely with coordinating the military space assets of NATO member states, and will coalesce around Space Force and the US Space Command.

The establishment of a future "Space NATO" is likely to expand with the inclusion of signatories to the Artemis Accords. Consequently, both NATO and the Artemis Accords will almost certainly become the backbone of a future military and civilian multinational space alliance that is designed to usher in this visionary Star Trek future as the optimal achievement. In the fictional Sci-Fi series *Star Trek*, Starfleet was the Earth-based military space entity that evolved into a multiplanetary alliance, which became the United Federation of Planets. Consequently, it is no stretch to say that the establishment of a NATO-like multinational space alliance that forms out of the Artemis Accords and NATO qualifies as an early form of Starfleet.

The similarities between the logos of Space Force and Starfleet is quite striking. It is therefore no great surprise that the creator of *Star Trek*, Gene Rodenberry, was allegedly given briefings by representatives of US naval intelligence about a future multinational military space alliance. In the *US Navy's Secret Space Program,* I described the unusual business relationship between Leslie Stevens IV and Rodenberry. After Rodenberry's failure with "The Lieutenant" television series that lasted only one season (1963-1964) it was Stevens who advised him to develop a Sci-Fi series. At the time, Stevens was the Director of the popular *The Outer Limits* which ran for two seasons (1963-1965) on ABC TV, and he allowed Rodenberry to sit in on the set of the second season to get ideas for a future Sci-Fi series.

Rodenberry's presence on the set of *The Outer Limits* was first revealed by Tom Seldon, one of the show's production assistants:

> Star Trek was in fact an outgrowth of The Outer Limits. Gene Roddenberry watched our dailies all the time and took a lot of phone calls from our screening room. He was spurring his imagination and checking on the incredible quality control we had. I wondered why he was there but he was there

more often than not during the time he was coming up with *Star Trek*.[341]

Chris Knowles, a media blogger who wrote a nine-part series of articles about the genesis of *Star Trek*, elaborates on Seldon's recollection, and asserts that Roddenberry and Leslie Stevens IV had secretly reached a business arrangement for the planned Sci-Fi series:

> Bearing in mind that Roddenberry was contracted to a rival studio and a rival network, the odds are essentially slim to none that the two men didn't have some kind of business arrangement, whether in writing or not. [342]

The highly unusual business relationship between Stevens and Rodenberry is also addressed by Gordon White, a book author who points to some hidden meaning:

> The case is convincingly made [by Knowles] that Leslie Stevens - rather than Roddenberry - was at the terrestrial epicentre of *Star Trek*'s prescient high strangeness, which it inherited from *The Outer Limits*. Having worked in broadcast production before, there really isn't any such thing as innocently sharing production resources. If Roddenberry was camped out with *The Outer Limits* team for a whole year, then that very much means something.[343]

Many *Star Trek* stars, such as William Shatner and Leonard Nimoy first appeared in multiple episodes of *The Outer Limits*. Most importantly, Steven's right hand man for *The Outer Limits*, Robert Justman, went on to direct, write and produce many Star Trek episodes and also served as Rodenberry's right-hand man. Justman could justifyingly lay claim as one Star Trek's creators. All this supported Knowles' claim that a secret agreement had been reached between Rodenberry and Stevens to share people and resources for the new show.

The vital key to unlocking the mystery of the business relationship between Rodenberry and Stevens is understanding that the latter was the son of Vice Admiral Leslie Stevens III who was a leading aeronautical engineer during World War II. Admiral Stevens was briefed about captured Nazi flying saucers and helped lead the Navy's reverse engineering efforts that would culminate in a Navy-led secret space program. In late 1949, he became the first head of "The Joint Subsidiary Plans Division," which was under the control of the Joint Chiefs of Staff, a position he held until at least early 1951 according to an official government document (see *Figure 31*). Army historian Alfred H. Paddock describes the mission of the Division:

> [To] coordinate the peacetime development of psychological warfare and covert operations capabilities within the Armed Services, coordinate detailed military plans and other agencies of the government, particularly with Department of State and the Office of Policy Coordination [CIA], and, in wartime, [to] become the means by which the JCS would provide continuous direction and guidance in these specialized fields to commanders under their control.[344]

In Admiral Steven's capacity as the head of the "The Joint Subsidiary Plans Division," he worked closely with the CIA in covert and psychological warfare operations. It is almost certain that during his time directing the Division, Admiral Stevens developed, with CIA leaders, a psychological warfare strategy for using movies and television to influence public perceptions on the flying saucer issue. This is evidenced in the January 1953, CIA-sponsored Robertson Panel report (the Durant Report), which recommended ridiculing the flying saucer phenomenon and the possibility of extraterrestrial life for national security reasons, and proposed the use of television and motion pictures for psychological warfare purposes. The Durant Report stated:

> The "debunking" aim would result in reduction in public interest in "flying saucers" which today evokes a strong psychological reaction. This education could be accomplished by mass media such as television, motion pictures, and popular articles. . . . Such a program should tend to reduce the current gullibility of the public and consequently their susceptibility to clever hostile propaganda.[345]

It is important to emphasize that the Admiral's son, Leslie Stevens IV, was himself a member of Army Air Force Intelligence during WWII, where his literary skills as a playwriter well suited him to psychological warfare operations. In the *Navy's Secret Space Program*, I make the case that Stevens (IV) may have even played a role in the Army's Interplanetary Phenomenon Unit, which involved a psychological warfare component.[346] Given Admiral Stevens' leadership position and close collaboration with the CIA in psychological warfare operations, it is reasonable to assume that the Admiral recruited his son as a valuable asset for disseminating key ideas (that were a part of psychological warfare operations) into the film and television industry, just as proposed by the Robertson Panel.

According to Knowles, this is a scenario which many had long suspected about Stevens IV:

Stevens, Sr. died in 1956 but his son was himself an intelligence agent during the Big One and almost certainly maintained his connections after the war. In fact, some believe he remained on the payroll throughout his Hollywood career.[347]

Approved For Release 2006/08/09 : CIA-RDP80R01731R000800060032-7

COPY #7

'NSC Declassification/   Release Instructions On File*

TS 43516

CENTRAL INTELLIGENCE AGENCY
Washington 25, D.C.

Office of the Director

8 January 1951

MEMORANDUM TO: EXECUTIVE SECRETARY
                    NATIONAL SECURITY COUNCIL

SUBJECT   :   Draft of NSC Directive on Covert Operations
                    and Clandestine Activities

1. On 14 December 1950, at my request, the National Security Council suspended paragraph 4 of NSC 10/2.

2. I am submitting herewith the draft of a directive for issuance by the National Security Council which clearly defines the responsibilities for covert operations and clandestine activities in peace or in war. This draft was prepared by representatives of this agency in consultation with Rear Admiral Leslie Stevens from the Joint Chiefs of Staff, Brigadier General John Magruder from the Office of the Secretary of Defense, and Mr. Robert Joyce from the Department of State.

3. It is my recommendation that this Directive be sent by the National Security Council to the Departments of State and Defense and the Joint Chiefs of Staff for comment.

4. A related subject which needs clarification is the distinction between covert operations such as may be planned and executed by this agency, and guerrilla warfare conducted by regular forces. I have directed that a paper on this subject be prepared for submission to the NSC.

/s/ WALTER B. SMITH
Director

MORI/CDF Pages 1/3/4

25X1

Approved For Release 2006/08/09 : CIA-RDP80R01731R000800060032-7

Figure 32. Document showing Admiral Leslie Stevens involved with CIA Covert Operations

It is highly likely that Stevens worked with his father and for the Pentagon's psychological warfare division, whereby he came up with ideas for "soft disclosure" of highly classified programs through the movie and television industry. The purpose appears to have been one of creating plausible deniability in order to protect a classified program from unauthorized disclosures, or to psychologically condition the public in a particular direction on the UFO and extraterrestrial issue as recommended by the Robertson Panel. Hiding the truth in plain sight through the entertainment industry had great benefit regarding anyone who made unauthorized disclosures. Such a person could be easily discredited by claiming that the idea was stolen from a movie or TV show.

Episodes of *The Outer Limits* were filled with concepts which can be directly linked to Top Secret Pentagon programs involving extraterrestrial life and technology that Stevens had very likely received briefings about. Among the more notable episodes was the pilot, "Galaxy Being," which introduced the idea of electronic visual communications with extraterrestrial beings. Episode 7, which introduced O.B.I.T. (Outer Band Individuated Teletracer), referred to extraterrestrial technology that could monitor real time human behavior anywhere in the world. Episode 20, "The Bellero Shield" introduced powerful laser weapons and electromagnetic shields that had been earlier theorized by the inventor Nikola Tesla as practical. Among the classified programs that would be protected through the "soft disclosure" method was a Navy-led secret space program. Consequently, Stevens helped Rodenberry come up with the idea of a "universe ruled over by a benevolent military dictatorship," as Knowles put it. [348]

According to Navy insider, William Tompkins, Stevens was authorized to brief Rodenberry about the US Navy's secret space program, which was under development at the time. In briefing Rodenberry, Stevens was passing on what Navy leaders thought would be the optimal future of the Navy's planned secret space program that would eventually be publicly disclosed. This means that the basic outline of the *Star Trek* series, born out of Rodenberry and Stevens collaboration on the set of the final season of *The Outer Limits*, was based on early Navy intelligence assessments of what the future held.

Vice Admiral Leslie Stevens, III   Leslie Stevens, IV.
Creator of the Outer Limits

Figure 33. Leslie Stevens III & IV.

An even more amazing possibility was brought up by Corey Goode in a discussion between us which was publicly released in video form on November 10, 2020. According to Goode, who says he first served in the Navy SSP from 1986 to 2007 in a "20 and back program," the Navy SSP uses recruits taken from earlier historical epochs going as far back as the 1930s. The Navy SSP recruits then undergo a "20 and back" term of service beginning in the 2030's or so, where time travel technology has been mastered, before being returned back to their point of departure. This is how Goode explained it:

> Let me blow your mind even more. The 20 and backs, all of the temporal travel that's going on, you have to visualize it this way. . . . Let's say in 2036,

Space Force develops the technology to travel back in time. Well, they're traveling back in time, and working with people back in the 30s, 40s, 50s, 60s, pulling them up into "20 and backs," working with them in these temporal groups. So that information, like the people going up and working in these "20 and backs," and working off planet for Space Force that's actually in the future, this is going into their consciousness so it's you know, it kind of bleeds out in different ways.

So I think there is a huge part of this puzzle that a lot of people really aren't paying enough attention to, and when all of this does come out, its gonna blow even the minds of people in ufology that have been covering, I know, about 58 different ET groups, I know about spacecraft that can fly from between here and the moon in a matter minutes, and they think they've got a good understanding, but when all of it does come out, the temporal aspect of it is going to be the mind-blowing part.[349]

I [MS] then asked Goode about the possibility of Rodenberry being recruited into the Navy SSP and serving for twenty years before being returned back in time in the manner Goode [CG] had just described:

[MS] So this pulling people out of historical epochs, the 1920s, 30s, 40s and pushing them into this kind of 20 year and back program . . . in the 2030s, 2040s, whatever, and after 20 years they get pushed back, well that raises the question, could Gene Rodenberry have been a "20 and back" in the Starfleet of the future?

[CG] Yeah, that's my question too.

[MS] OK, that's an interesting one.

[CG] He may have been influenced by someone who was.

[MS] Well I know he was actually directly influenced by Leslie Stevens who was the director of *The Outer Limits*. *The Outer Limits* was run by Leslie Stevens and he ran that from 64 to 66 [1963-1965], and Gene Roddenberry sat in on the second season of *The Outer Limits*. Now in the Navy Secret Space Program book I actually talked about Leslie Stevens' father who was the Vice Admiral. He was the guy that worked directly with [Rear Admiral] Rico Botta in setting up the Navy Secret Space Program. So, the son of Admiral Stevens was the guy that inspired or introduced Gene Roddenberry to a lot of these ideas. So, it's quite possible that maybe Leslie Stevens was one of these people pulled out and served in the 20 and back program, because Leslie Stevens doesn't just influence Gene Roddenberry with *Star Trek*, he also influenced Glen Larson who came up with the *Battlestar Galactica* series originally in the 70s . . .

[CG] *Battlestar Galactica* plays into the whole AI threat.

[MS] Exactly so that would make sense that Leslie Stevens was probably part of the 20 and back program . . .

[CG] You make an interesting argument.[350]

Evidence that Steven's father, the Admiral, was both involved in setting up the Navy's SSP and also in the psychological warfare operation to hide its existence, does raise the distinct possibility that his son was recruited into a future twenty and back Navy SSP, in the manner described by Goode. This would explain Stevens' extraordinary contribution to the science fiction genre through a succession of movies and TV shows, such as *The Outer Limits*, and also his ability to brief Gene Rodenberry sufficiently to help him create *Star Trek*.

All this would explain why, as Knowles explains, Stevens' involvement in the creation of *Star Trek* was deliberately downplayed despite the fact that actors, production staff and ideas were taken directly from the final season of *The Outer Limits* (1964-1965), and smoothly transferred over to Rodenberry's *Star Trek* series (1966-1969). In sum, either the *Star Trek* series was birthed out of early naval intelligence estimates of the secret space program the Navy would build in the next decade, or it was intelligence acquired by someone that had returned from a "20 and back" SSP assignment set in the future, Leslie Stevens IV being the most likely candidate. It is therefore no small irony that the 2019 Space Futures Workshop would create a Star Trek future as its optimal future scenario, whereby a powerful multinational space alliance—a Starfleet—would be created. The big question is what role does the Navy's secret space program play today in ushering in this Star Trek future?

According to William Tompkins, Corey Goode, and other insiders who have gone on the public record, the secret Navy Space Program was originally called Solar Warden. It comprises eight space battlegroups with kilometer-long space carriers, cruisers, destroyers, transports etc., that were first deployed in the early 1980s to patrol deep space and adjacent star systems. In a May 4, 2016, radio interview, Tompkins provided details about the construction facilities for these kilometers-long spacecraft first designed at Douglas Aircraft Company, and the aerospace companies involved in the subsequent construction process:

> One of the facilities that was used is east of the Wasatch Mountains in Utah. This was a very, very large cavern. It has smaller ones adjacent to it, but it's a massive one. And they were able to put together Lockheed space systems, Northrop-Grumman facilities, and even Boeing were involved in the actual construction of these kilometer-long spacecraft carriers that the Navy now has eight of these spacecraft carrier battle groups out in the galaxy.[351]

In the *Navy's Secret Space Program*, I provided extensive historical records and testimonies that support the remarkable claims that Solar Warden was created and continues to function today.

Significantly, in a private interview recorded on February 25, 2016, Tompkins told me about the Navy's current plan to replace its eight existing battle groups, which have become antiquated in comparison with other space programs, with twelve new battle groups. These are currently under development, and scheduled to become fully operational in the 2030's, replicating the fifty year life cycle of modern aircraft carriers. In the interview between Tompkins [WT] and myself [MS], he elaborated upon the Navy's future plans.

> [WT] All of the main eight Solar Warden battle groups are old, real old. They are in the process of being completely replaced by 12 new ones. Which is a major program going on, because they are very old.

[MS] So the current plan involves 12 battle groups under . . . development.

[WT] They are completely new, everything is new. Not just the ship . . . [new] hardware, everything.

[MS] When will they be deployed?

[WT] I think first deployment will be two [battle groups] in 2031, or close.

[MS] – They are under current design and manufacture . . .

[WT] It's all part of the stage. They have built a real fast program to get a prototype. They are four kilometers long rather that one kilometer.[352]

Even more incredible, Tompkins' asserted that the next generation space carrier battlegroups are being built at an off-planet location, in an adjacent star system with the help of friendly human looking Nordic extraterrestrials, rather than the previous construction site in Utah.

Given the Deep State's space programs, and how the Deep State has been secretly helping China develop a powerful space navy, it is understandable why the Navy's new space battle groups are being constructed in one or more off-planet facilities, for security reasons. The industrial espionage capabilities of China and the Deep State have reached a level of sophistication that any naval construction facility on Earth is vulnerable to having its secret blueprints stolen and replicated by China and/or the Deep State. Hence the need for off-planet construction facilities.

Let me bring all the main threads of this book together to understand the impending "Rise of Starfleet." We know that both the 2001 Space Commission Report and the Space Policy Directive-4 called for the creation of a Space Corps/Force under the

Department of the Air Force as a necessary first step towards the creation of a future Space Department within the Pentagon. President Trump made clear on several occasions that he desired to eventually create a Department of Space Force, which would be jointly controlled by elements drawn from the main military services: Air Force, Army, Marine Corps, Navy and Space Force. This is the only conceivable way in which the US Navy would ever disclose the existence of its secret space battle fleets, and delegate command and control to a new institution.

Space Force currently comprises space assets of the former Air Force Space Command, and the Earth-orbiting assets of the other military services. As I have described at length in earlier chapters, most of the antigravity spacecraft developed and deployed by Air Force Special Operations and the NRO/CIA are unlikely to find their way to Space Force for one reason or another. The former Air Force Space Command provided logistical and administrative support for squadrons of antigravity craft, but it was the NRO/CIA that historically exercised command and control. The latter will very likely emphasize its continued need for existing antigravity craft to conduct space surveillance missions under their jointly run Office of Space Reconnaissance (established 2014), which is institutionally located in the CIA, to keep the Director of National Intelligence out of the loop of its covert missions. Meanwhile, Air Force Special Operations will have its own need to use antigravity in its possession for covert operations both globally and in space. Consequently, Space Force will require aerospace contractors to build new squadrons of antigravity spacecraft, a time consuming and expensive process that will extend well into the 2020s.

Nevertheless, the foundations for the development of a multinational military space alliance which coalesces around Space Force and US Space Command has been established with the Artemis Accords, and NATO's creation of a Space Center at

Ramstein Air Base. In the immediate years ahead, it can be anticipated that Space Force will gradually acquire squadrons of antigravity spacecraft, and allied nations will do likewise in slowly building an expanded Space NATO to protect their respective GPS systems, space operations and commercial space activities. Towards the end of the current decade, a threshold will have been reached where the time is ripe for the US Navy to reveal the existence of its space battle fleets, and to integrate these with the multinational military space alliance. This is likely to occur around 2031 when the first two of new Navy space battle groups come online, according to Tompkins.

US Space Command has been set up in such a way that it is well suited to integrating the Navy's secret space fleets, alongside Space Force and space assets of other nations, for combined space operations. The institutional home of the Navy's space fleets, however, will almost certainly not be Space Force, as currently comprised as a military service under the direct authority of the Department of the Air Force. This is when the US Congress will need to step in and pass legislation creating a new military department for space towards the end of the 2020s. The new military space department is very likely going to be jointly controlled by commissioned officers drawn from the US Navy's SSP, Space Force, and military officers from allied nations. Given the incredible firepower and extensive force projection capabilities of the Navy's Solar Warden program, the future military space department will have a distinct naval flavor to it in terms of ranks, culture and operations. This means that the optimal Star Trek future desired by Air Force, NASA and other space professionals that participated in the Space Futures Workshop, is almost certainly going to give birth to a Starfleet.

The Rise of Starfleet will not be a smooth process since Space Force threatens many Deep State operations in space, which include false flag events, helping China carry out a Space Pearl

Harbor, facilitating forced labor on celestial bodies such as Mars and Ceres, and perpetuating a Galactic Slave Trade. The Deep State will fight desperately to maintain the status quo and sabotage Space Force and the Artemis multinational space alliance that it will coalesce around it. By the end of the 2020s, however, it can be anticipated that much of the Deep State's egregious space activities will have been exposed and finally ended. This will create the conditions, perhaps even required, for the Navy to announce the existence of its space battle fleets, and to integrate these with Space Force and the multinational space alliance.

A future Space Department (Starfleet) institutionally located within the Pentagon, is likely to work closely with friendly human-looking extraterrestrials that are helping the Navy build its next generation space carriers. This group of extraterrestrials very likely belong to the "Galactic Federation" described earlier by Prof. Eshed. Rodenberry's vision of a Starfleet—the fruit of a special business relationship with a Naval Intelligence operative and possible "20 and back" recruit, Leslie Stevens, IV—appears destined to become reality through the future integration of Space Force, the Artemis Accords, NATO, and the Navy's Solar Warden program. Not only will these combined events lead to the Rise of Starfleet but, even more incredibly, facilitate Earth's entry into a Galactic Federation comprising numerous extraterrestrial civilizations working with key governments around the globe, thereby fully manifesting our Star Trek Future.

Acknowledgements

Thanks to Mark McCandlish for his permission to reproduce the three "Alien Reproduction Vehicles" witnessed at Edwards Air Force Base in 1988. Many thanks also to JP for permission to include his photos of triangle, rectangle and saucer-shaped antigravity craft witnessed near MacDill Air Force Base and Orlando, Florida. I also grateful to Edgar Fouche for permission to use his illustration of a TR-3B flying triangle.

My deep appreciation to Rene McCann for generously donating her time and enthusiasm to create yet another inspiring book cover for this Secret Space Program series.

Finally, my heartfelt gratitude goes to my beautiful wife, Angelika Whitecliff, whose wise counsel and editorial skills have both greatly aided my research, writing and design of this book.

Michael E. Salla, Ph.D.
April 14, 2021.

About the Author

Dr. Michael Salla is an internationally recognized scholar in global politics, conflict resolution and U.S. foreign policy. He has taught at universities in the U.S. and Australia, including American University in Washington, DC. Today, he is most popularly known as a pioneer in the development of the field of 'exopolitics'; the study of the main actors, institutions and political processes associated with extraterrestrial life.

Dr Salla has been a guest speaker on hundreds of radio and TV shows including Ancient Aliens, Coast to Coast AM, and featured at national and international conferences. His Amazon bestselling *Secret Space Program* book series has made him a leading voice in the Truth Movement, and over 5000 people a day visit his websites for his most recent articles.

ENDNOTES

[1] *Executive Summary of the Report of the Commission to Assess United States National Security Space Management and Organization (Jan 11, 2001)* p. 22. Available online at: https://fas.org/spp/military/commission/executive_summary.pdf (accessed 10/1/2020).

[2] *Executive Summary of the Report of the Commission to Assess United States National Security Space Management and Organization,* p. 22.

[3] For US national policy makers attitudes towards China, see Michael Pillsbury, *The Hundred-Year Marathon: China's Secret Strategy to Replace America as the Global Superpower* (St Martin's Griffin, 2016).

[4] "President Clinton apologizes to Chinese leader for embassy bombing," https://www.history.com/this-day-in-history/clinton-apologizes-to-chinese-leader-for-embassy-bombing (accessed 12/15/2020).

[5] The "National Defense Authorization Act for Fiscal Year 2000" was signed into law on 10/5/1999. See https://www.congress.gov/bill/106th-congress/senate-bill/1059/text (accessed 12/15/2020).

[6] *Executive Summary of the Report of the Commission to Assess United States National Security Space Management and Organization,* p. vii. Available online at: https://fas.org/spp/military/commission/executive_summary.pdf (accessed 10/1/2020).

[7] *Executive Summary of the Report of the Commission to Assess United States National Security Space Management and Organization,* p. viii. Available online at: https://fas.org/spp/military/commission/executive_summary.pdf (accessed 10/1/2020).

[8] *Executive Summary of the Report of the Commission to Assess United States National Security Space Management and Organization,* pp. viii-ix. Available online at: https://fas.org/spp/military/commission/executive_summary.pdf (accessed 10/1/2020).

[9] *Executive Summary of the Report of the Commission to Assess United States National Security Space Management and Organization,* pp. 22-23. Available online at: https://fas.org/spp/military/commission/executive_summary.pdf (accessed 10/1/2020).

[10] *Executive Summary of the Report of the Commission to Assess United States National Security Space Management and Organization,* p. xv. Available online at: https://fas.org/spp/military/commission/executive_summary.pdf (accessed 10/1/2020).

[11] John A. Tirpak, "The Space Commission Reports," *Air Force Magazine* (3/1/2001): https://www.airforcemag.com/article/0301space/ (accessed 12/7/2020).

[12] John A. Tirpak, "The Space Commission Reports," *Air Force Magazine* (3/1/2001): https://www.airforcemag.com/article/0301space/ (accessed 12/7/2020).

[13] *Executive Summary of the Report of the Commission to Assess United States National Security Space Management and Organization,* p. xviii. Available online at: https://fas.org/spp/military/commission/executive_summary.pdf (accessed 10/1/2020).

[14] *Executive Summary of the Report of the Commission to Assess United States National Security Space Management and Organization,* p. 80.

[15] *Executive Summary of the Report of the Commission to Assess United States National Security Space Management and Organization,* p. 81.

[16] *Executive Summary of the Report of the Commission to Assess United States National Security Space Management and Organization,* p. 86.

[17] *Executive Summary of the Report of the Commission to Assess United States National Security Space Management and Organization,* p. 93.

[18] "Forgotten History - UFOs, Congress and Donald Rumsfeld," http://dbarkertv.com/1968%20UFO%20Congress%20Study.htm (accessed 10/10/20).

[19] See Duncan Phenix, "The Bolender Memo: Blue Book ended, but secret Pentagon study of UFOs continued," https://www.mysterywire.com/ufo/the-bolender-memo-blue-book-ended-but-secret-pentagon-study-of-ufos-continued/ (accessed 12/17/2020).

[20] See MeTV, "Let's talk about how Richard Nixon allegedly showed The Honeymooners' Jackie Gleason some aliens," https://www.metv.com/stories/let-s-talk-about-how-richard-nixon-allegedly-showed-the-honeymooners-jackie-gleason-some-aliens (accessed 12/17/2020).

[21] Clark McClelland, *Space! The Final Frontier* (Amazon, 2020) p. 11.

[22] Clark McClelland, *Space! The Final Frontier* (Amazon, 2020) p. 11.

[23] See Michael Salla, "Alleged Time Traveler Runs for U.S. President: Real Deal or CIA PsyOp?" https://exopolitics.org/alleged-time-traveler-runs-for-u-s-president-real-deal-or-cia-psyop/ (accessed 12/17/2020).

[24] Cited in Michael Salla, "Jump Room to Mars: Did CIA Groom Obama & Basiago as Future Presidents?" https://exopolitics.org/jump-room-to-mars-did-cia-groom-obama-basiago-as-future-presidents/ (accessed 12/17/2020).

[25] John A. Tirpak, The Space Commission Reports, *Air Force Magazine* (March 1, 2001). Available online at: https://www.airforcemag.com/article/0301space/ (accessed 10/4/2020).

[26] John A. Tirpak, The Space Commission Reports, *Air Force Magazine* (March 1, 2001). Available online at: https://www.airforcemag.com/article/0301space/ (accessed 10/4/2020).

[27] John A. Tirpak, The Space Commission Reports, *Air Force Magazine* (March 1, 2001). Available online at: https://www.airforcemag.com/article/0301space/ (accessed 10/4/2020).

[28] *Executive Summary of the Report of the Commission to Assess United States National Security Space Management and Organization,* pp. viii-ix.

[29] *Executive Summary of the Report of the Commission to Assess United States National Security Space Management and Organization,* pp. viii-ix.

[30] Donald Rumsfeld announces 2.3 Trillion missing from the Pentagon on September 10, 2001, YouTube: https://youtu.be/IVpSBUgbxBU (accessed 12/7/2020).

[31] Available online at https://exopolitics.net/Report-Black-Budget.htm (accessed 12/17/2020).

[32] "Rumsfeld VS the Military Industrial Complex," https://benedictkim.wordpress.com/2020/09/29/9-11-was-a-heist/ (accessed 10/10/2020).

[33] "Rumsfeld VS the Military Industrial Complex," https://benedictkim.wordpress.com/2020/09/29/9-11-was-a-heist/ (accessed 10/10/2020).

[34] Donald Rumsfeld speech September 10, 2001, https://www.c-span.org/video/standalone/?c4623026/user-clip-donald-rumsfeld-speech (accessed 10/10/2020).

[35] *9-11 Research*, "Multiple War Games Were Being Conducted on 9/11/01," https://911research.wtc7.net/planes/defense/wargames.html (accessed 10/9/2020).

[36] See *9-11 Research*, "NORAD Stand-Down," https://911research.wtc7.net/planes/analysis/norad/ (accessed 10/9/2020).

[37] See *9-11 Research*, "Building 7," https://911research.wtc7.net/wtc/attack/wtc7.html (accessed 10/9/2020).

[38] See Ian Harvey, Daily Commercial News, "World Trade Center 7 building did not collapse due to fire: Report," https://canada.constructconnect.com/dcn/news/others/2020/05/world-trade-center-7-building-did-not-collapse-due-to-fire-report (accessed 10/9/2020).

[39] Judy Woods, *Where Did the Towers Go? Evidence of Directed Free-energy Technology on 9/11* (The New Investigation, 2010).

[40] David Montgomery, "Trump's Excellent Space Force Adventure", *Washington Post* (12/3/2019) https://tinyurl.com/y4fxr9q7 (accessed 12/7/2020).

[41] CQ Staff, Air Force Opposes Creation of Space Corps, *Roll Call,* 6/22/2017): https://www.rollcall.com/2017/06/22/air-force-opposes-creation-of-space-corps/ (accessed 12/7/2020).

[42] CQ Staff, Air Force Opposes Creation of Space Corps, *Roll Call,* 6/22/2017): https://www.rollcall.com/2017/06/22/air-force-opposes-creation-of-space-corps/ (accessed 12/7/2020).

[43] Phillip Swarts, Space Corps proposal has murkier path forward in the Senate, *Space News* (7/14/2017): https://spacenews.com/space-corps-proposal-has-murkier-path-forward-in-the-senate/ (accessed 12/7/2020).

[44] Letter by James Mattis to Senator John McCain, https://tinyurl.com/y2ggtl3y (accessed 12/7/2020).

[45] General Robert Spalding's experiences at the NSC Trump White House through from 2017 to 2018 are detailed in his book, *Stealth War: How China Took Over While America's Elite Slept* (Portfolio, 2019).

[46] "Trump floats idea for a military 'space force'" https://www.youtube.com/watch?v=6lrJhatw3K4 (accessed 12/28/18).

[47] David Montgomery, "Trump's Excellent Space Force Adventure", *Washington Post* (12/3/2019) https://tinyurl.com/y4fxr9q7 (accessed 12/7/2020).

[48] John Gray, "What Sun Tzu knew," *New Statesman* (1/29/2020): https://www.newstatesman.com/sun-tzu-the-art-war-politics (accessed 12/18/2020).

[49] David Tweed, "This Is the Man Trump Described as 'The Leading Authority on China'", Bloomberg, 9/26/2018 https://www.bloomberg.com/news/articles/2018-09-27/trump-identifies-the-leading-authority-on-china-who-is-he (accessed 12/18/2020).

[50] Michael Pillsbury, *The Hundred Year Marathon China's Secret Strategy to Replace America as the Global Superpower* (Henry Holt and Co, 2015).

[51] I will discuss the Outer Space Treaty and its provisions dealing with the weaponization of space in chapter 10.

[52] See Robert Spalding, *Stealth War: How China Took Over While America's Elite Slept* (Portfolio, 2019).

[53] White House Fact Sheets, "President Trump is Building the United States Space Force for a 21st Century Military," https://www.whitehouse.gov/briefings-statements/president-donald-j-trump-building-united-states-space-force-21st-century-military/ (accessed 12/18/2020).

[54] For estimate of 80% of military space assets belonging to USAF see "Proposed Space Force to protect, expand U.S. cosmic capabilities," http://apgnews.com/community-news/proposed-space-force-to-protect-expand-u-s-cosmic-capabilities/ (accessed 4/21/19).

[55] *NBC News*, https://www.youtube.com/watch?v=5lEaLcumd08 (accessed 12/29/18).

[56] Oriana Pawlyk, "It's Official: Trump Announces Space Force as 6th Military Branch", https://www.military.com/daily-news/2018/06/18/its-official-trump-announces-space-force-6th-military-branch.html (accessed 12/28/18).

[57] "Final Report on Organizational and Management Structure for the National Security Space Components of the Department of Defense", p. 6. https://partner-mco-archive.s3.amazonaws.com/client_files/1533834803.pdf (accessed 12/27/18).

[58] "Text of a Memorandum from the President to the Secretary of Defense Regarding the Establishment of the United States Space Command," https://www.whitehouse.gov/briefings-statements/text-memorandum-president-secretary-defense-regarding-establishment-united-states-space-command/ (accessed 12/27/2018).

[59] James Mattis resignation letter is available at: https://www.pbs.org/newshour/politics/read-james-mattis-full-resignation-letter (accessed 12/18/2020).

[60] https://www.whitehouse.gov/presidential-actions/text-space-policy-directive-4-establishment-united-states-space-force/ (accessed 11/02/2020).

[61] https://www.whitehouse.gov/presidential-actions/text-space-policy-directive-4-establishment-united-states-space-force/ (accessed 11/02/2020).

[62] "President Donald J. Trump is Establishing America's Space Force," https://www.whitehouse.gov/briefings-statements/president-trump-establishing-americas-space-force/(accessed 2/19/19).

[63] See Michael Salla, *The US Navy's Secret Space Program and Nordic Extraterrestrial Alliance* (Exopolitics Consultants, 2017).

[64] Lara Seligman, "Before Resigning, Air Force Secretary Heather Wilson Irked Trump," *Foreign Policy* (3/8/2019). https://foreignpolicy.com/2019/03/08/before-resigning-air-force-secretary-heather-wilson-irked-trump-pentagon-mattis/ (accessed 12/18/2020).

[65] David Montgomery, "Trump's Excellent Space Force Adventure", *Washington Post* (12/3/2019) https://tinyurl.com/y4fxr9q7 (accessed 12/7/2020).

[66] Peter Garretson, "Air Force Suppressed Space Force Debate; Lt. Gen. Kwast Spoke Truth To Power," *Breaking Defense* (8/8/2019): https://breakingdefense.com/2019/08/air-force-suppressed-space-force-debate-lt-gen-kwast-spoke-truth-to-power/ (accessed 12/25/2020).

[67] Minnie L. Jones, "William 'Billy' Mitchell -- 'The father of the United States Air Force'," https://www.army.mil/article/33680/william_billy_mitchell_the_father_of_the_united_states_air_force (accessed 12/25/2020).

[68] Lt. Gen. Steven L. Kwast, "Space diplomacy: A better way to combat China's challenge," *The Hill* (03/19/2019) https://thehill.com/opinion/national-security/434651-space-diplomacy-a-better-way-for-a-new-era (accessed 12/25/2020).

[69] Peter Garretson, "Air Force Suppressed Space Force Debate; Lt. Gen. Kwast Spoke Truth To Power," *Breaking Defense* (8/8/2019): https://breakingdefense.com/2019/08/air-force-suppressed-space-force-debate-lt-gen-kwast-spoke-truth-to-power/ (accessed 12/25/2020).

[70] Air Force Space Command, "Remarks by Gen. Jay Raymond at the 35th Space Symposium, Colorado Springs, Colorado," https://www.afspc.af.mil/News/Article-Display/Article/1813636/remarks-by-gen-jay-raymond-at-the-35th-space-symposium-colorado-springs-colorado/ (accessed 12/25/2020).

[71] Heather Wilson's termination of Steven Kwast's appointment is discussed by Ambassador Harry Cooper in "Crucial Decisions Needed on Space Force," *Newsmax* (08/06/2019): https://www.newsmax.com/henryfcooper/edtf-kwast-sdi-sda/2019/08/06/id/927495/ (accessed 12/25/2020).

[72] Frank Gaffney, "Steven Kwast Is the General Trump Has Been Seeking," Breitbart (8/1/2019): https://www.breitbart.com/politics/2019/08/01/frank-gaffney-steven-kwast-is-the-general-trump-has-been-seeking/ (accessed 12/25/2020).

[73] "Open Letter in Support of Establishing the U.S. Space Force," http://highfrontier.org/wp-content/uploads/2019/05/USSF-LETTER-FINAL-2.pdf (accessed 12/25/2020).

[74] See Ambassador Harry Cooper, "Crucial Decisions Needed on Space Force," *Newsmax* (08/06/2019): https://www.newsmax.com/henryfcooper/edtf-kwast-sdi-sda/2019/08/06/id/927495/ (accessed 12/25/2020).

[75] Secretary of the Air Force Public Affairs, "The Air Force We Need: 386 Operational Squadrons," https://www.af.mil/News/Article-Display/Article/1635070/the-air-force-we-need-386-operational-squadrons/ (accessed 12/25/2020).

[76] See Nellie Andreeva, "'Space Force' Workplace Comedy Series From 'The Office's Steve Carell & Greg Daniels Ordered By Netflix," https://deadline.com/2019/01/space-force-workplace-comedy-series-steve-carell-star-greg-daniels-netflix-the-office-reunion-1202535944/ (accessed 12/21/2020).

[77] Bryan Bender, "Progressives to Biden: Kill Space Force," *Politico* (11/17/2020): https://www.politico.com/newsletters/morning-defense/2020/11/17/progressives-to-biden-kill-space-force-791698 (accessed 12/21/2020).

[78] Space Force Act, Title IX. Subtitle D. Sec.951, https://docs.house.gov/billsthisweek/20191209/CRPT-116hrpt333.pdf (accessed 11/3/2020).

[79] Sandra Erwin, "Following standup of U.S. Space Force, Air Force bases could be renamed as space bases," *SpaceNews* (12/20/2019) https://spacenews.com/following-standup-of-u-s-space-force-air-force-bases-could-be-renamed-as-space-bases/ (accessed 11/3/2020).

[80] *Breaking Defense*, "16,000 AFSPC Head to Space Force; What About The Rest?" https://breakingdefense.com/2019/12/16000-afspc-head-to-space-force-what-about-the-rest/ (accessed 11/3/2020).

[81] The 18 month transition period is described in "About the Space Force," https://www.spaceforce.mil/About-Us/About-Space-Force/ (accessed 11/3/2020).

[82] Space Force Act, Title IX. Subtitle D. Sec.951, https://docs.house.gov/billsthisweek/20191209/CRPT-116hrpt333.pdf (accessed 11/3/2020).

[83] Space Force Act, Title IX. Subtitle D. Sec.953, https://docs.house.gov/billsthisweek/20191209/CRPT-116hrpt333.pdf (accessed 11/3/2020).

[84] Colin Clark, "Chinese ASAT Test Was 'Successful:' Lt. Gen. Raymond," Breaking Defense (4/14/2015): https://breakingdefense.com/2015/04/chinese-asat-test-was-successful-lt-gen-raymond/ (accessed 12/21/2020).

[85] Air Force Space Command, "Remarks by Gen. Jay Raymond at the 35th Space Symposium, Colorado Springs, Colorado," https://www.afspc.af.mil/News/Article-Display/Article/1813636/remarks-by-gen-jay-raymond-at-the-35th-space-symposium-colorado-springs-colorado/ (accessed 12/25/2020).

[86] See "Combatant Commands", https://www.defense.gov/Our-Story/Combatant-Commands/ (accessed 11/3/2020).

[87] "USSPACECOM makes history with first change of command," https://www.spacecom.mil/News/Article-Display/Article/2320283/usspacecom-makes-history-with-first-change-of-command/ (accessed 12/21/2020).

[88] Jim Garamone, "Space Force Leader to Become 8th Member of Joint Chiefs," https://www.spaceforce.mil/News/Article/2452955/space-force-leader-to-become-8th-member-of-joint-chiefs/ (accessed 12/21/2020).

[89] Kyle Mizokami, "The Space Force Will Become the Sixth Branch of the U.S. Military" *Popular Mechanics* (12/11/2019): https://www.popularmechanics.com/military/a30184766/space-force-official/ (accessed 11/4/2020).

[90] Space Force Act, Title IX. Subtitle D. Sec.951, https://docs.house.gov/billsthisweek/20191209/CRPT-116hrpt333.pdf (accessed 11/3/2020).

[91] Joshua Philipp, "New Chinese Weapons Threaten Every Satellite in Orbit, Says US General," Epoch Times (April 17, 2015): https://www.theepochtimes.com/new-chinese-weapons-threaten-every-satellite-in-orbit-says-us-general_1323124.html (accessed 11/3/2020).

[92] Bill Gertz, *Deceiving the Sky: Inside Communist China's Drive for Global Supremacy* (Encounter Books, 2019) p. 53.

[93] Brett Tingley, "Recently Retired USAF General Makes Eyebrow Raising Claims About Advanced Space Technology," https://www.thedrive.com/the-war-zone/31445/recently-retired-usaf-general-makes-eyebrow-raising-claims-about-advanced-space-technology (accessed 11/3/2020).

[94] Space Daily "US Air Force Head mulls declassifying secret programs to gain support for Space Force in Congress" (12/11/2019): https://tinyurl.com/y64x4rs3 (accessed 11/3/2020).

[95] See Michael Salla, *The US Air Force Secret Space Program: Shifting Extraterrestrial Alliances & Space Force* (Exopolitics Consultants, 2019).

[96] See U.S. Air Force Scientific Advisory Board, Overview of the Scientific Advisory Board (9/28/2020): https://www.scientificadvisoryboard.af.mil/Studies/Fact-Sheets/Display/Article/461161/overview-of-the-scientific-advisory-board/ (accessed 11/5/2020).

[97] Graham Simons, *Operation Lusty: The Race for Hitler's Secret Technology* (Pen and Sword Aviation, 2016).

[98] Richard Sauder discusses W.O. Schumann's name among Operation Paperclip scientists in *Hidden in Plain Sight: Beyond the X-Files* (Keyhole Publishing, 2011); and "Vorticular Madness Of The Dark Magicians," https://truthtalk13.wordpress.com/category/operation-paperclip/ (accessed 11/06/2020).

[99] See Michael Salla, *Antarctica's Hidden History: Corporate Foundations of Secret Space Programs* (Exopolitics Consultants, 2018).

[100] For detailed discussion of what occurred with the US Army Air Force flying saucer press release and retraction, see Thomas Carey and Donald Schmidt, *Witness to Roswell, Revised and Expanded Edition: Unmasking the Government's Biggest Cover-Up* (New Page Books, 2009).

[101] A leaked September 24, 1947, Memorandum from President Truman confirms the creation of "Operation Majestic Twelve". Memo https://majesticdocuments.com/pdf/truman_forrestal.pdf (accessed 11/26/2020).

[102] See Michael Salla, *Kennedy's Last Stand: UFOs, MJ-12 & JFK's Assassination* (Exopolitics Institute, 2013).

[103] See Thomas Valone, *Electrogravitics Systems: Reports on a New Propulsion Methodology*, 2nd Edition (Integrity Research Institute, 1995).

[104] Alex Hollings, "Kelly Johnson: The man who designed the future of military aviation" (8/19/2020): https://www.sandboxx.us/blog/kelly-johnson-the-man-that-designed-the-future-of-military-aviation/ (accessed 11/5/2020).

[105] See Robert Lazar, *Dreamland: An Autobiography by Bob Lazar* (Interstellar, 2019).

[106] Peter W. Merlin, "Taking E.T. Home: Birth of a Modern Myth," *Sunlight: Shedding some light on UFOlogy and UFOs,* Vol 5, No. 6 (2013): http://home.comcast.net/~tprinty/UFO/SUNlite5_6.pdf (accessed on 7/14/15).

[107] Ralph Blumenthal and Leslie Kean, No Longer in Shadows, Pentagon's U.F.O. Unit Will Make Some Findings Public" New York Times (7/23/2020): https://www.nytimes.com/2020/07/23/us/politics/pentagon-ufo-harry-reid-navy.html?searchResultPosition=1 (accessed 11/5/2020).

[108] See Michael Salla, "Bombshell document confirms Navy Admiral was denied access to UFO crash retrieval program," https://exopolitics.org/bombshell-document-confirms-navy-admiral-was-denied-access-to-ufo-crash-retrieval-program/ (accessed 11/26/2020).

[109] For discussion of FBI documents containing witness accounts of flying saucers sighted in Nazi Germany, see Henry Stevens, *Hitler's Flying Saucers: A Guide to German Flying Disks of the Second World War* (Adventures Unlimited Press, 2003) pp. 144-65.

[110] See Henry Stevens, *Hitler's Flying Saucers,* pp. 55-68.

[111] See Michael Salla, *Antarctica's Hidden History,* pp. 56-71. A brief biography of Vladimir Terziski is available online at: http://www.whale.to/b/terziski_h.html (accessed on 11/14/17).

[112] Vladimir Terziski presented his findings in a 1992 workshop available online at: https://youtu.be/MPBvHjuJtB8

[113] *Earthfiles,*http://www.earthfiles.com/news.php?ID=1503&category=Real+X-Files (accessed 9/24/14).

[114] *Earthfiles,*http://www.earthfiles.com/news.php?ID=1501&category=Real+X-Files_(accessed on 11/14/17).

[115] See Michael Salla, *US Air Force Secret Space Program,* pp. 250-62.

[116] Global Security, "Air Force Plant 42," https://www.globalsecurity.org/military/facility/afp-42.htm (accessed 11/08/2020).

[117] See Michael Salla, *US Air Force Secret Space Program,* pp. 250-62.

[118] Dr Steven Greer, "Testimony of Mr. Mark McCandlish, US Air Force," *Disclosure: Military and Government Witnesses Reveal the Greatest Secrets in Modern History*, pp. 500-01, 504.

[119] *The US Air Force Secret Space Program*, pp. 258-63.

[120] "US Space Force enters 'Year 2' with momentum and soaring expectations," https://www.spacewar.com/reports/US_Space_Force_enters_Year_2_with_momentum_and_soaring_expectations_999.html (accessed 12/23/2020)

[121] Michael Salla, *US Air Force Secret Space Program,* pp. 269-78.

[122] Edgar Fouche's documents are available online at: http://www.checktheevidence.com/pdf/Edgar%20Fouches%20Military%20Documents.pdf (accessed 1/2/2019).

[123] Edgar Rothschild Fouche, "Secret Government Technology," https://tinyurl.com/y4avzh3u (accessed on 6/12/15).

[124] See "TR-3B Questions & Answers – Edgar Fouche" https://tinyurl.com/yxu28j6g (accessed on 11/30/18).

[125] See "TR-3B Questions & Answers – Edgar Fouche" https://tinyurl.com/yxu28j6g (accessed on 11/30/18).

[126] Peter W. Merlin, "Taking E.T. Home: Birth of a Modern Myth," *Sunlight: Shedding some light on UFOlogy and UFOs,*Vol 5, No. 6 (2013), http://home.comcast.net/~tprinty/UFO/SUNlite5_6.pdf (accessed on 7/14/15).

[127] See "TR-3B Questions & Answers – Edgar Fouche," https://tinyurl.com/yxu28j6g (accessed on 11/30/18).

[128] See Courtney V.K. Homer, *Spies in Space: Reflections on National Reconnaissance and the Manned Orbiting Laboratory (*Center for the Study of National Reconnaissance, May 2019).

[129] See "TR-3B Questions & Answers – Edgar Fouche" https://tinyurl.com/yxu28j6g (accessed on 11/30/18).

[130] See "TR-3B Questions & Answers – Edgar Fouche" https://tinyurl.com/yxu28j6g (accessed on 11/30/18).

131 Ronald Reagan, *The Reagan Diaries* (Harper Perennial, 2009) p. 334.

132 See "Sunday Express Newspaper Article," September 17, 1995. http://www.ufoevidence.org/documents/doc418.htm (accessed on 6/20/15).

133 See Edgar Rothschild Fouche, "Secret Government Technology," https://tinyurl.com/y4avzh3u (accessed on 6/18/15).

134 The photos and stories about them can be found on my website at: https://exopolitics.org/jp-articles-photos-videos/ (accessed 11/08/20).

135 I first wrote about JP's photos and skype messages about the October 19, 2017 photos in "Covert Disclosure of Antigravity Craft near MacDill AFB" http://www.exopolitics.org/disclosure-of-antigravity-craft-near-macdill-afb/ (accessed 12/21/18).

136 For a video showing close ups of the October 19, 2017 photos, go to: https://www.youtube.com/watch?v=PPGvBfW1-CY (accessed 12/21/18).

137 I first wrote about JP's October 23, 2017 photos and encounter in "Covert Disclosure of Antigravity Rectangle Weapons Platforms by USAF Special Operations," https://www.exopolitics.org/covert-disclosure-rectangle-craft-usaf-spec-ops/ (accessed 12/21/18).

138 Michael Salla, *US Air Force Secret Space Program,* pp. 371-76.

139 Sandra Erwin, "Air Force Special Operations Command officer named to senior post in U.S. Space Force," *SpaceNews* (1/31/2020): https://spacenews.com/air-force-special-operations-command-officer-named-to-senior-post-in-u-s-space-force/ (accessed 11/6/2020).

140 Sandra Erwin, "Following standup of U.S. Space Force, Air Force bases could be renamed as space bases," Space News (12/20/2020): https://spacenews.com/following-standup-of-u-s-space-force-air-force-bases-could-be-renamed-as-space-bases/ (accessed 11/6/2020).

141 Air Force Special Operations Command, https://www.afsoc.af.mil/About-Us/Fact-Sheets/Display/Article/560215/air-commandos/ (accessed 11/6/2020).

142 Space Force personnel were given the official name "Guardians" on December 19, 2020. https://www.defense.gov/Explore/News/Article/Article/2452910/space-force-personnel-to-be-called-guardians/ (accessed 12/23/2020).

143 See "Space Force leads first training exercise since its inception," https://www.spacewar.com/reports/Space_Force_leads_first_training_exercise_since_its_inception_999.html (accessed 11/08/2020).

144 See Stephen Losey, "The Air Force we can afford: The 386-squadron goal appears out of reach," *Air Force Times* (2/24/2020): https://www.airforcetimes.com/news/your-air-force/2020/02/24/the-air-force-we-can-afford-the-386-squadron-goal-appears-out-of-reach/ (accessed 12/23/2020).

145 Clayton D. Laurie, *Congress & the National Reconnaissance Office* (Center for the Study of National Reconnaissance, 2001) pp. 9-10.

[146] *Executive Summary of the Report of the Commission to Assess United States National Security Space Management and Organization (Jan 11, 2001)* p. xxiii.

[147] Commission on the Roles and Capabilities of the United States Intelligence Community, *Preparing for the 21st Century: An Appraisal of U.S. Intelligence* (March 1996) p. 121. https://tinyurl.com/y2b7nw58 (accessed 11/23/2020).

[148] Clayton D. Laurie, *Congress & the National Reconnaissance Office,* pp. 16-17.

[149] Tim Weiner, "A Secret Agency's Secret Budgets Yield Lost Billions, Officials Say," *New York Times* (1/30/1996) https://tinyurl.com/y4stp7fc (accessed 11/24/2020).

[150] Clayton D. Laurie, *Congress & the National Reconnaissance Office,* p. 17.

[151] Commission on the Roles and Capabilities of the United States Intelligence Community, *Preparing for the 21st Century: An Appraisal of U.S. Intelligence* (March, 1996) pp. 122-23. https://tinyurl.com/y2b7nw58 (accessed 11/23/2020).

[152] 50 United States Code (U.S.C.) 403-4(c) up to its amendment in 2004. Available at: https://tinyurl.com/y5vgnael (accessed 11/23/2020).

[153] See Michael E. DeVine, "The Director of National Intelligence (DNI)," Congressional Research Service (5/10/2019) https://fas.org/sgp/crs/intel/IF10470.pdf (accessed 11/23/2020).

[154] See Michael E. DeVine, "Intelligence Community Spending: Trends and Issues," Congressional Research Service (11/6/2019). https://fas.org/sgp/crs/intel/R44381.pdf (accessed 11/23/2020).

[155] See Michael E. DeVine, "Defense Primer: National and Defense Intelligence," Congressional Research Service (1/24/2020): https://fas.org/sgp/crs/natsec/IF10525.pdf (accessed 11/23/2020).

[156] See Michael E. DeVine, "Intelligence Community Spending: Trends and Issues," Congressional Research Service (11/6/2019): https://fas.org/sgp/crs/intel/R44381.pdf (accessed 11/23/2020).

[157] See Michael E. DeVine, "Intelligence Community Spending: Trends and Issues," Congressional Research Service (11/6/2019): https://fas.org/sgp/crs/intel/R44381.pdf (accessed 11/23/2020).

[158] Tim Weiner, "A Secret Agency's Secret Budgets Yield Lost Billions, Officials Say," *New York Times* (1/30/1996) https://tinyurl.com/y4stp7fc (accessed 11/24/2020).

[159] 50 USC 3510 (b): https://uscode.house.gov/view.xhtml?req=granuleid:USC-prelim-title50-section3510&num=0&edition=prelim (accessed 11/24/2020).

[160] 50 USC 3517 (b)(3): https://uscode.house.gov/view.xhtml?req=(title:50%20section:3517%20edition:prelim) (accessed 11/24/2020).

[161] See Michael Salla, "The Black Budget Report: An Investigation into the CIA's 'Black Budget' and the Second Manhattan Project," https://exopolitics.net/Report-Black-Budget.htm (accessed 11/24/2020).

162 CIA involvement in the international drug trade is documented in Gary Webb, *Dark Alliance: The CIA, the Contras, and the Cocaine Explosion* (Seven Stories Press, 1999).
163 For an overview of the CIA's National Clandestine Service, see "Role and Mission of the CIA National Clandestine Service," https://www.ciaagentedu.org/national-clandestine-service/ (accessed 11/24/2020).
164 See Michael Salla, "The Black Budget Report: An Investigation into the CIA's 'Black Budget' and the Second Manhattan Project," https://exopolitics.net/Report-Black-Budget.htm (accessed 11/24/2020).
165 House Committee on Appropriations, "Appropriations Committee Releases Fiscal Year 2021 Defense Funding Bill," https://appropriations.house.gov/news/press-releases/appropriations-committee-releases-fiscal-year-2021-defense-funding-bill (accessed 11/24/2020).
166 "UQ Wire: What's Up With the Black Budget?" https://www.scoop.co.nz/stories/HL0209/S00126.htm (accessed 11/24/2020).
167 See "MOL Program Perspective" http://www.nro.gov/Portals/65/documents/foia/declass/mol/736.pdf (accessed 2/8/2021).
168 "Air Force to Develop Manned Orbiting Laboratory," http://www.nro.gov/Portals/65/documents/foia/declass/mol/6.pdf (accessed 11/6/2018).
169 See President Johnson's Statement on MOL, http://www.nro.gov/Portals/65/documents/foia/declass/mol/129.pdf (accessed 11/6/2018).
170 See March 10, 1964 letter to Major General Ben L. Funk, http://www.nro.gov/Portals/65/documents/foia/declass/mol/15.pdf (accessed 11/6/2018).
171 "DORIAN Optical Studies," http://www.nro.gov/Portals/65/documents/foia/declass/mol/93.pdf (accessed 11/6/2018).
172 Astrospies, http://www.pbs.org/wgbh/nova/military/astrospies.html (accessed 7/28/2015).
173 James Outzen, ed., *The Dorian Files Revealed: A Compendium of the NRO's Manned Orbiting Laboratory* Documents (Center for the Study of National Reconnaissance, 2015) p. xiv.
174 Mark Erickson, *Into the Unknown Together: The DOD, NASA, and Early Spaceflight*, p. 343. Available online at: https://tinyurl.com/y76onu7q (accessed 10/31/2018).
175 Letter from George E. Mueller, http://www.nro.gov/Portals/65/documents/foia/declass/mol/3.pdf (accessed 11/6/2018).

[176] Von Braun Station http://astronautix.com/v/vonbraunstation.html (accessed 11/6/2018).

[177] When combined with the Gemini 2 capsule, the MOL had a total length of 72 feet (22 meters), see http://www.astronautix.com/m/mol.html (accessed 11/7/2018).

[178] "MOL Directive No. 67-4, MOL Program Advanced Planning Approved by Gen. Ferguson," http://www.nro.gov/Portals/65/documents/foia/declass/mol/353.pdf (accessed 11/7/2018).

[179] "Draft Memorandum for the President, Subject: MOL," http://www.nro.gov/Portals/65/documents/foia/declass/mol/709.pdf (accessed 11/9/2018).

[180] "The Department of Defense has Terminated the Air Force MOL Program," http://www.nro.gov/Portals/65/documents/foia/declass/mol/742.pdf (accessed 11/9/2018).

[181] "Terminate MOL Except for the "Automatic" Camera System," http://www.nro.gov/Portals/65/documents/foia/declass/mol/737.pdf (accessed 11/9/2018).

[182] "Advanced MOL Planning: Missions and Systems," p. 17, available at: http://www.nro.gov/Portals/65/documents/foia/declass/mol/794.pdf (accessed 11/17/2018).

[183] Ronald Reagan, *The Reagan Diaries* (Harper Perennial, 2009) p. 334.

[184] Available online at: http://www.nro.gov/Portals/65/documents/foia/declass/mol/737.pdf (accessed 11/17/2018).

[185] See MSFC History Office, https://history.msfc.nasa.gov/vonbraun/bio.html (accessed 11/17/2018).

[186] See Michael Salla, "Secret NRO Space Stations to be Revealed in Limited Disclosure Plan," https://www.exopolitics.org/secret-nro-space-stations-to-be-revealed-in-limited-disclosure-plan/ (accessed 12/31/2018).

[187] Ronald Reagan, *The Reagan Diaries* (Harper Perennial, 2009) p. 334.

[188] See *Report of the National Commission for the Review of the National Reconnaissance Office: The NRO at the Crossroads*, (November 2000). Available at: https://fas.org/irp/nro/commission/exec_sum.htm (accessed 11/24/2020).

[189] Clayton D. Laurie, *Congress & the National Reconnaissance Office*, p. 58.

[190] Clayton D. Laurie, *Congress & the National Reconnaissance Office*, p. 60.

[191] *Report of the National Commission for the Review of the National Reconnaissance Office*, https://fas.org/irp/nro/commission/exec_sum.htm (accessed 11/24/2020).

[192] *Report of the National Commission for the Review of the National Reconnaissance Office*, https://fas.org/irp/nro/commission/exec_sum.htm (accessed 11/24/2020).

[193] *Department of Defense Directive* 5105.23 (10/.29/2015) p. 14 https://tinyurl.com/y2fq6ek5 (accessed 11/24/2020).
[194] Douglas Pasternak, "Lack of Intelligence: America's secret spy satellites are costing you billions," (US News (08/11/03) https://freerepublic.com/focus/f-news/957239/posts (accessed 11/24/2020).
[195] House Hearing, 114 Congress, U.S. Government Publishing Office, https://www.govinfo.gov/content/pkg/CHRG-114hhrg20062/html/CHRG-114hhrg20062.htm (accessed 11/24/2020).
[196] "DNI Clapper Statement on President Obama's Intent to Appoint the Chief Information Officer of the Intelligence Community," https://tinyurl.com/y338dwp4 (accessed 11/24/2020).
[197] United States Space Force, "Space Capstone Publication: Spacepower Doctrine for Space Forces," (June 2020) p. xiv: https://tinyurl.com/y46upoqt (accessed 11/28/2020).
[198] United States Space Force, "Space Capstone Publication: Spacepower Doctrine for Space Forces," (June 2020) p.iii. https://tinyurl.com/y46upoqt (accessed 11/29/2020).
[199] "Chief of Space Operations Planning Guidance", p. 1. https://media.defense.gov/2020/Nov/09/2002531998/-1/-1/0/CSO%20PLANNING%20GUIDANCE.PDF (accessed 11/29/2020).
[200] United States Space Force, "Space Capstone Publication: Spacepower Doctrine for Space Forces," (June 2020) p.xiv. https://tinyurl.com/y46upoqt (accessed 11/29/2020).
[201] United States Space Force, "Space Capstone Publication: Spacepower Doctrine for Space Forces," (June 2020) p.12. https://tinyurl.com/y46upoqt (accessed 11/29/2020).
[202] United States Space Force, "Space Capstone Publication: Spacepower Doctrine for Space Forces," (June 2020) p.14. https://tinyurl.com/y46upoqt (accessed 11/29/2020).
[203] Brittany De Lea, "Space race: The next trillion-dollar economy?" *Fox Business* (12/3/2019) https://www.foxbusiness.com/markets/space-trillion-dollar-economy (accessed 11/28/2020).
[204] United States Space Force, "Space Capstone Publication: Spacepower Doctrine for Space Forces," (June 2020) p. 7. https://tinyurl.com/y46upoqt (accessed 11/29/2020).
[205] 1st Chief of Space Operations, *Chief of Space Operations Planning Guidance* (2020) p. 1. https://tinyurl.com/y2bve87f (accessed 12/8/2020).
[206] See Jean-Michel Stoulig, "Rumsfeld Commission Warns Against 'Space Pearl Harbor'," *Space Daily* (1/11/2001): https://www.spacedaily.com/news/bmdo-01b.html (accessed 12/8/2020).
[207] See Michael Pillsbury, *The Hundred Year Marathon: China's Secret Strategy to Replace America as the Global Superpower* (St. Martin's Griffin, 2016).

208 United States Space Force, "Space Capstone Publication: Spacepower Doctrine for Space Forces," (June 2020) p. xiii. https://tinyurl.com/y46upoqt (accessed 11/29/2020).
209 "Treaty on Principles Governing the Activities of States in the Exploration and Use of Outer Space, including the Moon and Other Celestial Bodies" (aka Outer Space Treaty), Article IV: https://www.unoosa.org/oosa/en/ourwork/spacelaw/treaties/outerspacetreaty.html (accessed 11/30/2020).
210 United States Space Force, "Space Capstone Publication: Spacepower Doctrine for Space Forces," (June 2020) p. xiv. https://tinyurl.com/y46upoqt (accessed 11/29/2020).
211 1st Chief of Space Operations, *Chief of Space Operations Planning Guidance* (2020) p. 1. https://tinyurl.com/y2bve87f (accessed 12/8/2020).
212 1st Chief of Space Operations, *Chief of Space Operations Planning Guidance* (2020) p. 2. https://tinyurl.com/y2bve87f (accessed 12/8/2020).
213 1st Chief of Space Operations, *Chief of Space Operations Planning Guidance* (2020) p. 2. https://tinyurl.com/y2bve87f (accessed 12/8/2020).
214 For comparison of the worlds top economies by Nominal GDP and by PPP in 2019 see *Investopedia*, "The Top 20 Economies in the World," https://www.investopedia.com/insights/worlds-top-economies/ (accessed 12/8/2020).
215 United States Space Force, "Space Capstone Publication: Spacepower Doctrine for Space Forces," (June 2020) pp. 16-17. https://tinyurl.com/y46upoqt (accessed 11/29/2020).
216 United States Space Force, "Space Capstone Publication: Spacepower Doctrine for Space Forces," (June 2020) p. 21. https://tinyurl.com/y46upoqt (accessed 11/29/2020).
217 1st Chief of Space Operations, *Chief of Space Operations Planning Guidance* (2020) p. 9. https://tinyurl.com/y2bve87f (accessed 12/8/2020).
218 See Presidential Memoranda, "Text of Space Policy Directive-4: Establishment of the United States Space Force," (2/19/2019): https://www.whitehouse.gov/presidential-actions/text-space-policy-directive-4-establishment-united-states-space-force/ (accessed 12/8/2020).
219 1st Chief of Space Operations, *Chief of Space Operations Planning Guidance* (2020) p. 9. https://tinyurl.com/y2bve87f (accessed 12/8/2020).
220 Cited by Nathan Strout, "Barrett, Rogers consider declassifying secretive space programs," https://www.defensenews.com/smr/reagan-defense-forum/2019/12/08/barrett-rogers-plan-to-declassify-black-space-programs/ (accessed 12/8/2020).
221 See "Text of Space Policy Directive-4: Establishment of the United States Space Force," https://www.whitehouse.gov/presidential-actions/text-space-policy-directive-4-establishment-united-states-space-force/ (accessed 11/28/2020).

[222] Air Force Space Command, *Future of Space 2060 and Implications for U.S. Strategy: Report on the Space Futures Workshop* (5 September 2019) p. 9. https://s3.amazonaws.com/images.spaceref.com/news/2019/USAFSpace.pdf (accessed 11/02/2020).

[223] See Nathan Strout, "Barrett, Rogers consider declassifying secretive space programs," https://www.defensenews.com/smr/reagan-defense-forum/2019/12/08/barrett-rogers-plan-to-declassify-black-space-programs/ (accessed 12/8/2020).

[224] For fiscal year 2020, the number of patents withheld due to secrecy orders is 5,915, see Invention Secrecy Activity, https://fas.org/sgp/othergov/invention/stats.html (accessed 12/8/2020).

[225] *Future of Space 2060 and Implications for U.S. Strategy,* p. 9.

[226] *Future of Space 2060 and Implications for U.S. Strategy,* p. 9.

[227] "Treaty on Principles Governing the Activities of States in the Exploration and Use of Outer Space, including the Moon and Other Celestial Bodies" (aka Outer Space Treaty): https://www.unoosa.org/oosa/en/ourwork/spacelaw/treaties/outerspacetreaty.html (accessed 11/30/2020).

[228] Michael Listner, "The Moon Treaty: failed international law or waiting in the shadows?", *The Space Review*, October 24, 2011: https://www.thespacereview.com/article/1954/1 (accessed 10/30/2020)

[229] *Future of Space 2060 and Implications for U.S. Strategy,* p. 12.

[230] *Future of Space 2060 and Implications for U.S. Strategy,* p. 9.

[231] *Future of Space 2060 and Implications for U.S. Strategy,* p. 10.

[232] *Future of Space 2060 and Implications for U.S. Strategy,* p. 10.

[233] *Future of Space 2060 and Implications for U.S. Strategy,* p. 11.

[234] *Future of Space 2060 and Implications for U.S. Strategy,* p. 10.

[235] "Treaty on Principles Governing the Activities of States in the Exploration and Use of Outer Space, including the Moon and Other Celestial Bodies" (aka Outer Space Treaty) Article IV: https://www.unoosa.org/oosa/en/ourwork/spacelaw/treaties/outerspacetreaty.html (accessed 11/30/2020).

[236] "Steven Kwast - The Urgent Need for a U.S. Space Force," https://youtu.be/KsPLmb6gAdw?t=1139 (accessed 12/12/2019).

[237] Dr. James Sheehy's letter to Philip J. Bonzell, https://tinyurl.com/y67bp42e (accessed 9/23/2019).

[238] *Future of Space 2060 and Implications for U.S. Strategy,* p. 15.

[239] *Future of Space 2060 and Implications for U.S. Strategy,* p. 16.

[240] "Space Policy Directive-1 of December 11, 2017: Reinvigorating America's Human Space Exploration Program." https://fas.org/irp/offdocs/nspm/spd-1.pdf (accessed 11/01/2020).

[241] Jim Bridenstine, *@JimBridenstine*,
https://twitter.com/JimBridenstine/status/1128086110247235584 (accessed 11/01/2020)

[242] See Joey Roulette, "'Star Trek, not Star Wars:' NASA releases basic principles for moon exploration pact," https://www.reuters.com/article/us-space-exploration-artemis/star-trek-not-star-wars-nasa-releases-basic-principles-for-moon-exploration-pact-idUSKBN22R2Z9 (accessed 11/02/2020).

[243] See Joey Roulette, "'Star Trek, not Star Wars:' NASA releases basic principles for moon exploration pact," https://www.reuters.com/article/us-space-exploration-artemis/star-trek-not-star-wars-nasa-releases-basic-principles-for-moon-exploration-pact-idUSKBN22R2Z9 (accessed 11/02/2020).

[244] Ryan Britt, "3 Ways NASA's Artemis Accords want to create a Star Trek utopia," https://www.inverse.com/entertainment/star-trek-nasa-artemis-accords (accessed 11/02/2020).

[245] "The Artemis Accords: Principles for Cooperation in the Civil Exploration and Use of the Moon, Mars, Comets, and Asteroids for Peaceful Purposes," https://www.nasa.gov/specials/artemis-accords/img/Artemis-Accords-signed-13Oct2020.pdf (accessed 11/02/2020).

[246] Matthew Ehret, "Can NASA's Artemis Accords Spark a U.S.-Russia Alliance," *Strategic Culture Foundation*, https://www.strategic-culture.org/news/2020/05/25/can-nasa-artemis-accords-spark-us-russia-alliance/ (accessed 11/01/2020).

[247] TASS, "Russia will not accept attempts to privatize the Moon," says Roscosmos CEO: https://tass.com/science/1159969 (accessed 11/01/2020).

[248] Eva Dou, "China and Russia to open moon base, expanding space cooperation," *Washington Post* (3/10/2021), https://tinyurl.com/4ntwk4yx (accessed 11/01/2020).

[249] The Artemis Accords Principles for Cooperation in the Civil Exploration and use of the Moon, Mars, Comets, and Asteroids for Peaceful Purposes, p. 1. https://www.nasa.gov/specials/artemis-accords/img/Artemis-Accords-signed-13Oct2020.pdf (accessed 12/01/2020).

[250] The five treaties have been compiled in a booklet titled *International Space Law: United Nations Instruments* (2017) authored by the United Nations Office for Outer Space Affairs. Available online at: https://tinyurl.com/y6mwewxu (accessed 10/29/2020).

[251] Michael Listner, "The Moon Treaty: failed international law or waiting in the shadows?" *The Space Review*, October 24, 2011: https://www.thespacereview.com/article/1954/1 (accessed 10/30/2020)

[252] White House, "Executive Order on Encouraging International Support for the Recovery and Use of Space Resources." https://www.whitehouse.gov/presidential-actions/executive-order-encouraging-international-support-recovery-use-space-resources/ (accessed 11/01/2020).

[253] The Artemis Accords Principles for Cooperation in the Civil Exploration and use of the Moon, Mars, Comets, and Asteroids for Peaceful Purposes, p. 1. https://www.nasa.gov/specials/artemis-accords/img/Artemis-Accords-signed-13Oct2020.pdf (accessed 12/01/2020).

[254] The Artemis Accords Principles for Cooperation in the Civil Exploration and use of the Moon, Mars, Comets, and Asteroids for Peaceful Purposes, p. 2. https://www.nasa.gov/specials/artemis-accords/img/Artemis-Accords-signed-13Oct2020.pdf (accessed 12/01/2020).

[255] The Artemis Accords Principles for Cooperation in the Civil Exploration and use of the Moon, Mars, Comets, and Asteroids for Peaceful Purposes, p. 4. https://www.nasa.gov/specials/artemis-accords/img/Artemis-Accords-signed-13Oct2020.pdf (accessed 12/01/2020).

[256] Michael Listner, "The Moon Treaty: failed international law or waiting in the shadows?" *The Space Review*, October 24, 2011: https://www.thespacereview.com/article/1954/1 (accessed 10/30/2020)

[257] White House, "Executive Order on Encouraging International Support for the Recovery and Use of Space Resources." https://www.whitehouse.gov/presidential-actions/executive-order-encouraging-international-support-recovery-use-space-resources/ (accessed 11/01/2020).

[258] TASS, "Russia will not accept attempts to privatize the Moon", says Roscosmos CEO: https://tass.com/science/1159969 (accessed 11/01/2020)

[259] "Treaty on Principles Governing the Activities of States in the Exploration and Use of Outer Space, including the Moon and Other Celestial Bodies," (aka Outer Space Treaty): https://www.unoosa.org/oosa/en/ourwork/spacelaw/treaties/outerspacetreaty.html (accessed 11/30/2020).

[260] Ronald Reagan, "Address to the Nation on Defense and National Security" (3/23/1983): https://tinyurl.com/yxjakmls (accessed 12/1/2020).

[261] CDx Diagnostics, "What do you get when you cross Star Wars missile defense technology with the pap smear? https://www.cdxdiagnostics.com/blog/star-wars-technology (accessed 12/1/2020).

[262] Dr. Peter Beter, "Audio Letter 26," (9/30/1977) https://drpeterbeter.blogspot.com/2014/10/dr-peter-beter-audio-letter-26.html (accessed 12/1/2020).

[263] Dr. Peter Beter, "Audio Letter 26," (9/30/1977) https://drpeterbeter.blogspot.com/2014/10/dr-peter-beter-audio-letter-26.html (accessed 12/1/2020).

[264] See David Vine, "War and Forced Migration in the Indian Ocean: The US Military Base at Diego Garcia," *International Migration* 42:3 (2004): pp. 111-43. https://tinyurl.com/yyp4y3zk (accessed 10/31/2020).

265 Dr. Peter Beter, "Audio Letter 26," (9/30/1977): https://drpeterbeter.blogspot.com/2014/10/dr-peter-beter-audio-letter-26.html (accessed 12/1/2020).

266 Dr. Peter Beter, "Audio Letter 26," (9/30/1977): https://drpeterbeter.blogspot.com/2014/10/dr-peter-beter-audio-letter-26.html (accessed 12/1/2020).

267 Dr. Peter Beter, "Audio Letter 26," (9/30/1977): https://drpeterbeter.blogspot.com/2014/10/dr-peter-beter-audio-letter-26.html (accessed 12/1/2020).

268 Dr. Peter Beter, "Audio Letter 26," (9/30/1977): https://drpeterbeter.blogspot.com/2014/10/dr-peter-beter-audio-letter-26.html (accessed 12/1/2020).

269 "Report that UR Destroyed Secret US Base on Moon," (1/24/1979): https://wikileaks.org/plusd/cables/P790011-1247_e.html (accessed 12/1/2020).

270 See Robert Spalding, Stealth War: How China Took Over While America's Elite Slept (Portfolio, 2019); and Michael Pillsbury, The Hundred Year Marathon: China's Secret Strategy to Replace America as the Global Superpower (St Martin's Griffin, 2016).

271 Office of the Secretary of Defense, Military and Security Developments Involving the People's Republic of China 2020: Annual Report to Congress, p. 14. https://media.defense.gov/2020/Sep/01/2002488689/-1/-1/1/2020-DOD-CHINA-MILITARY-POWER-REPORT-FINAL.PDF (accessed 10/31/2020).

272 Office of the Secretary of Defense, Military and Security Developments Involving the People's Republic of China 2020: Annual Report to Congress, p. ii. https://media.defense.gov/2020/Sep/01/2002488689/-1/-1/1/2020-DOD-CHINA-MILITARY-POWER-REPORT-FINAL.PDF (accessed 10/31/2020).

273 See Hui Zhang, "Chinese Perspectives on Space Weapons," https://www.amacad.org/publication/russian-and-chinese-responses-us-military-plans-space/section/4 (accessed 10/30/2020).

274 Office of the Secretary of Defense, Military and Security Developments Involving the People's Republic of China 2020: Annual Report to Congress, p. viii. https://media.defense.gov/2020/Sep/01/2002488689/-1/-1/1/2020-DOD-CHINA-MILITARY-POWER-REPORT-FINAL.PDF (accessed 10/31/2020).

275 "GPS celebrates 25th year of operation," https://www.spaceforce.mil/News/Article/2166101/gps-celebrates-25th-year-of-operation/ (accessed 10/30/2020).

276 Elizabeth Howell, "China launches final Beidou satellite to complete GPS-like navigation system," https://www.space.com/china-launches-final-beidou-navigation-satellite.html (accessed 10/30/2020).

277 The Artemis Accords Principles for Cooperation in the Civil Exploration and use of the Moon, Mars, Comets, and Asteroids for Peaceful Purposes, p. 7.

https://www.nasa.gov/specials/artemis-accords/img/Artemis-Accords-signed-13Oct2020.pdf (accessed 12/01/2020).

[278] The Artemis Accords Principles for Cooperation in the Civil Exploration and use of the Moon, Mars, Comets, and Asteroids for Peaceful Purposes, p. 5. https://www.nasa.gov/specials/artemis-accords/img/Artemis-Accords-signed-13Oct2020.pdf (accessed 12/01/2020).

[279] The Artemis Accords Principles for Cooperation in the Civil Exploration and use of the Moon, Mars, Comets, and Asteroids for Peaceful Purposes, p. 5. https://www.nasa.gov/specials/artemis-accords/img/Artemis-Accords-signed-13Oct2020.pdf (accessed 12/01/2020).

[280] The Artemis Accords Principles for Cooperation in the Civil Exploration and use of the Moon, Mars, Comets, and Asteroids for Peaceful Purposes, p. 5. https://www.nasa.gov/specials/artemis-accords/img/Artemis-Accords-signed-13Oct2020.pdf (accessed 12/01/2020).

[281] The Artemis Accords Principles for Cooperation in the Civil Exploration and use of the Moon, Mars, Comets, and Asteroids for Peaceful Purposes, p. 6. https://www.nasa.gov/specials/artemis-accords/img/Artemis-Accords-signed-13Oct2020.pdf (accessed 12/01/2020).

[282] White House, "National Space Policy of the United States of America" (Dec 9, 2020) pp. 3-4. https://www.whitehouse.gov/wp-content/uploads/2020/12/National-Space-Policy.pdf (accessed 12/11/20).

[283] "Online press conference by NATO Secretary General Jens Stoltenberg following the first day of the meetings of NATO Defence Ministers," https://www.nato.int/cps/fr/natohq/opinions_178946.htm (accessed 11/02/2020).

[284] I discuss the credentials of William Tompkins, Edgar Fouche, Clark McClelland, and Emery Smith in the US Air Force Secret Space Program: Shifting Extraterrestrial Alliances and Space Force (Exopolitics Consultants, 2019).

[285] I discuss the backgrounds of Kewper, JP and Corey Goode in the US Air Force Secret Space Program: Shifting Extraterrestrial Alliances and Space Force.

[286] Biographical information on Professor Haim Eshed found at: https://tinyurl.com/yyxs3nje (accessed 12/8/2020).

[287] Cited by David Israel, "Former Head of Israel's Space Program: The Aliens Asked Not To Be Revealed, Humanity Not Yet Ready," Jewish Press (12/5/2020): https://tinyurl.com/yxop6tv5 (accessed 12/8/2020).

[288] Cited by David Israel, "Former Head of Israel's Space Program: The Aliens Asked Not To Be Revealed, Humanity Not Yet Ready," Jewish Press (12/5/2020): https://tinyurl.com/yxop6tv5 (accessed 12/8/2020).

[289] Theodore Roosevelt, "The Progressive Covenant with the People," https://www.loc.gov/collections/theodore-roosevelt-films/articles-and-essays/sound-recordings-of-theodore-roosevelts-voice/ (accessed 12/2/2020).

[290] Cited in Colonel John Hughes-Wilson, JFK An American Coup D'ETAT: The Truth Behind the Kennedy Assassination (Kings Road Publishing, 2013).

[291] Gary Benoit, Introduction to Alex Newman, *Deep State: Pulling the Strings From Behind the Scenes* (The John Birch Society, 2018).

[292] For discussion of the Sumerian King's List see Michael Salla, Antartica's Hidden History: Corporate Foundations of Secret Space Programs (Exopolitics Consultants, 2018) pp. 318-19.

[293] Manetho, Book I, p. 2, https://tinyurl.com/y5z95jfh (accessed 12/8/2020).

[294] "The Book of Enoch," http://www.markfoster.net/rn/texts/AllBooksOfEnoch.pdf (accessed 11/1/17)

[295] Jim Marrs, *Rule by Secrecy: The Hidden History That Connects the Trilateral Commission, the Freemasons, and the Great Pyramids* (William Morrow, 2001).

[296] William Bramley, *The Gods of Eden* (Avon, 1993).

[297] David Icke, *The Biggest Secret: The Book That Will Change the World* (David Icke Books, 1999).

[298] Fritz Springmeier, *Bloodlines of the Illuminati* (Spring Arbor Distributors, 1998). Cited from online copy at: https://tinyurl.com/y2wclejl (accessed 12/8/2020).

[299] The entire dialogue has been archived at the following location: http://www.illuminati-news.com/00363.html (accessed 12/8/2020).

[300] Cited from "Dialogue with "Hidden Hand", Self-Proclaimed Illuminati Insider," http://www.illuminati-news.com/00363.html (accessed 12/8/2020).

[301] Cited from "Dialogue with "Hidden Hand", Self-Proclaimed Illuminati Insider," http://www.illuminati-news.com/00363.html (accessed 12/8/2020).

[302] Cited from "Dialogue with "Hidden Hand", Self-Proclaimed Illuminati Insider," http://www.illuminati-news.com/00363.html (accessed 12/8/2020).

[303] I discuss the German flying saucer flights over US territory and the humiliating defeats suffered by the US (Army) Air Force in the *US Air Force Secret Space Program: Shifting Extraterrestrial Alliances and Space Force* (2019), pp. 109-22.

[304] See Missy Sullivan, "In 1952, 'Flying Saucers' Over Washington Sent the Press Into a Frenzy," https://www.history.com/news/ufos-washington-dc-news-reports (accessed 12/8/2020).

[305] Burned Memo is available online at https://majesticdocuments.com/pdf/burnedmemo-s1-pgs1-2.pdf . For analysis of the Burned Memo and its connection to Allen Dulles, see Michael Salla, *Kennedy's Last Stand: Eisenhower, UFOs, MJ-12 & JFK's Assassination* (Exopolitics Institute, 2013) pp. 115-21.

[306] For discussion on the Apollo Program and how it was run by the Fourth Reich, see Michael Salla, *US Air Force Secret Space Program,* pp. 207-24.

[307] See Michael Salla, *Insiders Reveal Secret Space Programs* (Exopolitics Institute, 2015) pp. 179-96.

[308] See Sam Keen, *Faces of the Enemy: Reflections of the Hostile Imagination* (Harper & Row, 1991).

[309] Judy Woods, *Where Did the Towers Go? Evidence of Directed Free-energy Technology on 9/11* (The New Investigation, 2010).

[310] "Watch, Read: Defense Secretary Esper's Keynote at AFA's vASC 2020," https://www.airforcemag.com/watch-read-defense-secretary-espers-keynote-at-afas-vasc-2020/ (accessed 12/4/2020).

[311] See Michael Salla, *US Air Force Secret Space Program: Shifting Extraterrestrial Alliances and Space Force,* pp. 343-57.

[312] See Mac Slavo, "Are Directed Energy Weapons Starting Fires in California and Oregon," https://tinyurl.com/yytccg5d (accessed 12/8/2020).

[313] Laura Eisenhower, "2012 and the Ancient Game: Venus–Sophia and Recruitment to Mars," https://sites.google.com/site/lauramagdalene/home/2012-and-the-ancient-game (accessed 12/8/2020).

[314] See Corey Goode, "Joint SSP, Sphere Alliance & ICC Leadership Conference & Tour of Mars Colony on 6.20.2015," https://tinyurl.com/y6op77d6 (accessed 12/8/2020).

[315] Richard Hollingham "How to Overthrow a Martian Dictatorship BBC," (6/22/2015): https://www.bbc.com/future/article/20150619-how-to-overthrow-a-martian-dictatorship (accessed 12/4/2020).

[316] See U.S., Department of Justice, "Involuntary Servitude, Forced Labor, and Sex Trafficking Statutes Enforced" https://www.justice.gov/crt/involuntary-servitude-forced-labor-and-sex-trafficking-statutes-enforced (accessed 12/8/2020).

[317] Alfred P. Rubin, "The hostages: international law to the rescue?" The Christian Science Monitor (1/9/1981): https://www.csmonitor.com/1981/0109/010925.html (accessed 12/8/2020).

[318] "Treaty on Principles Governing the Activities of States in the Exploration and Use of Outer Space, including the Moon and Other Celestial Bodies," https://www.unoosa.org/oosa/en/ourwork/spacelaw/treaties/outerspacetreaty.html (accessed 12/5/2020).

[319] "Treaty on Principles Governing the Activities of States in the Exploration and Use of Outer Space, including the Moon and Other Celestial Bodies," https://www.unoosa.org/oosa/en/ourwork/spacelaw/treaties/outerspacetreaty.html (accessed 12/5/2020).

[320] Michael Salla, "Questions for Corey Goode on SSP Conflicts and Human Slave Trade – May 29/30, 2015," https://exopolitics.org/galactic-human-slave-trade-ai-threat-to-end-with-full-disclosure-of-et-life/ (accessed 12/4/2020).

[321] Michael Salla, "Questions for Corey Goode on SSP Conflicts and Human Slave Trade – May 29/30, 2015," https://exopolitics.org/galactic-human-slave-trade-ai-threat-to-end-with-full-disclosure-of-et-life/ (accessed 12/4/2020).

[322] Michael Salla, "Questions for Corey Goode on SSP Conflicts and Human Slave Trade – May 29/30, 2015", https://exopolitics.org/galactic-human-slave-trade-ai-threat-to-end-with-full-disclosure-of-et-life/ (accessed 12/4/2020).

[323] For interview details see "20 Years a Slave in Secret Space Programs", https://exopolitics.org/20-years-a-slave-in-secret-space-programs-abduction-programming/ (accessed 12/5/2020).

[324] Private email received from Tony Rodrigues on August 16, 2015.

[325] Deborah Byrd, "Ceres' bright spots come from salty water below" Earth Sky (8/14/2020): https://earthsky.org/space/bright-areas-dwarf-planet-ceres-salty-water-below (accessed 12/10/2020).

[326] See "William Pawelec Interview," https://www.youtube.com/watch?v=9OiZRr9V7Z4 (accessed 12/10/2020).

[327] "William Pawelec Interview," https://youtu.be/9OiZRr9V7Z4?t=686 (accessed 12/10/2020).

[328] "William Pawelec Interview," https://youtu.be/9OiZRr9V7Z4?t=840 (accessed 12/10/2020).

[329] "William Pawelec Interview," https://youtu.be/9OiZRr9V7Z4?t=1308 (accessed 12/10/2020).

[330] "William Pawelec Interview," https://youtu.be/9OiZRr9V7Z4?t=1312 (accessed 12/10/2020).

[331] Gina Dimuro, "The West Africa Squadron: The British Royal Navy's Deadly Battle To End The Slave Trade"(3/21/2019): https://allthatsinteresting.com/west-africa-squadron (accessed 12/10/2020).

[332] "Steven Kwast - The Urgent Need for a U.S. Space Force," https://youtu.be/KsPLmb6gAdw?t=1139 (accessed 12/12/2019).

[333] See Michael Salla, *Rise of the Red Dragon*, pp. 235-38.

[334] Ryan Pickrell, "China is the world's biggest shipbuilder, and its ability to rapidly produce new warships would be a 'huge advantage' in a long fight with the US, experts say," *Business Insider* (9/8/2020): https://www.businessinsider.com/china-has-advantage-over-the-us-in-shipbuilding-2020-9 (accessed 12/10/2020).

[335] Cited by Ryan Pickrell, "China is the world's biggest shipbuilder, and its ability to rapidly produce new warships would be a 'huge advantage' in a long fight with the US, experts say," *Business Insider* (9/8/2020): https://www.businessinsider.com/china-has-advantage-over-the-us-in-shipbuilding-2020-9 (accessed 12/10/2020).

[336] Joshua Philipp, "For China, Space Is About Politics and War," https://www.theepochtimes.com/for-china-space-is-about-politics-and-war_2877600.html (accessed 9/23/2019).

[337] Chris Knowles, "Secret Star Trek, Part 9: Levels Above Human," http://thesecret-sun2.blogspot.com/2013/07/secret-star-trek-part-9-levels-above.html (accessed 12/5/2020).

[338] Air Force Space Command, *Future of Space 2060 and Implications for U.S. Strategy: Report on the Space Futures Workshop* (5 September 2019) p. 9. https://s3.amazonaws.com/images.spaceref.com/news/2019/USAFSpace.pdf (accessed 11/02/2020).

339 "The Artemis Accords: Principles for Cooperation in the Civil Exploration and Use of the Moon, Mars, Comets, and Asteroids for Peaceful Purposes," https://www.nasa.gov/specials/artemis-accords/img/Artemis-Accords-signed-13Oct2020.pdf accessed 11/02/2020)

340 "Online press conference by NATO Secretary General Jens Stoltenberg following the first day of the meetings of NATO Defence Ministers," https://www.nato.int/cps/fr/natohq/opinions_178946.htm (accessed 11/02/2020).

341 Chris Knowles, "Secret Star Trek, Part 8: Daystar Trek and the Majestic Nine," http://thesecret-sun2.blogspot.com/2013/07/secret-star-trek-part-8-daystar-trek.html (accessed 12/5/2020).

342 Chris Knowles, "Secret Star Trek, Part 8: Daystar Trek and the Majestic Nine," http://thesecret-sun2.blogspot.com/2013/07/secret-star-trek-part-8-daystar-trek.html (accessed 12/5/2020).

343 Gordon White, "Apolalypse Puja," http://runesoup.com/2013/08/apocalypse-puja/ (accessed 3/8/2021)

344 Alfred H. Paddock, Jr., *US Army Special Warfare: Its Origins: Psychological and Unconventional Warfare, 1941-1952* (National Defense University Press, 1982), 78-79.

345 Cited from online version of Robertson Panel at: http://www.cufon.org/cufon/robertdod.htm (accessed 3/8/2021)

346 See Michael Salla, US Navy's Secret Space Program, pp. 107-108.

347 Chris Knowles, "Secret Star Trek, Part 8: Daystar Trek and the Majestic Nine," http://secretsun.blogspot.co.uk/2013/07/secret-star-trek-part-8-daystar-trek.html (accessed 3/8/2021).

348 Chris Knowles, "Secret Star Trek, Part 9: Levels Above Human," http://thesecret-sun2.blogspot.com/2013/07/secret-star-trek-part-9-levels-above.html (accessed 12/5/2020).

349 SphereBeing Alliance, "Israeli Ex-Mil Space Chief: US & ALIEN Galactic Federation Deal (Human Experiments) & Mars Base," https://youtu.be/c7OwPpc4cLA?t=3236 (accessed 12/11/2020).

350 SphereBeing Alliance, "Israeli Ex-Mil Space Chief: US & ALIEN Galactic Federation Deal (Human Experiments) & Mars Base," https://youtu.be/c7OwPpc4cLA?t=3329 (accessed 12/11/2020).

351 Rense Radio Interview with William Tompkins with Maj. George Filer & Frank Chille – May 4, 2016 http://spherebeingalliance.com/blog/the-amazing-story-continues-part1.html

352 Unpublished Recorded Interview, February 25, 2016

Index

CPSIA information can be obtained
at www.ICGtesting.com
Printed in the USA
FSHW021255200921
84883FS